Mass Communication in Japan

Mass Communication in Japan

Anne Cooper-Chen

with Miiko Kodama

Iowa State University Press

Ames

Anne Cooper-Chen is professor and director of the Institute for International Journalism at the E. W. Scripps School of Journalism at Ohio University. The former head of the International Communication Division of the Association for Education in Journalism and Mass Communication (AEJMC), Cooper-Chen worked in Japan for the *Asahi Evening News* for two years and returned to Japan as a Fulbright Senior Research Scholar to work on this book.

Miiko Kodama is professor of journalism at Musashi University, Tokyo.

© 1997 Iowa State University Press, Ames, Iowa 50014
All rights reserved

Authorization to photocopy items for internal or personal use, or the internal or personal use of specific clients, is granted by Iowa State University Press, provided that the base fee of $.10 per copy is paid directly to the Copyright Clearance Center, 27 Congress Street, Salem, MA 01970. For those organizations that have been granted a photocopy license by CCC, a separate system of payments has been arranged. The fee code for users of the Transactional Reporting Service is 0-8138-2710-8/97 $.10.

∞ Printed on acid-free paper in the United States of America

First edition, 1997

Library of Congress Cataloging-in-Publication Data

Cooper-Chen, Anne
    Mass communication in Japan/Anne Cooper-Chen, with Miiko Kodama.—1st ed.
    Includes bibliographical references and index.
    ISBN 0-8138-2710-8
    1. Mass media—Japan.   I. Kodama, Miiko.   II. Title.
    P92.J3C67   1997
    302.23′0952—dc21   97-9167

Last digit is the print number: 9 8 7 6 5 4 3 2 1

The four characters on the cover represent the four syllables ma su ko mi *(mass communication in Japanized English).*

To my husband, Charles Chin-tse Chen,
and in memory of
Deborah Ann Chen Russ
(1965–1995)

PREFECTURES AND MAJOR CITIES

Prefectures and major cities of Japan. From *A Day in the Life of Japan* (1985),
New York: William Collins.

Contents

Preface

According to one of the few scholars writing in English about Japan's mass media, Roya Akhavan-Majid (1990, 1006), "Despite the growing importance of Japan on the international scene, the last five decades have seen few analytical investigations of the postwar mass media in Japan." This book seeks to remedy that situation.

Various authors have told parts of Japan's mass communications story. But the book in your hands is the only work in English that treats all of Japan's allied media industries, explains how they relate to each other and puts their functioning in a context. Thus it does not contain exhaustive detail about any one topic, but neither does it oversimplify or pander. Its sources range from research studies in academic journals to newspaper articles written for a general audience.

I learned about Japan's mass media from the inside out, by working for the *Asahi Shimbun*, Japan's only "great daily" (Merrill 1990; Merrill and Fisher 1980). In September 1966, I traveled alone to Japan to work for two years at the *Asahi Shimbun*'s English-language sister daily, the *Asahi Evening News* (AEN). The experience changed my life.

Thus in a sense I have been working on this book for 30 years. The chance to return in 1992–93 as a Fulbright Senior Research Scholar landed me in a wealthier and somehow calmer Japan, where even though all my favorite *kissaten* [coffee shops] had long since disappeared, the train stations and aspects of the mass media remained.

A gratifying aspect of this research was meeting again a colleague who still works for the *Asahi Evening News*: Isamu Ebitsubo, now AEN's editorial director. In addition to talking with him, I conducted nearly 100 formal interviews in Japan—too many people to mention individually. All those people who took the time to talk to me, many of whose names appear in the text, have my unending thanks.

The late Professor Hiroshi Kawakami of Seijo University, formerly a reporter for the *Sankei Shimbun*, originally collaborated with me on this project. Not only did Professor Kawakami lend insights about the mass media, but he also did generous amounts of videotaping.

My present collaborator, Miiko Kodama, a professor at Musashi University, patiently read and suggested changes in this manuscript, saving me from inconsistencies, omissions and downright mistakes. Any remaining errors, however, are mine. She and I form the perfect cross-cultural team: her background in broadcasting, as a former anchorwoman for Fuji Television, complements mine in print.

I concentrated my interviews in the Tokyo and Nagoya areas. A former student at Ohio University, Drew Freyman, contributed interviews in the Osaka area. Mr. Freyman, fluent in Japanese, happened to be in Kobe during the January 1995 earthquake and wrote a moving account of that tragedy.

This book would not be in your hands without the support of the Japan–United States Educational Commission, which administers the Fulbright program. My contact and handholder, Teruyo Kuramoto, and the then-director, Carolyn Matano Yang, pointed me in the right direction (literally) countless times.

Friends at Chubu University, a sister school of Ohio University since 1973, distinguished themselves as the perfect hosts and helpers. Special thanks go to Tomoyasu Tanaka, Sumiko Tanaka and Noriko Tanaka Mukai, as well as Hiromi Imamura, Hiroshi and Megumi Katsumori, Mizuo Kaneshige, Musuo Murase and President Kazuo Yamada. Also in Japan, Kenji Yamada, Bradley Martin, Hideko Takayama, Hideo Takeichi, Satomi Tsutsui, William May and Youichi Ito gave generous help that I will never forget.

Friends at and graduates of Ohio University also contributed in inestimable ways. Luckily for me, Michiyo Tanaka, Tsutomu Kanayama, Reiko Sato, Fumiko Yoshimura, Debra Yamashita Traynor and Hiroshi Suzuki chose OU as the place at which they wanted to study. Mary Ann and Don Flournoy, Ralph and Janet Izard, Felix Gagliano, Josep Rota and Paul Nelson helped clear logistical hurdles. At other universities, I owe thanks to Kyu Ho Youm of Arizona State, Louisa Ha of Oklahoma and Charles Self of Texas A&M.

Gretchen Van Houten, formerly acquisitions editor and now editor-in-chief at Iowa State University Press, has worked with me for five years on this project. Her support and flexibility have been a godsend.

Most of all, without my husband, Charles Chen, a professor of physics and native speaker of Japanese, this book would not exist. When we first met, on Halloween eve in 1985, I wore as my costume my favorite kimono, which served as a conversation starter. In addition to high-level expertise, he lent help inputting tabular data and typing TV schedules.

Finally, a few notes regarding style. The order of names gives family name last (Western style). The exchange rate is based on $1 to ¥100. The Japanese "o" or "u" held for two beats is transliterated as ō or ū (but not in proper names, such as Tokyo).

I hope this book finds an audience on both sides of the Pacific, and I welcome any comments you, valued readers, may have.

Part 1
Introduction

1
East-West
Communication

It's time in Japan for the nightly TV weather report, including the precipitation, sunshine and temperature forecasts. But what are those other symbols on the local map? They look like T-shirts with percentages emblazoned upon them: "30%" for Nagoya, "70%" for Gifu City, and so on.

In fact, the T-shirts represent laundry, and the percentages combine sunshine and humidity factors to let viewers know whether tomorrow will bode well for hanging out the wash. In Japan, people prefer sun drying to expensive, small-capacity electric dryers, so the T-shirt numbers help them plan the next day's activities.

From February to June, the weather forecasts add yet another symbol: pink flowers to track the northward movement of the cherry blossom front. The first pink blossoms in the Japanese archipelago appear in Okinawa. In late March, the first trees that bloom in Tokyo attract not only weather-report coverage but on-location reporting within the main news as well. This year, did the blooms occur earlier or later than last year? Will winds blow them away quickly, or will they stay long enough for the traditional under-tree drinking parties? Indeed, reporters stake out likely early bloomers so as not to miss the grand opening. Coverage ends for the season in May when, for one glorious week, the *sakura* trees sport full blooms on the northern island of Hokkaido.

The transitory cherry blossoms have had cultural meaning from ancient times to modern. "Fall gallantly, like cherry blossoms in spring" runs an ancient saying. As the flowers lent themselves to art and poetry in the past, today they make the quintessential TV story in the visually oriented, seasonally conscious Japanese society. In a larger sense, they reflect a preoccupation with nature—heightened by a sense of loss and nostalgia on the part of the 58.2 percent of Japanese who live in cities (only 25.4 percent in the United States) as they view the natural world on the small screen. According to Itoh and Clark (1983, 14), "For centuries the Japanese people have closely observed the cycle of the seasons, gradually developing the wisdom necessary to cope with the changes of each of the four."

Like Japan itself, for which Benedict (1946) created the double metaphor of the chrysanthemum and the sword in her book of the same title, Japan's mass media embrace a web of influences. Chapter 2 will further analyze the interplay of Japanese cultural values and the mass media. This chapter will create the context for that analysis by starting from familiar territory and making comparisons with Japan.

Like Benedict's (1946) juxtaposition of a flower and a sword, we find stories about space travel and *sakura* side by side on Japanese television. On December 3, 1990, to celebrate the 40th anniversary of commercial broadcasting in Japan, the Tokyo Broadcasting System (TBS) sponsored the launch of one of its reporters, Toyohiro Akiyama, into space. Nine supporting companies absorbed almost half of the ¥5 billion ($50 million) cost of the mission, during which the crew made a rendezvous with the Soviet *Mir* space station, from where Akiyama reported for days (and racked up TV ratings of 36 percent).

Later, Mamoru Mohri, the first Japanese national on a U.S. space shuttle mission (the *Endeavor* voyage of September 12–21, 1992), also broadcasted from space. So did Chiaki Mukai, M.D., Japan's first woman astronaut, who chalked up the longest flight record of any woman to that time (more than 14 days) for her 236 earth orbits on *Columbia*, launched on July 8, 1994. Yet the history books will record that Japan's first astronaut was a TV journalist—as if Walter Cronkite rather than John Glenn Jr. had gone aloft as the first American in orbit. (To date, a teacher and a congressman but no journalist has blasted into orbit on a U.S. space mission.)

The prominence in Japanese life of the TV set, which stays on in the average household for more than eight hours a day, as well as the strength of commercial TV broadcasting, made the launch of journalist Akiyama fit just as naturally into Japan's media agenda as the nightly cherry blossom reports. By contrast, a Westerner might see the four months of cherry blossom coverage as media overkill and the launch of a TV reporter as gimmickry.

One way for Westerners to begin to understand is to make connections with what we know. With apologies to our non-U.S. readers, we will draw some comparisons between the world's two largest economic powers.

Contrasts and Convergences

According to former U.S. ambassador to Japan Mike Mansfield, the U.S.-Japan relationship is the single most important bilateral relationship in the world. The Japanese $3 trillion economy and the U.S. $5 trillion economy together make up 42 percent of the world's gross national product (Maloney 1991b).

By the year 2000, the Pacific Rim will generate more than half of the world's goods and services, with Asia producing 25 percent and the United States and Canada producing 30 percent. If Eastern Europe emerges as a lucrative market, Western Europe will benefit more than the United States or Japan; in any case, the United States' ties with Asia already surpass those with Europe. By the mid-1990s, Pacific-U.S. trade will probably equal twice the U.S.–Western Europe trade (Wood 1991).

When Westerners first come to Japan, presumably to one of that nation's large cities, they see similarities to the West: modern buildings, efficient subways, stores with abundant consumer goods. The cleanliness and safety, as well as the absence of potholes, recall the best of the cities back home. For Americans, even the climate feels familiar; geographically, Japan and the United States lie at exactly the same latitudes, resulting in a range of weather from the chilly north (Maine/Hokkaido) to the mild south (Georgia/Kyushu).

But stay awhile. Soon, differences emerge. The school year begins April 1, not in the fall. Transactions most commonly occur with cash, not checks. The paper available in copiers comes in varied sizes, but not 8½×11 inches. People don't sign documents; they use a stamp. Table 1.1 shows larger-scale contrasting and converging social characteristics between the two countries.

Social/Cultural Profiles

Culturally, most observers (e.g., Fallows 1989) find more differences than similarities. Each society, believes van Wolferen (1993, 11), belongs to "an altogether different frame of reference." Indeed, in a chapter titled "Cultural Similarities and Differences Between the United States and Japan," Gudykunst and Nishida (1994) almost exclusively explore differences. Drawing inspiration from Hofstede (1984) and Hall (1976), Gudykunst and Nishida (1994, 19) have identified five "dimensions of cultural variability":

1. Individualism (United States), which embraces self-realization and personal well-being, vs. collectivism (Japan), which means attachment to an in-group; it involves the concepts of *wa* [oneness and harmony], *amae* [a trustful dependence] and *enryo* [restrained conformity]. The United States ranked 91, while Japan ranked only 46, on Hofstede's individualism scale.

2. Low-context (United States) vs. high-context (Japan) communica-

Table 1.1. Social characteristics: Japan and the United States

	Japan	United States
Urban population	58.2% total population	25.4% total population
Single households	21.0% total households	24.0% total households
Age first married	F: age 26; M: age 29	F: age 23.5; M: age 26
Divorces	1.25/1,000 population	4.75/1,000 population
Birth rate	1.53 babies/woman	1.87 babies/woman
Single women	1.0% of all births	24.5% of all births
Senior citizens	20.0% total population (2010)	13.9% total population (2010)
Working women	40.1% total labor force	44.9% total labor force
Women's wages	50.7% of men's wages	70.2% of men's wages
Elected women	2.4% House of Representatives	5.7% House of Representatives
Homicides	1.4/100,000 people	10.2/100,000 people
Rapes	2.2/100,000 people	36.4/100,000 people
Lawyers	11.7/1,000 population	273.8/1,000 population
Two incomes	52.3% of famililes	71.2% of families
Own home	61.4% of families	64.0% of families
House size	89.9 sq. meters	149 sq. meters
House cost	$652,500 (Tokyo)	$149,000 (Nebraska)
Food intake	2,061 calories/day	3,500 calories/day
College entry	M: 35.2%; F: 37.4%	M: 37.9%; F: 42.3%
High School dropouts	2.2%	28.4%
MDs	1.6/1,000 population	2.5/1,000 population
Health care	4.9% of GNP	11.1% of GNP

Figures are from 1988–90.

Source: JETRO, *US and Japan in Figures,* 1991; K. Ito (1994).

tion, whereby information is conveyed in direct, explicit messages or implicitly, with *awase* [adjusting messages to the people listening, assuming they will "catch on"].

3. Low (United States) vs. high (Japan) uncertainty avoidance, whereby dissent, emotionalism and deviant behavior are either accepted or avoided; in Japan, certainty is achieved by obeying rules and behaving in an orderly way. On Hofstede's scale, Japan scored high (92) and the United States scored low (46) on this dimension.

4. Power distance, which can be low (needing reasons for following a superior's orders) or high (accepting orders without question). On Hofstede's power distance scale, Japan scored higher (54) than the United States (40).

5. Masculinity-femininity. On Hofstede's masculinity scale, Japan ranked highest of all 40 countries studied, with a 95 score. By contrast, the United States scored a middle-range 62. In cultures like Japan's, women and men occupy different places; few women hold professional

or technical jobs, and they tend to be segregated from men in education. Indeed, women tend to enroll in junior colleges, while 82 percent of four-year college students are men.

Table 1.2 shows the imbalance (in Japan's favor) in flows of goods and people between the two countries. As a counterweight, information flows more strongly from the United States to Japan. The world's two largest economies both support mass media systems that serve the information/entertainment needs of mature consumer societies. And they both face similar problems, such as TV saturation and declining newspaper readership among the young.

Two Information Societies

Japan and the United States (as well as other developed societies) share a common economic profile. By the 1980s, almost 40 percent of workers in Japan, and more than 40 percent in the United States, dealt with information–office workers, teachers, journalists and others. Just as the change began, some writers realized its implications. The *jōhō shakai* [information society] concept began independently in Japan and the United States in the 1960s–about 10 years earlier than in Europe. While Machlup (1962) in the United States discussed "production of knowledge," Umesao's (1963) writing on "information industries" spurred Japan to enter an "information society boom" of thinking and planning (Ito 1991). Later, Bell (1973) developed the idea of the "postindustrial society," and still later in Japan, Sakaiya (1985) predicted a revolution whereby economic growth would derive from information and *chika* [intangible value] (Ito 1991a).

Table 1.2. Interchanges: Japan and the United States

	Japan	United States
Tourists	Sends 3,122,503 to U.S.	Sends 244,152 to Japan
Students*	Sends 45,276 to U.S.	Sends 1,400 to Japan
Enterprises	Operates 1,777 in U.S.	Operates 507 in Japan
Imports	$52,841 million from U.S.	$93,070 million from Japan
Exports	To U.S.=31.7% world total	To Japan=12.3% world total

Figures are from 1988–90, except for students (1994–95).

Source: JETRO, *US and Japan in Figures,* 1991.

*Institute for International Education.

In the United States, the transformation to an industrial and then information society occurred slowly, spanning a century, as agricultural workers declined from 40 to 10 percent of the work force. In Japan, the process of agriculture's decline from the largest to the smallest sector took only 25 years. Now, in both Japan and the United States, manufacturing and services constitute the middle segments between the information and agricultural sectors.

With the mass media, the amount of information stock (information available through reading, watching, hearing) has increased exponentially, doubling at ever-shorter intervals. The multiplying effect of mass media means that one created original message can convey information efficiently to large numbers of people and increase the volume of information in circulation. The amount of information amassed from the dawn of history to the first century doubled by 1750; then it doubled again around 1900; then again in 1950; and again in 1960.

Japan's transformation into an information society in the late 1960s and early 1970s was similar to Japan's industrialization in the late 19th century (Ito, 1991a and b). In both cases, the mass media aided the rapid diffusion of new ideas because of Japan's high literacy and educational levels. Japan's motivation to catch up to the West, especially the United States, spurred development in both periods of change. Overall, Japanese attitudes toward the United States have gone through swings ranging from admiration to disdain.

The Japanese View of the United States

In 1853, Commodore Matthew C. Perry amazed and awed the Japanese with his fleet of imposing, gun-equipped "black ships" that steamed up Tokyo Bay against the wind. The Edo (Tokyo) government had no choice but to sign an unequal treaty with the United States, granting provisioning privileges at two ports.

Japan, having been opened to the West after 200 years of isolation, then embarked on "a virtual craze for almost anything Western" (Reischauer 1981, 125). Beginning in 1859, hundreds of U.S. missionaries set up schools and taught a myriad of subjects, even though the ban on Christianity did not end officially until 1873. In the 1870s and 1880s, translations of Western books fed the hunger for *bummei kaika* [civilization and enlightenment]. By the 1920s, not just serious works of science and learning but also U.S. popular culture had invaded Japan, according to former U.S. Ambassador to Japan Edwin O. Reischauer (1981, 173): "As in the United States, the symbol of the twenties was the 'flapper,' called by the Japanese the *moga*, a contraction of the English words 'modern girl.' Moving pictures, made either in Hollywood or in Japan on

Hollywood patterns, had a tremendous vogue, and American jazz and Western social dancing became popular with the more sophisticated."

Moreover, the Japanese enthusiastically adopted the Western sports of tennis, golf, and track and field. But the greatest fervor went to the U.S. national sport of baseball; university and high school games drew tremendous crowds of devoted fans.

Then in the 1930s, after a systematic process of rapidly learning from the West, Japan used its modern might to try to realize its "dream of hegemony over the whole of East Asia" (Reischauer 1981, 208). The "striving for international political power and the frustration Japan experienced in international treaty making were among the factors that led up to the surprise bombing of Pearl Harbor on December 7, 1941," write DeVos and Bock (1974, 25). But Japan misjudged the United States. According to Reischauer (1981, 210), in 1941 the Japanese military underestimated America, "which they believed to be corrupted by too much luxury. They were convinced that Americans did not have the will to fight a long war." After the U.S. bombing of Hiroshima on August 6, 1945, and Nagasaki on August 9, the emperor used the mass medium of radio to broadcast the surrender on August 14.

The American influence during the Occupation, 1945–52, was monumental. Until then, no foreign power had had any influence over Japan's internal policies. The dependent relation that continued even after the Occupation had formally ended went through another swing in the late 1970s. According to Reischauer (1981, 367), the Japanese wondered if they could join the elite group of nations or remain on the outside looking in: "To them, the complaints of others seemed to be essentially that the Japanese worked harder and were more disciplined and efficient—or perhaps simply that they were different and spoke a strange language. Japanese felt that the others did not appreciate their country's great economic vulnerabilities."

The trade imbalance crisis that began in the 1970s remains with us 20 years later. Indeed, in 1995, for the fifth straight year, Japan remained "the world's wealthiest nation in terms of overseas net assets" ("Japan remains" 1996). Japan's overseas assets minus liabilities put it $720 billion in the black, whereas the U.S. net deficit totaled $63.45 billion in the red.

Regarding the imbalance, the Japanese feel put upon partly because, with Japan having half the U.S. population, "Japanese demands in such fields could never grow large enough to bring the trade statistics into balance" (Reischauer 1981, 368). Are we to be penalized, they wonder, because of our industrial success and our more highly educated labor force? Japan felt proud that it had "taken what it wanted from the West . . . but without losing its own identity. It had shown that a non-Western land could be thoroughly modern without losing its soul. . . . it appeared to some that the time had come for the student to change roles with the teacher" (Reischauer 1981, 371).

Ever since the 1600s, Japanese have tended to "understand many things in terms of the positions of sumo wrestlers (*banzuke-hyo*)," so they see nations as either ascending or descending (Ito 1993c, 162). Indeed, a 1990 *Business Week* poll revealed that much of the Japanese public thinks the United States has begun an irreversible decline. Ironically, this same attitude led to Japan's World War II defeat. At the same time, ever since 1981, Japan's answer to the poll question "Which country do you like?" consistently and by a large margin has been, "the United States." Conversely, half of the Japanese named Russia (in March 1994) as the country they disliked (Ladd 1995, 19).

Consider the special place of English, one of three components on college entrance exams, and the heavy usage of adapted English words, such as *rienji* [reengineering], *salaryman* and *OL* [office lady] in Japanese mass media and everyday conversation (Nakazawa 1993; Reid 1995a). While France and other countries are legislating to rid their language of the feared English invasion, the Japanese feel so secure that no one even suggests that English will threaten their self-identity.

According to a 1992 *Time* poll, the dominant characteristic that the Japanese associate with U.S. citizens is friendliness (only 15 percent saw Americans as hardworking) (Hillenbrand 1992). Japanese admired Americans' freedom of expression (89 percent), leisure time (88 percent), variety of lifestyles (86 percent) and treatment of women (68 percent) (Murrow 1992).

Mass media may play a role in reinforcing these attitudes. For example, Saito (1994) found that heavy TV viewers in Japan associate the United States with a positive image of gender equality. Saito (1995, 18) also found that "television may not necessarily cultivate negative perceptions of American society." The term "*gaijin* complex" (Christopher 1983)–a mixture of superior and inferior feelings–sums up Japan's contradictory attitudes toward the United States. Such complexity also holds true in reverse.

The U.S. View of Japan

Van Wolferen (1993, 4) decries Americans' "one-sided ignorance" of Japan, whereby the country "is still treated as a curiosity." Lionel Tiger, an anthropologist ("Images of Japan" 1996), goes even further: "Every culture has its monsters . . . as a kind of demonic threat, for economic purposes . . . the Japanese have been very successful." How did such a view develop?

Attitudes

A brief overview of U.S. attitudes can logically begin in 1853 with Commodore Perry's arrival. Perry and his sailors found the Japanese unfailingly polite but prone to lies and evasion–a dichotomy that "helped set a pattern of American thinking about Japanese that has persisted for a century" (Dulles 1965, 68–69).

From 1885 to 1924, Japanese laborers flooded into Hawaii and the West Coast, such that by the 1920s, nearly half of Hawaii's population was first-generation (*issei*) or second-generation (*nisei*) Japanese. U.S. fears of loyalty to immigrants' home countries did not apply equally to all ethnic groups. Anti-Japanese sentiments, which ran especially high, derived from Japan's military strength and its enlarged territory after World War I as well as the high numbers of Japanese residents in U.S. lands. The Hawaiian government, for example, "feared the *nisei* generation would mature into a majority bloc of voting citizens who still paid homage to Japan" (Brislin 1995, 1). Many "yellow peril" cartoons and articles appeared in the mainstream U.S. press (Brislin 1995).

Racism reached a peak in 1924 when Congress reversed U.S. immigration policy, excluding all Asians. Concurrently, the Washington and London naval conferences limited Japan's naval strength relative to the West. Relations entered a negative phase.

In 1941, even though "the Americans were willing to go part way to compromise, they would not consider giving the Japanese a free hand in China" (Ambrose 1988, 13). The attack on Pearl Harbor followed. Ten weeks after the Japanese attack, President Roosevelt issued Executive Order 9066, resulting in the internment of 80,000 U.S. citizens of Japanese descent and 30,000 Japan-born residents in California, Washington and Oregon. Although not one person was charged with espionage or disloyalty, they were held in guarded camps for three years.

During 1941–42, not one West Coast newspaper opposed the internment in editorials. Chiasson (1991, 104) concluded that many of the 27 newspapers he studied in that pre-TV era "seem not to have evaluated governmental policy, but blindly supported it . . . [conveying] messages based upon rumour and not fact."

If the press fanned existing anti-Japanese feeling, what role did racism play in the dropping of the atomic bomb? The "racial factor in the decision cannot be ignored," believes Ambrose (1988, 51), but "the simplest explanation is perhaps the most convincing. The bomb was there. Japan was not surrendering."

Hatred arising from feelings of racial superiority against Asians in general and mistrust of the Japanese in particular as a legacy of Pearl Harbor and World War II is layered with contemporary hatred arising from feelings of economic vulnerability. In recent years, Vincent Chin (mistaken for a Japanese) was killed by two Detroit auto workers, and businessman Yasuo Kato was killed in Los Angeles by a man who blamed Japan for the loss of his job.

But all during the Cold War, the role of Japan as an ally counterbalanced the image of Japan as an economic threat. The "great divide about the Americans' perception of Japan," according to Yoshi Tsurumi ("Images of Japan" 1996), occurred in about 1989, with the fall of the Berlin Wall.

As the 1990s opened, Japan replaced the Soviet Union as America's chief antagonist. A 1989 poll revealed that 68 percent of Americans feared Japan's economic threat more than Russia's military threat. "The Cold War is over," said Paul Tsongas during the 1992 presidential primaries, "and Japan won." It looked as if a trade war might replace the Cold War. Early in his presidency, Bill Clinton took a hard line in attempting to open up Japan's markets to U.S. trade. Trade statistics revealed a $59.3 billion trade surplus with the United States. Still, the United States actually had more trade disputes with Canada than Japan.

Possibly because of media emphasis on Japan, Americans cling to misconceptions about the volume of trade with Japan. U.S. news media cover Japan much more extensively than Canada. For example, the three weekly newsmagazines carried only 24 stories on Canada during 1990–91 but almost five times that many (117) on Japan (Flournoy et al 1992). Erroneously, 78.1 percent of respondents thought in 1991 that the United States imported more from Japan than from Canada, when in fact in 1990 the value of imports from both countries was about the same. When the question turned to free trade, cultural biases were evident. Free trade with Canada was favored by 81.0 percent; with Mexico, by 69.7 percent; but with Japan, by only 58.5 percent (Flournoy et al 1992).

By 1996, attitudes had mellowed toward Japan, which experienced a recession in the early 1990s and lost some of its demonic luster. Meanwhile, trade disputes with a new adversary, China, reached epic proportions. A series of ABC-TV polls shows a dramatic shift in Americans' attitudes ("Images of Japan" 1996). Questions and shifting answers include the following:

1. Are U.S.-Japanese relations good or poor?
   1994: poor, 58 percent; good, 38 percent; 1996: good, 53 percent; poor, 42 percent
2. Are anti-Japanese feelings rising or declining?
   1992: rising, 65 percent; 1996: rising, 23 percent

3. Does Japan practice fair trade with the United States?
1994: yes, 16 percent; 1996: yes, 24 percent

Two East Asia experts agree with this sampled assessment that Japan remains somewhat intransigent on trade but that other issues loom larger than trade. George Packard of Johns Hopkins University believes that the "idea of Japan as a threat is gone," whereas Professor Ezra Vogel of Harvard believes that in about 1994 "both sides realized that we had to continue working with each other, we were partners in world activity" ("Images of Japan" 1996).

Some observers say that with so much media and political attention going to China, "instead of Japan-bashing . . . now we're doing Japan-passing, that we're not paying attention at all" ("Images of Japan" 1996). In fact, the U.S. mass media have never paid a great deal of attention to Japan.

Media Coverage

The United States does not think about Japan as much as Japan thinks about the United States. A report covering 1979–84 found that the Japanese newspaper *Asahi Shimbun* had 671 international articles, of which 42.6 percent dealt with the United States. By contrast, of the *New York Times'* 382 international articles, only 10.2 percent dealt with Japan (Takeichi 1991, 73). Likewise, on television, during a period from fall 1992 to spring 1993, Japan had 37 hours of news relating to the United States, whereas U.S. television had only three hours of news about Japan. Japan focused on U.S. society and culture, and the United States focused on Japanese economics and politics. Similarly, during three months in 1993, TBS covered 15 stories from the United States, whereas CBS covered only three stories from Japan (Cooper-Chen and Sims 1996).

Of all countries, Japan maintains the largest U.S.-based press corps (Germany runs a close second) (U.S. Information Agency 1993). At an average of three correspondents per bureau, Japan has more than 300 people covering the United States, which for its part has only 185 people covering Japan (Kliesch 1991). Thus, the "coverage imbalance" mirrors other imbalances (see Table 1.2): Japan sends more reporters, goods and international students to the United States than vice versa.

The analogy goes even further. Like U.S. businesspeople, journalists complain of formal and informal barriers. Problems include access to public figures, a lack of "bang-bang" (spot news), the reluctance of Japanese sources to do interviews by phone, the need to build rapport over many meetings, and the lack of substance in interviews because Japanese "shy away from accepting responsibility or going out on a limb" (Shifrel 1988, 28). According to Bradley Martin, former *Newsweek* Tokyo bureau chief, who has covered a half-dozen Asian nations, "This country is the most difficult and challenging place to find out what's happening. . . . Not in terms of what so-and-so said, but what is really happening" (Shifrel 1988, 28).

Given these barriers, the U.S. press corps does not cover Japan as well as it should. According to van Wolferen (1993, 305), the foreign press corps (and diplomatic community) rely heavily on the local press. But the corps should use "suspicious scrutiny" in picking apart the constructed (but false) reality the press presents.

Part of the fault emanates from the home front: editors who don't "get it" and readers used to "cherry blossom journalism." According to Bradley Martin, newspapers used to "do the 'gee-whiz, isn't this a peculiar country?' story. . . . The reader didn't notice because there weren't many readers" (Shifrel 1988, 26).

Which U.S. newspapers cover Japan most? With business and economics as the big story, not surprisingly, Flournoy et al (1992) found that the *Wall Street Journal* carried more than twice as many items (news stories, editorials and columns) about Japan (2,284) as did the next most attentive newspaper, the *New York Times* (1,225 items). The *Los Angeles Times* had 843, the *Washington Post* had 660, and all other papers in the study had fewer than 500 during January 1990–September 1991.

What pictures of Japan do U.S. TV networks provide? During 1972–81, Japan ranked 10th in the number of video reports originating from overseas–just behind Poland and just ahead of Italy (Larson 1984). Okabe (1991), who studied CBS coverage of Japan in 1987, found the major portion of newscasts to be neutral but with a larger portion negative than positive. As for topics, economics stood out as far and away *the* Japan story on CBS, with politics barely making a showing on the news.

Even as U.S.-Japan relations become closer, communication becomes more problematic. According to van Wolferen (1993, 6), "The communication gap, dating from the early 1970s, that separates Japan from the West . . . appears to be widening." To begin closing that gap by understanding key concepts and values is the goal of the next chapter.

2
Mass Media: Origins and Functions

The Japanese characters for Nihon mean "sun" and "origin." (The English word "Japan" comes from the South Chinese pronunciation of the characters.) From continental Asia, the sun does appear to rise in the Japanese archipelago. *Asahi* [morning sun] serves as the name of Japan's most prestigious newspaper, the *Asahi Shimbun* (Merrill 1990), as well as a popular brand of beer and numerous other products.

The earliest Japanese chronicle, the *Kojiki* (712 A.D.), tells of a supreme sun goddess, Amaterasu, mythical ancestor of the imperial family line. In the fifth and sixth centuries, worship of the Sun Goddess and other deities was part of a reverence for nature that later coalesced as the Shinto religion. Layered over Shinto and early social practices, Buddhism and Confucianism entered from China.

Along with religion, as a byproduct, Japan also borrowed (and adapted) China's writing system, but its spoken language resembles no other. The Japanese have shared a language and elements of a common culture from prehistoric Jomon times, beginning about 800 B.C. Asserts Reischauer (1981, 8), "the Japanese probably face a bigger language barrier between themselves and the rest of the world than any other major national group." Conversely, outsiders can rarely attain native fluency in Japanese. Today, Westerners seem to bridge the culture of other Asian societies much more easily than Japan's.

Since language renders Japan's mass media inaccessible, most Westerners lose valuable insights about contemporary Japanese life. As with any culture, to understand one facet, one must dig down to see the interplay of influences.

Ten Roots of *Masu Komi*

Today, Japan has one of the world's highest newspaper circulation rates (581 copies per 1,000 people) and highest TV viewing rates (three hours, 32 minutes per person per day). Its rich mass media scene combines Eastern, Western and modern, universal elements. Even the phrase "mass communication" has been borrowed but adapted. The syllabic Japanese language, with vowels attached to each consonant, would make the phrase an unwieldy eight syllables long (the final "n" is one syllable): *ma su ko myu ni ke shyo n.* Every Japanese understands the shorter phrase *ma su ko mi.*

The functioning of Japan's *masu komi* reflects the interplay of sociology, technology and culture. For example, the traditional reverence for nature and an attunement to the changing seasons have an effect on TV content (see Chapter 1). For that matter, the long-standing visual orientation of the Japanese helped make the very acceptance of television smooth and enthusiastic (Head 1985, 22; Kitamura 1987, 144). The ideographic writing system, the rich tradition of painting and wood-block printing, the variety of ceramic and fabric designs, the importance of artistic food and flower arrangements, the attention to packaging—all underscore the observation that "of the five senses, sight is most important in Japan" (Kitamura 1987, 144).

To pull apart the roots of a functioning organism is difficult, but we will draw on the work of experts who have previously identified specific factors that characterize Japanese society. Below, we highlight 10 that have particular relevance to Japan's mass media.

Insularity/Uniqueness

Japan lies 100 miles from Korea and 500 miles from China—in ancient times, truly at the end of the earth. This isolation meant that "the borrowed culture had more chance to develop along new and often unique lines" (Reischauer 1981, 7), free from hordes of invaders. Japan's clothing, cuisine and architecture (including *tatami* mats, *tokonoma* alcoves, *shōji* sliding doors and *hibachi* braziers) diverge from those of all other cultures, including China's.

Japan today "constitutes what may be the world's most perfect nation-state: a clear-cut geographical unit containing almost all the people of a distinctive culture and language and virtually no one else" (Reischauer 1981, 8). The "homogeneity of Japanese society leaves little room for incorporating outside elements, its fabric intricately and finely interwoven to a negative extreme" (Nakane 1988, 6).

While the Japanese "face no problem of national identity" (Reischauer 1981, 6), they carry a negative image as a closed, exclusionary society. Antagonism toward outsiders derives from scarce land and a high population, believes Nakane (1988). Who wants to share one's meager piece of the pie? Regarding Chinese, Koreans and Southeast Asians, Japanese exhibit "ethnocentrism that does not tolerate the way other Asians approach life" (DeVos and Bock 1974, 25). Reischauer (1981, 8) concurs, asserting that the Japanese are "somewhat tense in their contacts with foreigners and they have shown relatively little sensitivity to the feelings and reactions of other people."

To counteract Japan's geographical and psychological insularity, *kokusaika* [internationalization] has "become a sincere goal of Japanese governmental, cultural and educational leaders" (Wray 1990, 17). But, cautions Nakane (1988, 6): "It is the fashion in Japan today to declaim the necessity for 'internationalization.' This I take to be a sure indication that Japan is still a closed society. If it were an open one, there would be no need to talk about internationalization."

Despite a large overseas Japanese press corps (U.S. Information Agency 1993), little overseas coverage reaches the small screen in Japan. Newspapers do a somewhat better job than television in reporting overseas events. But van Wolferen (1993) believes that all mass media reinforce the Japanese sense of uniqueness to a negative degree. "In the absence of an intellectual tradition that vigorously analyses the conventional certainties" (van Wolferen 1993, 356), the media fail to criticize the literature of *Nihonjinron* [theorizing about the Japanese], a genre of writing that explores the supposedly special traits of the Japanese psyche.

In the 1980s, the idea of a "pure" Japanese race resurfaced, for example, in TV serials that portrayed Japanese encounters with foreigners. This purity myth is "accompanied by an increased use in the media of the term *minzoku* to denote the Japanese people" and is related to "the myth of homogeneity" (van Wolferen 1993, 352, 350).

Homogeneity

Conspicuous wealth or poverty makes Japanese uncomfortable. Wealth is more evenly distributed in Japan than in the United States. A person in top management makes 17 times the salary of a typical factory worker in Japan, whereas in the United States the figure for executives is 85 to 100 times that of a factory worker (Maloney 1991a, 6). Senior company executives even use public transportation to get to work (it's faster and easier than driving). An annual government survey revealed that since the mid-1960s, a majority of Japanese—by the 1980s, more than 90 percent—identify themselves as middle class (van Wolferen 1993, 351).

This broad middle class does not concern itself much with distinctions between high and low culture. In Japan, according to Kato (1988, 315), "intellectual snobbery is almost nil . . . conspicuous non-ownership of television . . . is totally alien in Japanese society." Narrowcasting, such as on U.S. cable systems with up to 95 channels, does not exist in Japan. Thus a few broadcast outlets can serve large audiences. For somewhat different reasons, only a few national newspapers dominate the print field. Van Wolferen's (1993, 304) equating of the Japanese press with "the controlled press of the Communist world" glosses over grave differences on specific issues. Yet in general, its sameness can pass for harmony.

Harmony

Japanese stress harmony between the individual and society. Personality attributes such as independence, assertiveness and outspokenness, often positive values in the West, are de-emphasized in favor of working smoothly with others, self-restraint and reticence. Thus the maverick investigative reporter finds minimal respect and encouragement in Japan.

But there is a dark side to harmony, in that "those who publicly express controversial or provocative views here do so increasingly at their own risk" (Jameson 1992). Yasuhiro Okudaira, a professor at International Christian University, Tokyo, elaborates (Jameson 1992): "The media quickly start self-restraint when protests occur. They refuse to take risks. . . . Official freedom of speech is well developed. But socially, Japanese don't have freedom of speech. . . . From the Tokugawa era, Japanese society has been organized on the lines of a village in which it is thought that any different kind of person must be assimilated into a single society. . . . The stronger the wind blows, the more likely the mass media will bend."

The media bend to create a "malleable" reality that "consists not so much of the results of objective observation as of an emotionally constructed picture in which things are portrayed the way they are supposed to be" (van Wolferen 1993, 10)–that is, as harmonious. "Because the Japanese media believe it is their task to help defuse conflict rather than reflect it, much remains unreported" (van Wolferen 1993, 439).

Shusuke Nomura, a self-proclaimed nationalist, decries how media ignore unpopular minority viewpoints that do not fit the "reality" of a harmonious country: "In Japan, freedom of speech doesn't exist. . . . You can speak out, but the Establishment suppresses the dissemination of what is spoken. Journalism should have a critical spirit against those in power" (Jameson 1992).

Keiichi Katsura, a professor at Ritsumeikan University, believes that profits rather than conspiracy or a sense of mission lie behind Japan's bland, homogenized media: "If something really different is taken up, newspapers fear their circulations will drop; TV networks fear sponsors will stop advertising" (Jameson 1992).

Feldman (1993, 199) offers another explanation for harmonious, uncontroversial content: Politics is still a very sensitive issue in Japan, so a story that oversteps a certain line can anger some groups on the left and the right who "will resort to intimidation or even violence against reporters. . . .To avoid such attacks, reporters and desk members are often purposely vague."

Violence

Rates of rape and other violent crimes in Japan are the lowest in the developed world (see Table 1.1), but a swath of violence cuts through Japanese history. Benedict (1946) chose the sword, not just the chrysanthemum, as a symbol for Japan. The Three Imperial Regalia, supposedly of divine origin (but actually dating from about 400 B.C.), are a bronze mirror; a small, comma-shaped gemstone; and a long, iron sword. During the 1400s, the "finely laminated steel swords of Japan, in fact, were the best the world had ever seen and were in great demand abroad" (Reischauer 1981, 65). Today, swords are a weapon of choice for those with violent intent.

In 1994 a man wielding a sword and another toting a gun, both members of the right-wing Taihikai group, took two hostages at the *Asahi Shimbun*'s Tokyo office to protest postwar reporting; no one was injured. Other journalists have not been so lucky. In 1987 one *Asahi Shimbun* reporter was killed and another critically injured by a gunman reportedly allied to an extreme rightist group.

During the 1980s, the Japanese right numbered about 120,000, in some 800 different groups, some of whom rode around in speaker trucks, with flags and banners, booming out military music. In 1989, the Dai Nippon Seisanto, which is linked with the former Black Dragon Society, attacked all the national newspapers for disrespect in minutely covering Emperor Hirohito's last illness (Feldman 1993, 198–99).

Organized crime, religious groups and disgruntled celebrities also lash out at the media. In 1994, a man fired shots in a *Mainichi Shimbun* office because of a Sunday *Mainichi* article on a gang. Earlier, the director of a movie critical of gangsters was slashed in the face and neck. After a magazine ran a story about a star's personal life, the star and 11 friends inflicted bodily injury to the editors (Jameson 1992; Sakata 1995).

Fear of retribution has dampened coverage of gang violence. In January 1990, for example, a war between two organized crime groups broke out in Tokyo's Hachiōji district "with such intensity that riot police were mobilized, shops were shuttered"; however, "little attention was given to the ferocious war between two of Japan's largest crime syndicates" (Hadfield 1991, 16).

Fictional depictions of violence may compensate for a tameness in media portrayals of life which, despite isolated incidents, remains safe and placid. Media aimed at men traditionally serve up graphic, gratuitous gore.

Gender Differentiation

In boys' and men's comic books, or *manga*, one finds page after page of "heads rolling, eyes gouged out and showers of blood" (Schodt 1986, 124). Also in these *manga*, in stories involving women, "rape, incest, lynching, murder, kidnapping, violence and sexual harassment are common scenarios" (Ito, Kinko, 1994, 87) (see Chapters 6 and 12). One comic called "Rape-Man" was finally discontinued (Kristof 1995). Women have an entire comic book industry all to themselves. A minor ripple includes some stories depicting rape fantasies (Kristof 1995), but most spin out starry-eyed romances in exotic or historic settings (see Chapter 6).

As Chapter 1 noted, Japan ranked the highest (95) of all countries on Hofstede's (1984) masculinity scale, indicating extreme gender role differentiation. The separation of gender roles affects mass media in a myriad of ways, from the almost total male domination of reporting as a profession to women's habits as media consumers to the media's portrayal of women.

Popular female stars (*tarento*) do not cultivate overt sexiness, which men find threatening and young women do not wish to emulate. According to Kinoshita (1991, 92): "Just barely past puberty, a *tarento* is a young girl who is plucked from the ranks of amateur beauty pageants and made into a star, with a recording contract, TV appearances, and ad campaigns. No need to be able to sing or act: these girls have the only thing that matters—*kawaii* [cuteness]."

The cult of *kawaii* extends throughout the mass media: cute stuffed animals awarded as prizes on TV quiz shows, cartoonlike voices announcing station breaks, soft-sell commercials showing smiling babies. From their homes in Nagoya, twin sisters Gin ("Silver") Kanie and Kin ("Gold") Narita streaked into local, then national, media prominence after their 100th birthdays on August 1, 1992 ("Kin and Gin" 1992). Asking any Japanese to describe the ancient, diminutive sisters will elicit a one-word answer: *"kawaii!"*

Media sociologist Hidetoshi Kato (personal communication, June

1993) believes the disposable income of young working women, who revel in the cult of *kawaii*, affects the content of all Japanese popular culture. The chapter in *Women, Media and Consumption in Japan* that explains why young women's freedom devised from their oppression is called "Cuties in Japan" (Skov and Moeran 1996). Living with their parents until they marry, single women can enjoy all the affluence of contemporary urban Japan.

Urbanization

Rural Japan has almost ceased to exist. In 1991, 58.2 percent of Japanese lived in cities of 100,000 or more, with half of Japan's population living in just three urban areas: Tokyo, Osaka and Nagoya. Thus newspapers can reach millions of readers through home delivery without the expense of far-flung rural motor routes. With 92.6 percent of newspapers delivered rather than purchased at a newsstand, the subscriber base is stable and the newspaper habit ingrained.

Tokyo, the political and economic capital of Japan, also serves as the media capital. Its urban area of more than 20 million (8.2 million people within the city limits) generates more news than any other region. Also, organizations of all types in Tokyo place bulk subscription orders. And finally, more than 15 percent of the population lives there, representing well over 15 percent of purchasing power.

Of the nation's 125 dailies, the Tokyo Big Three—the *Asahi, Yomiuri* and *Mainichi*—account for 45 percent of daily newspaper circulation. Add in the *Nihon Keizai Shimbun* (a business/economics paper) and *Sankei Shimbun*, likewise published in Tokyo, and those five papers account for 52 percent of circulation. The *Yomiuri* had a 1994 circulation of 9.9 million; the *Asahi*, 8.3 million; and the *Mainichi*, 4.0 million (morning editions only). The TV networks, major advertising and PR agencies and magazine publishing conglomerates likewise have their central headquarters in Tokyo.

Centralization/Concentration

Another form of centralization characterizes Japanese industries, including mass media enterprises: concentration of ownership. In theory, regulations limit newspaper holdings in broadcasting to 10 percent. In practice, however, newspaper subsidiaries' ownership of pieces of a broadcasting group circumvents the rules against cross-ownership. For example, the *Yomiuri Shimbun* owns 10 percent of Nihon TV (NTV); family members of the *Yomiuri* "clan" own percentages individually;

Yomiuriland, a theme park, owns a small percentage; and so on up to a controlling interest by the Yomiuri group of more than 50 percent.

Under similar arrangements, *Mainichi* partly owns the Tokyo Broadcasting System (TBS); *Sankei* owns Fuji TV; *Asahi* owns ABC; and *Nihon Keizai* owns TV Tokyo. Moreover, the newspaper groups own sports dailies, weekly papers, magazines, book enterprises and new media companies. Beyond media, they own such endeavors as sports teams, musical groups and theme parks.

Likewise, to encourage diversity, regulations bar Tokyo TV stations from forming networks throughout Japan. But although local stations have a *tatemae* [surface appearance] of independent operation, the *honne* [underlying truth] reveals that the "key" stations do in fact provide the local stations with more than 80 percent of their programming.

Finally, despite regulations to the contrary, interlocking directorships exist between newspapers and TV stations. At the head of each of the five mass media giants, one person often simultaneously serves as chair of the key TV station and president of the newspaper.

Akhavan-Majid (1990, 1008) warns that control over information flow to the many in the hands of a few means that the "executives and managing editors of these conglomerates hold the power to cover up or reveal any political scandal or to campaign for or against any interest." Lines of allegiance, favoritism and obligation do not include the average citizen.

Loyalty

Japanese live in concentric circles of groups to which they must show loyalty. Japan's vertical system of human relations (Nakane 1970) remains today as a legacy from the structure of early clans. In the family, members traditionally had clear role obligations and a defined place in the family hierarchy, but the father's unquestioned authority has eroded in the past 30 years.

Government bureaucracies and large companies, including mass media organizations, mimic the hierarchical family structure more closely than smaller firms and newer industries. As DeVos and Bock (1974, 17) explain: "Given the familial structure of companies, the advantage of seniority and the strong sense of identity with the organization, it is not surprising that there is little movement from one company to another in Japan. In their hiring practices, companies also find it to their advantage to hire the young and inexperienced, who will then approach their jobs as a lifetime commitment." Lifetime employment affects only those in larger corporations (and applies almost exclusively to male employees, not female).

Once on the job, one's identity rests with the firm. Thus norms of what "a real journalist" should do have less meaning than what a loyal employee should do: work long hours, avoid embarrassment for the firm, get along with one's lifetime colleagues.

The equating of journalism with confrontation does not exist in Japan at the large media companies. The *kisha* club system (discussed below) shows this tendency at its zenith. The covered and the coverers together form a tight group, excluding all others; loyal group members do not tell tales out of school (i.e., print disloyal investigative stories). Even for those journalists (print and broadcast) who do not belong to a club, getting along with one's colleagues counts for more than self-aggrandizement, making waves, writing exposés or crusading for the public.

Loyalty to the firm "has served many Japanese companies and institutions well," but it means that journalists feel allegiance to their employers and colleagues; they "are not seen as independent professionals working in the public interest" (Vanden Heuvel and Dennis 1993, 72–73). Much like bureaucrats, journalists work their way up the promotion ladder, preferring to follow majority opinion and directives from above rather than risk antagonizing lifelong colleagues. Since few free-lance journalists exist in Japan, an outcast reporter literally has nowhere to go (Takeichi 1991).

Education

High school completion rates (see Table 1.1) dramatically delineate the differences between U.S. and Japanese attitudes toward education: 28.4 percent of students drop out in the United States, compared with only 2.2 percent in Japan. Since there are virtually no functional illiterates in Japan, everyone can understand the print media. And because of a longer school year and other factors, high school graduation in Japan indicates a higher level of achievement than in the United States.

Once students pass the grueling entrance examination for the university of their choice, their future is "virtually sealed. The most prestigious companies [including media companies] hire almost exclusively from the top universities, and relationships formed through school ties are important connections to carry through life" (DeVos and Bock 1974, 20). Moving from one school to another is not common in Japan. Thus journalists, politicians and CEOs who attended class together share a lifetime bond. The graduates of Tokyo, Kyoto, Waseda, Keio and certain other top universities, whether working for big media, big industry or big government, form an integrated elite power structure (Akhavan-Majid 1990, 1008).

Getting a job resembles getting into a university. Part of the application involves taking a series of tests. For example, the test to join the *Asahi Shimbun*'s staff of about 10,000 journalists is so difficult that only one in 100 applicants passes.

Since the firm prefers to train (some might say indoctrinate) its own employees, a journalism major with a list of internships has no hiring advantage; indeed, the opposite may hold true. Thus only a few schools offer journalism majors, and none publishes a daily newspaper or requires internships. So new hires, whose university looms larger than their major subject, lack a sense of the profession beyond the culture of their particular organization (see Chapter 11).

Sports and *Seishin*

The culture of most organizations includes golf as a business perk for cementing ties with associates and clients. But with the advent of the five-day work week, Japanese have begun to engage in sports for recreation and golf for non-business purposes. With women jumping onto the sports bandwagon, about 20 percent of Japanese now actively participate in physical activities.

A *Yomiuri Shimbun* poll of March 1992 (Takabatake 1993, 42) revealed sumo as the most popular spectator sport by far, watched by 66 percent of respondents; tournament tickets are sold out for years in advance. Other top sports were professional baseball, 51 percent; marathon and stage relay road races, 43 percent; high school baseball tournaments, 40 percent; volleyball, 27 percent; golf, 21 percent; skiing and skating, 16 percent; gymnastics, 15 percent; and others.

All branches of media feed the hunger. Tokyo has six daily sports newspapers, some with regional editions (which now carry general entertainment news as well as sports). Live TV coverage of the 1992 Olympics surpassed 20 percent, despite the broadcast times of midnight and later.

The abundant and often fawning sports coverage in the mainstream press and on the commercial TV networks results partly from the "strange tie between the nation's newspapers and baseball" (Tokuoka 1983, 6). *Yomiuri* owns the Yomiuri Giants, and *Asahi* and *Mainichi* sponsor high school baseball tournaments; these newspapers in turn each control a TV network. The 4 million–circulation Nagoya-based *Chūnichi Shimbun* owns the Chunichi Dragons. In journalism's baseball "sanctuary," reporters "present as good as possible images of their pet players" (Tokuoka 1983, 6).

Even the 7–8 p.m. national news of the non-commercial Japan Broadcasting Corp. (NHK, Japan's equivalent of the non-commercial BBC) includes 15 minutes of sports; imagine PBS's "McNeil-Lehrer News Hour" devoting 25 percent of its time to sports. Moreover, NHK broadcasts live each of the six yearly 15-day sumo tournaments. Since NHK assumes the role of "Japanifying" rather than internationalizing its audience (Cooper-Chen 1995), NHK finds this ancient sport appropriate fare. Its highest sumo rating, a phenomenal 64.2 percent, occurred in January 1992 when two ōzeki [champions] from opposing stables fought each other.

But sports reporting does not dwell exclusively on winning. A competitor need not win an Olympic medal as long as he or she has *seishin*. This set of qualities, meaning literally "mind" or "spirit," is "an elusive and elastic set of ideas that make up an integral part of the Japanese cultural identity" (May 1988, 2). According to Reischauer (1981, 210), exaggeration of the importance of *seishin* played a part in the unrealistic expectations Japan harbored before and during World War II. The Japanese "counted heavily on their own moral superiority, the 'Japanese spirit.'"

That same spirit has propelled Japan to its position as the world's second greatest economic power. As some would have it, its sterling economy far outdistances its mediocre politics.

Mass Media and Politics

The Japanese describe themselves as "a country with a first-rate economy and third-rate politics" (Ito 1993b, 77). To this assessment some would add, "and a second-rate media." A media-government coziness exists that surprises most Westerners, creating "a significant difference between what they [Westerners] call journalism and what exists in Japan" (Vanden Heuvel and Dennis 1993, 72–73).

The Power of the Press

Japan ranks as one of 67 countries in the world—and one of a handful in Asia—with a free press system (Sussman 1993). Some writers even categorize Japan as Western (e.g., Stevenson 1993). However, Akhavan-Majid (1990, 1006) cautions against an "almost Western" assessment of Japan's press system, which has "inherent structural differences with the Libertarian model"; Japan's "altogether different" press exercises "reverse control on the ruling elite, even as it is controlled by it."

In some countries, journalists stand on the outside looking in, hoping to arouse or alert the public, whose voices in turn might change government policy. In Japan, the press–by virtue of its "integration into the elite power structure"–exercises "direct participation in government policy-making structures and process" (Akhavan-Majid 1990, 1006). Mechanisms of centralization/concentration and the bond of education (see above) enhance the political power of the industry.

For example, a revolving door system of personnel exchanges, called *amakudari* [descent from heaven], exists involving regulators and those they formerly regulated. Commonly, retired high-level bureaucrats from the Ministry of Posts and Telecommunications (MPT) move into top executive positions in the media industry, cementing the "overlap between various elite power groups in Japan" (Akhavan-Majid 1990, 1009).

The press in Japan traditionally has stood on the inside, allied with the government, looking out at the public. From time to time, however, certain issues have divided the press and the government (see Chapter 3). Previously, when "public political consciousness was relatively low," Japan had a "bipolar system of the government versus the press" (Tsujimura 1994, 25). Today, a tripolar system with a stronger role for the public is emerging (Tsujimura 1994; Ito 1993c, 1994).

People, Press and Politics

At this writing, Japan's politics and political news-gathering system are both in a state of flux. Postwar Japan used to be described as a country with a one-and-a-half party system (all opposition parties counted for half against the Big One, the Liberal Democratic Party, or LDP). Then in Japan's July 1993 election, the most important since the end of the war, the LDP lost its 38-year hold on power. (It remained a part of the Murayama cabinet and a leading party in the House of Representatives. In 1996, an LDP man, Ryutaro Hashimoto, once again held the prime minister's post.)

In 1995, the July 23 upper house election showed the Japanese voters' continuing "depth of antipathy for the Liberal Democratic Party" (Barr 1995, 5); instead of the LDP, the New Frontier Party, just seven months old, took first place in the balloting. However, most citizens simply stayed away from the polls on election day, perhaps because "they were too disgusted with politics to vote" (Barr 1995, 5).

In a free society, citizens do have to make political decisions. Yet Japanese lack direct knowledge of politics, since the level of active participation in politics is generally low (Kawakami and Feldman, 1988).

Because of "a long history of feudalism, the Japanese, especially in rural constituencies, tend to leave decisions on difficult matters to *okami* [people above us]" (Ito 1993b, 73). Also, reticence and unwillingness to go out on a limb to express opinions (Gudykunst and Nishida 1994) mean Japanese do not usually have arguments or discussions about politics. Thus compared with other countries, people in Japan rely more heavily on mass media for political information (Edelstein, Ito and Kepplinger 1989, 206).

But Japanese, especially younger Japanese, have well nigh given up on the media, according to a poll taken in April 1993. Half of respondents (51 percent) said newspapers were pursuing their watchdog role over politics reasonably well, whereas 46 percent said they were not (3 percent didn't know). Older people held more favorable opinions, but 60 percent of people younger than 30 held a negative view. Similarly, more than half of people in their 20s and 30s said newspapers did not provide enough information to judge politics and scandals (overall, 56 percent found such information adequate).

Citizens are cynical about and uninvolved in politics because of journalistic practices, says Feldman (1993, 201): "The lack of detailed coverage of political events and the difficulty in understanding stories tends to divert readers from political stories to the easier ones, such as social reportage." Critics concur that the people's need to know often gets short shrift: "The Japanese press will usually decide what is or is not news by reference to 'the national interest' rather than to the public's right to know. In this sense, little has changed since the days of press censorship during the war" (Hadfield 1991, 15–16). The citizen/consumer's low rank in the "need to know" hierarchy prompts van Wolferen (1993, 132) to complain that the press reacts only "to such excesses as actually threaten to disturb the social order."

A Japanese media analyst, Takeshi Maezawa, thinks that loyalty (see above) explains journalists' disregard for the public. Maezawa (Vanden Heuvel and Dennis 1993, 76) asks journalists not for "an end to loyalty but a switching of loyalties"–from sources and colleagues to readers and viewers.

Covering Nagatacho

Hordes of political reporters roam around Nagatacho, Tokyo, the Capitol Hill of Japan. Located here are the national Diet (the main body of power), the prime minister's official residence, the offices of Diet members, the Diet Press Club and the headquarters of the major political parties. Badges on their lapels and special photo ID cards permit reporters to move freely around the huge Diet Building complex: in and out of various committee rooms, the plenary chamber and even the restaurant. All day and into the night, in the three huge seven-story office buildings across the road behind the Diet Building, journalists visit with members of the House of Representatives and House of Councilors (Feldman 1993, 33).

"Nagatacho" is a synonym for Japanese politics in general. Not surprisingly, Western journalists (Shifrel 1988; Hadfield 1991; Sherman 1990; van Wolferen 1993) equate the coziness between Japanese journalists and the political establishment as a process of covering *up* rather than covering Nagatacho.

In Japan, when it comes to investigative reporting, bigger does not by a long stretch mean better. The influential and enormous NHK, with its 16,000 employees, traditionally exercised clout "simply by failing to challenge the powers that be. . . . Some staff members at the NHK complex in Tokyo used to refer to the evening news as 'The LDP Hour'" (Sanger 1993).

Similarly, the Big Five newspapers deign not to challenge the political powers that be. They have been scooped "on several of the biggest political stories in the post-war era–scooped, moreover, by weekly magazines . . . out of the mainstream" (Sherman 1990, 37). The magazines provide most of the raw, political backroom stories, or *ura*, that reach the public. By contrast, the mainstream media provide the "Nagatacho *gyōkaishi*" [the Industry Pages of Nagatacho]–coverage of routine political activities in the Nagatacho district of Tokyo, such as regular sessions of the Diet, important committee meetings, press conferences and activities of Diet members (Feldman 1993, 196). Thus the concepts of *tatemae* [surface presentation, public face] and *honne* [real intentions, inner thoughts] as practiced in interpersonal communication (Lebra 1976) have their counterparts in political reporting.

The penchant of the Japanese press for not naming sources makes many readers "wonder about the real intentions of the anonymous source" (Feldman 1993, 200). Often such information comes from a *kishakon* [off-the-record meeting], a *memokon* [meeting in which reporters cannot use a tape recorder or video camera but can take notes] or *hikōshiki hatsugen* [an informal statement from the source that is not supposed to be published]. The ubiquitous phrase *suji mono* [according to the related people] serves as "the source for nearly 90 percent of all political stories" (Feldman 1993, 201). Other weasel words used to protect sources include *seifu shuno* [a top government official], *gaimusho shuno* [a top official in the Ministry of Foreign Affairs], *tōshuno* [a leader of a political party], *seifu suji* [a source within the government], *zaikai kankeisha* [a source related to economic circles] and *shushō shūhen* [a source close to the prime minister].

In addition to anonymous attribution, readers have to put up with murky writing, overly general descriptions of the political process and events and tortured syntax. Common expressions include *nariso* [it looks as if], *to iwareru* [it is said that] and *to mirareru* [it can be said to appear as if]. A reporter may even resort to a cumbersome phrase such as "the conditions are getting stronger toward a direction such as" (Feldman 1993, 196–97).

Reporters seem to be writing for political insiders rather than the average reader. They use vague language in their stories not only to protect sources but also so as not to anger fellow journalists. After all, they belong, literally, to the same club.

The *Kisha* Club System

The *kisha* club system absorbs the lion's share of criticism about the mass media's political function. "We call the press clubs geisha clubs," says Takeshi Maezawa, a media critic, "because some years ago most geisha girls had sponsors in Japanese society. In the *kisha* clubs, the sponsors are the politicians and the *kisha* play the role of geishas" (Sherman 1990, 39).

Not wishing to alienate sponsors or cut off information flow, reporters avoid scoops like the plague. Without equivocation, Dutch journalist Karel van Wolferen states that "nowhere else in the industrialized world is self-censorship so systematic" (Vanden Heuvel and Dennis 1993, 73). Yet almost with a touch of pride, Hoshiyama (1994, 29) says that the *kisha* club system "has no parallel in the world" and is difficult for foreigners to understand. Hirose (1994, 73) points out two merits of the system: its efficiency as a news diffusion mechanism and the "collective security" it gives to reporters who know they will not miss a story. On the other hand, the system promotes laziness, reduces journalists to message carriers and creates uniformity of content.

Japanese reporters themselves have mixed feelings about the clubs. In a November 1993 poll of 1,735 journalists by the Japan Newspaper Editors and Publishers Association (Nihon Shimbun Kyokai, or NSK) (Akao 1995), 40.9 percent said the system should probably or definitely continue; 27.2 percent said it should probably or definitely be abolished; and 30.9 percent were ambivalent. What is this system that less than half of journalists themselves support?

Structure and Operations

More than 1,000 entities in Japan (400 in Tokyo alone) each allocate a large room for use by reporters on that beat: the national Diet, regional assemblies, police, political parties and major economic organizations. The most important clubs, with membership in the hundreds, cover the prime minister (the Nagata Club) and the LDP (the Hirakawa Club).

The 15 major Japanese news media companies dominate the clubs: the Big Five newspapers; three bloc newspapers (Hokkaido, Chunichi and Nishi Nippon groups); five television networks (NHK and four commercial companies); and two news agencies (Kyodo and Jiji). Each company pays a monthly membership fee per reporter (*kurabu kaihi*). Only journalists who work for the 114 member companies of the NSK and Nihon Minkan Hoso Renmei (The National Association of Commercial Broadcasters in Japan) may join the clubs. Reporters who work for political parties, religious organizations, unions, periodicals and magazines may not join the clubs (Feldman 1993, 70).

Reporters from the same news media company assigned to the same press club constitute a team (*chimu*), which operates from its own minioffice at the press club. An experienced team member, the captain (*kyappu*), supervises the writing of stories. After arriving at the club directly from their homes in the late morning, the reporters hold a daily team meeting. They keep in contact with their headquarters by telephone but work autonomously. Although at times the desk assigns stories, the team largely decides what to cover and how to cover it (Feldman 1993, 74).

When team members get wind of scandals, loyalty to their sources precludes them from revealing the story. In fact, according to Maezawa, "major scandals over the past two decades were first disclosed by other media, such as magazines, or the foreign media" or police (Vanden Heuvel and Dennis 1993, 73). The foreign media's stories about Japan both benefit and worry Japanese journalists, so the *kisha* clubs for many years kept foreigners at arm's length.

Finally, in response to years of complaints, on November 12, 1992, the Kasumi Club, attached to the Ministry of Foreign Affairs, admitted the Associated Press and Reuters as regular members, as long as they asked all questions in Japanese. Then on June 10, 1993, NSK's Editorial Affairs Committee approved a new guideline, stating, "The Kisha Clubs, as a matter of principle, should grant full membership to foreign correspondents who wish to join." And even though Japanese magazines are barred, "special consideration is sought for foreign magazines that report news as their primary task" (Hoshiyama 1994, 30).

After the change, foreign reporters eagerly joined the Kunai Kisha Kai of the Imperial Household Agency, the Kabuto Club of the Tokyo Stock Exchange, the Kinyu Club of the Bank of Japan, the Keizai Kenkyukai of the Economic Planning Agency, the Zaisei Kenkyukai of the Ministry of Finance and the Kisha Kai of the Ministry of International Trade and Industry.

In July 1993, the century-old system (it started in 1890 when the national Diet was established) experienced a further shake-up when the LDP lost its postwar political dominance (see Chapter 3). Because a coalition government took power, "the number of reporters allocated to each political party's press club changed greatly" (Hirose 1994, 72). Some press clubs even abolished the *kondan* [background talks] (discussed below). But the system itself remained in place; if anything, it grew more complex than the processes described below.

Inside the *Ban*

The *ban kisha* [beat or watch reporters], who represent the Big Five newspapers and often also one reporter from each wire service, are a special Japanese "in" group. The core group of five or seven, which follows one particular person all day long and into the night, can grow to as many as 15 when a hot issue develops.

Each *ban* has a secretary who arranges group meetings with the Diet members that the group is covering. Usually, a *ban* has two or three secretaries appointed for a term of two months, one from a newspaper and the other from an "unconnected" (no cross-ownership ties) TV network.

Among *ban* within the Nagata Club are the *kanbofukuchokan-ban*, covering the deputy chief cabinet secretary, the *kanbochokan-ban*, covering the chief cabinet secretary and, most important, the *sōri ban* or *shushō ban*, covering the *sōri* (prime minister). A rookie reporter normally serves in this *ban* from 12 to 18 months. According to Feldman (1993, 82): "During this time, the reporter's ability to gather information and write stories is carefully examined and judged by the captain of the team, the desk members, and the political editor. Once reporters are evaluated as fitting to serve on the political section, they will be given their next assignment, usually for one or two years."

Serving as pool reporters, two men from the Kyodo News Service and Jiji Press even follow the prime minister's car whenever he drives through the streets of Tokyo with his bodyguards (Feldman 1993, 83).

Press conferences, held for press club members, provide the *tatemae* [surface account] for public consumption. In addition, Diet members often give *kondan* [background talks] in their own offices for a few reporters. Equally as useful for gaining *honne* [the underlying truth] are *yo uchi* [night attacks], which take place at about 8–10 p.m. at a Diet member's home, with whiskey or snacks served by the Diet member's wife; thus reporters have several hours to write stories before morning edition deadlines. Although reporters are prohibited from entering Diet members' homes unless invited, they wait obtrusively near the gate, such that as Diet members gain power, they feel more and more like captives of the press.

In the mid-1980s, Feldman (1993) interviewed both Diet members and reporters in person and with questionnaires. Reporters told him that press conferences provide them with about 20 percent of the information concerning a given issue, and the *kondan* and the night attack provide them with the other 80 percent. According to a reporter: "The information that I bring to the desk, claiming it was obtained at a kondan (or 'night attack'), will be evaluated more highly than information obtained at regular press conferences. Editors tend to publish such information without hesitation or further verification" (Feldman 1993, 92).

Newspapers view the informal channels as so important that they provide cars and drivers to chauffeur reporters from one source's home to another for the late night chats and snacks. Such close, sustained contact with politicians in a comfortable, men's club atmosphere has made reporters participants in rather than just observers of Japan's political process. During negotiations, when politicians need to hammer out an agreement or build a consensus, reporters serve as go-betweens. A reporter may well ask a colleague at his newspaper to carry a message from "his" source to the colleague's source. As one Diet member, the leader of a large faction, put it: "People tend to think that our faction consists of 120 members, but actually we have 125; the other five are the reporters from the 'big five' newspapers who cover our faction [and give] useful personal counsel and suggestions" (Feldman 1993, 178).

The power to affect the destiny of the nation gives Japanese journalists a special brand of Potomac (or Sumida River) fever that can pale beside the reporting of routine news. The press club system bestows on them political clout but restricts their freedom to report to the public.

However, the limitations of the club system do not mean a complete absence of investigative reporting. Reporters on non-government beats often write about events and trends of social significance. Moreover, mass media often criticize the government despite the restrictions of the club system. Criticism can come from non-staff pundits who write columns or voice opinions on television.

Still, ordinary citizens do not benefit from "the sensitivity shown by the major media to officialdom" (Sherman 1990, 40). On the other hand, when private people become caught up in public matters, the media take a no-holds-barred approach. Chapter 3 will put this idea and others from Chapter 2 into perspective by looking at events that the media both reported and helped to shape.

3
Case Studies: News in the 1990s

As Chapter 2 explained, values, institutions and practices affect the reporting of news stories. Some practices are universal, such as the need to meet deadlines, and some are unique to Japan, such as the way the *kisha* club system functions. This chapter will discuss six major occurrences in Japan in the 1990s and show how the factors described in Chapter 2 impinged on the reporting process and product.

Making News

Major news stories of the past can provide a context for recent events. Using *Asahi Shimbun* editorials to represent "the press" and *Asahi Shimbun* polls to represent "public opinion," Tsujimura (1994) found various degrees of public/press concord and discord with government. Even though poll taking is "not compatible with either the Japanese character or the Japanese language" (Nishihara 1987, 166), the people of Japan, ever curious to know what others think, love to read poll results. Newspapers, which still conduct more than half of national polls, took the lead in instituting public opinion surveys (the *Mainichi Shimbun* took the first nationwide poll, on middle school entrance examinations, in May 1940).

Quite often, the three forces of press, government and the public will all favor a course of action, such as long-standing support for reclaiming territories from the Soviet Union that Japan lost at the end of World War II. In another possible pattern, the government and public can line up against the press, as when the *Asahi Shimbun* opposed terms of the 1952 peace treaty that officially ended World War II. Alternatively, the government might find itself opposing both the press and the public (e.g., regarding the U.S.-Japan Security Treaty in 1960). Or the press might support a movement that the government and public oppose (e.g, the *Asahi* stood behind striking railway workers in 1975). In a much more rare situation, the public can stand opposed to the press and the government (e.g., on the restoration of Japan-China diplomatic relations in 1972).

The Tanaka scandal of the 1970s holds some valuable lessons about what happens when the press and the public confront the government. In August 1972, a month after Kakuei Tanaka assumed the prime minister's post, he registered the highest popularity (62 percent) ever recorded by a postwar prime minister. However, in 1974, articles by Takashi Tachibana and Takaya Kodama in the magazine *Bungei Shunjū* exposed Tanaka's shady financial land deals. The mainstream press broached the topic only after the magazine articles came out.

The mainstream press "took advantage of rising public opinion instead of taking the leadership in urging the Prime Minister to resign" (Tsujimura 1994, 39). The popularity of the Tanaka cabinet plunged to 27 percent as early as April 1973 and then nosedived in November, before he resigned, to only 12 percent. The Kishi cabinet during the 1960 Japan-U.S. Treaty turmoil had the same low rank. In the Tanaka case, the non-mainstream press, then public opinion and finally the mainstream press converged against the government.

Since the group-oriented *kisha* system discourages scoops, individual journalists can use its "pack" mentality creatively by tipping off a non-establishment mass medium to push a story into the public domain. "Non-establishment" usually means Japanese magazines, foreign newspapers or both.

In 1989, the *Mainichi Shimbun* learned that Prime Minister Sosuke Ono had a mistress but did not break the story. Instead, it passed it along to the related *Sunday Mainichi* magazine, whose reporters do not belong to any *kisha* clubs. The mainstream press still did nothing until *Mainichi* editor Shuntaro Torigoe faxed the story to foreign bureaus, whereupon the *Washington Post* picked it up. Then Manae Kubota, a female Socialist Diet member, cited the *Post* article in a speech, eventually causing Ono to resign for bringing shame to the Japanese nation.

A type of non-political reporting whereby the press leads public opinion is called in Japan a *mondai* [problem, issue or question]: "From time to time, the Japanese nation throws itself on a particular subject with a real vengeance as the media hit it day after day" (van Wolferen 1993, 130). One *mondai*, school bullying, surfaces frequently. A middle school student suffocated in 1993 when classmates, who had teased him constantly, wrapped him up in a mat and did not let him out. However, "Most press-generated mondai are on the front pages for a couple of months at the most. But during this time it is predictable what coffee shop and bar conversations will be. Alternative opinions about the mondai of the month, other than those the media make current, would be surprising" (van Wolferen 1993, 130).

The following cases represent a mixture of important political, natural disaster, crime and nationhood issues. However, lest we leave the wrong impression of a press always concerned with weighty matters, we must mention a penchant in the Japanese mass media for domestic trivia, which often swamp more substantive stories.

In 1993, in a Tokyo park, a reporter spotted a duck that someone had shot with an arrow. The arrow had pierced the duck in such a way that it missed vital organs and spared the duck's life; it was even able to fly. As officials tried to capture the duck, the story grew bigger and bigger, often leading the TV national news. Likewise, newspapers "gave the poor duck the kind of attention that Madonna's publicity managers only dream of" (Fukunaga 1993, 5).

On February 12, 1993, the duck was captured and the arrow successfully extracted. TBS-TV led its national newscast with a five-minute report of the incident, including models of the duck, X-rays of the arrow and two on-location reporters. Japan Broadcasting Corp. (NHK) had the *yagamo* [arrow duck] as its sixth story on February 12, giving it a generous two minutes, 16 seconds.

On February 15–possibly as an echo of the injured duck story–TBS devoted one minute, 34 seconds of its national newscast to video of a cat that had injured its foot when it got caught in a trap. On February 15, no news from anywhere outside Japan appeared on TBS. A magazine editor (Fukunaga 1993, 5) decries this "insane rush to cover a minor story, then blow it up out of all proportion and keep it in the public eye day after day. . . . The fault lies not with the general public, but with the media which are supposed to serve them."

But do they? The following cases will delve into the relations among the mass media, the public and the government.

1990: Japanese Forces to Kuwait?

Article 9 of the Japanese "peace" Constitution reads:

> Aspiring sincerely to an international peace based on justice and order, the Japanese people forever renounce war as a sovereign right of the nation and the threat or use of force as means of settling international disputes.
>
> In order to accomplish the aim of the preceding paragraph, land, sea, and air forces, as well as other war potential, will never be maintained. The right of belligerency of the state will not be recognized.

Chapter 7, Article 43, of the U.N. charter authorizes U.N. forces for peacekeeping missions. Japan belongs to the United Nations and, according to political leader Ichiro Ozawa, U.S. Ambassador Walter Mondale and many others, deserves a seat on the Security Council. But can it take such a seat without committing its own people? And can it send forces overseas when its Constitution forbids the use of force? Japanese governments "traditionally have taken the view that the activities of the Japanese Self Defense Force is limited to pure self-defense against direct attack and participation in the UN Forces is not allowed" (Ito 1993c, 274).

After Iraq invaded Kuwait on August 2, 1990, President George Bush asked Japan for help. By way of an answer, Prime Minister Toshiki Kaifu proposed and the cabinet approved a new law to permit Japanese peacekeeping activities, such as surveillance and medical services, outside of Japan. It was then sent to the Diet.

The fate of the bill rested on the three poles described above: press, public and political. To discern how the political wind would blow, the *Asahi Shimbun* sent questionnaires to all 510 lower house Diet members, with a 78 percent response rate. Results showed that 11 percent of Liberal Democratic Party (LDP) members and 100 percent of opposition members opposed the bill.

The press itself was split. The *Asahi* and *Mainichi* "are close to leftist opposition parties" (Ito 1993a, 276), whereas the *Yomiuri* and *Keizai* are close to the LDP–attitudes clearly reflected in their editorials. The editorials in the *Yomiuri* supported the bill, and the *Asahi* opposed it. The *Keizai* was neutral. The *Mainichi*'s stance was not clear.

Public opinion was against the bill. In October 1990, an *Asahi* survey found that 21 percent supported the U.N. Peace Cooperation bill, whereas 58 percent opposed it. Women opposed the bill in greater numbers than men. The Kaifu government also lost popularity because of the bill. Supporters dropped from 60 to 48 percent between July and November. On November 5, Kaifu and the LDP dropped the bill.

The dominant *kuuki* [air, atmosphere] created by the three poles or sectors blew against the bill. *Kuuki* "is a kind of pressure that has direction and intensity. It makes people with minority opinions silent" (Ito 1994, 16). After the Gulf War ended, the *kuuki* changed (Ito 1994). Kaifu dispatched minesweepers to the Persian Gulf in April 1991 with only minor resistance. In June 1992, under the Miyazawa Administration, the U.N. Peace Keeping Operation Cooperation Bill (PKO) was passed. Under this bill, a construction unit of the Self Defense Force went to Cambodia in September 1992. One Japanese policeman and one civilian volunteer working as an election monitor were killed.

1991: Volcanic Disaster on Kyushu; 1995: The Kobe Earthquake

Mt. Fugendake, a volcano in Nagasaki Prefecture on Kyushu (Japan's southernmost main island), started erupting in November 1990, after having lain dormant for about 200 years. Suddenly, on June 3, 1991, a pyroclastic flow of ashes, hot rocks and gas raced down the side of the volcano at 60 miles per hour, killing 43 people, including 16 reporters and cameramen and taxi drivers they had hired.

The victims, engulfed in just seconds, had assembled every day at a vantage point that offered an excellent view of the active volcano—even though the spot had been designated as an off-limits evacuation zone. Reporter Tsugikazu Tainaka of the *Yomiuri*'s Osaka bureau, who took a photo a moment before he died, posthumously received a Japan Newspaper Editors and Publishers Association (NSK) 1991 Photography Award. One of the most lethal assignments ever for Japanese journalists, "this disaster has taught a lesson to the Japanese press as to the need to pay more attention to safety precautions" (Yamada 1992, 17).

Local residents suffered not only from the volcano but from the journalists who descended on the Unzen area and stayed until about June 12. Had media people not ignored warnings about restricted areas, volunteer firefighters, who assisted them and had to guard the empty houses of evacuees, might have survived. Four people told the magazine *Hōsō Report* ("*Dai ka sairyu*" 1992, 2–6) about the journalists' insensitive, unprofessional and downright life-threatening behavior. Two complained about press vehicles parked illegally on roadways, even though residents had to put their cars in certain parking lots so that police and fire vehicles could get around. But the parked press vehicles obstructed them. An owner of a house burned by the volcanic flow stated, "When I returned to my home to fetch something, a media car was parked in front of it. Since the car had no key in it, I couldn't move it, so it took me a long time to take out my things from the house." Another villager complained that three TV satellite trucks were parked in front of the Shimabara City Hall.

Villagers felt the media people took advantage of them. Some used phones and electricity in empty houses without getting permission. According to one woman, "One TV crew member used my phone 40 minutes and gave me only a telephone card, worth about 500 or 1,000 yen. At the beginning, I trusted them, but I found out that they were using our naivete (*sobokusa*)."

As the subjects of media reports, the residents took issue with the techniques and approaches of the press. After the June 3 disaster, according to one woman: "Media people kept asking survivors only 'How do you feel now?' . . . When famous public figures came to see us at an evacuation center, reporters and cameramen followed them, standing in our way and making it unable for us to see them speaking. I was also annoyed at the same questions by different reporters of the same news-gathering company. I said, 'Don't you pass over information to your colleagues with each other?'"

One man felt that when they "took pictures of angry, sobbing, or confrontational people," the media made "evacuees' stress and dissatisfaction" even worse. And missing were reports showing people what to do in a similar disaster. Said one person: "This type of problem is not only applicable to Shimabara, but also to Japan itself, which is an archipelago with volcanoes. I would like media people willingly to release the information they had acquired."

The villagers' impressions of the noisy, trespassing, penny-pinching media people ranged from "my hatred for media wouldn't diminish for the rest of my life" to "I was very angry at media" to "the worst part of this disaster was the mass media."

Putting citizens at the bottom of the pecking order and treating them shabbily when disaster strikes has been a long-standing problem (Nakasa 1987, 45–46). When a Japan Air Lines jumbo jet crashed in August 1985, reporters swarmed around bereaved families and the four survivors. Suicides of young students routinely bring hordes of journalists interviewing the victims' classmates.

The mass media did a better job when an earthquake of magnitude 7.2 jolted central Japan, including the city of Kobe, at 5:46 a.m. on January 17, 1995. The quake killed about 5,500 people, destroyed or damaged more than 150,000 homes and forced more than 200,000 people to take shelter.

Initially, radio proved a godsend, according to 56 local residents interviewed after the quake (February 26 to March 1). As power was restored, survivors turned to television for up-to-the-minute information (Takagi 1995, 35). With NHK leading the way by mobilizing 1,000 employees, TV networks told survivors who was safe, who was seeking relatives, which supermarkets were operating and which trains had returned to service.

Newspapers played a unique role. As one survivor said, "The first thing I checked is how the railway is being restored and the time at which the bus comes around. I do not have to put it down on paper. I just clip it and use it" (Takagi 1995, 35). The *Kobe Shimbun* even managed to get an evening paper out on January 17 by using the facilities of the *Kyoto*

Shimbun under the terms of a contingency plan already in place. The experience prompted other local papers to reach agreements with those nearby.

To distribute the news in the absence of open freeways, newspapers used boats, helicopters and anything else that moved. To gather news, reporters used motorbikes, bicycles and even helicopters. However, some complained that helicopters muffled the cries for help of people trapped under the rubble.

Victims also criticized photographers for pointing cameras at them without getting consent, and shelter workers and municipal officials complained of too many telephone calls from the mass media at a time when they were the busiest right after the earthquake. Finally, readers said stories on relief measures should clearly distinguish between definite decisions, pending decisions and possible decisions.

1991–93: The Prince Seeks a Princess

Who would be the future empress of Japan? Since the mid-1980s, newspapers, television, and weekly and monthly magazines had been "engaged in [a] news-gathering and reporting competition" (Yamada 1993, 16) regarding the marriage plans of Crown Prince Naruhito. The extreme deference the mass media showed to the imperial family had its mirror opposite in the treatment of commoners who had not yet stepped behind the sheltered "chrysanthemum curtain" that surrounded the imperial family. Indeed, some potential brides reportedly dropped out of the "competition" because the press hounded them mercilessly.

When Japan's most eligible bachelor began to seriously search for a mate (his younger brother having already married), the Imperial Household Agency, which closely controls information flow about the imperial family, wanted its *kisha*–about 450 reporters–to step away from their biggest story. Thus in July 1991, Shoichi Fujimori, grand steward of the Imperial Household Agency, appealed to the NSK for "a quiet and restrained atmosphere," citing "a lot of private factors such as a meeting between two people and cultivating understanding between them" (Yamada 1993, 16). Back in 1958, the press had agreed to do just that when the present emperor was courting the present empress (they married on April 10, 1959).

After an airing of "violent arguments both pro and against" (Yamada 1993, 16), NSK finally in February 1992 agreed (1) not to report on possible bride candidates or details of the selection processes for three months, and (2) to respect the rights and the privacy of any bride candidate. After the National Association of Commercial Broadcasters in Japan (NAB) and the Japan Magazine Publishers Association concluded similar agreements, all princess bride stories stopped.

For its part, the Imperial Household Agency agreed to brief NSK members at least once a month on how the selection was progressing. But it did not hold up its end of the bargain. Briefings gave no hint of progress, when in fact the prince, 32, had proposed to Masako Owada, 29, on October 3. The agency got three extensions of the blackout, yet "had not even dropped a hint" (Yamada 1993, 16) about the course of events even after the couple got engaged on December 12, 1992–rendering the ban an anachronism.

Some Japanese reporters had learned the happy news, but they continued to honor the embargo. On January 6, 1993, the *Washington Post*, not covered by the agreement, carried a report from Tokyo that Owada has been informally picked as the bride for the crown prince and that the Imperial Household Council might meet on January 19 to formalize the engagement. Reuters, The Associated Press and other foreign news agencies picked up the story with a sense of déjà vu; the foreign media had also broken the story of the present emperor's engagement in 1958.

NSK held an emergency meeting the same day and decided to withdraw the agreement as of 8:45 p.m., whereupon "the stunning energy of Japan's mass media kicked into high gear" (Watanabe 1993, 5). Some 300 reporters camped outside the Owada home, where the Harvard graduate lived with her family. TV stations interrupted programming, and newspapers–even sports tabloids–put out special editions. The two appeared together for the first time at a press conference, televised live, on January 19 after the Imperial Household Council had approved the engagement that morning.

With the same details repeated by all stations, many people got bored and watched alternate programming. Yet among all the words, none broached "such sensitive questions as whether the worldly career woman really fell for the prince or just succumbed to ferocious pressure to sacrifice herself for the national interest," underscoring "how carefully Japan's journalists must tread when it comes to the royal family" (Watanabe 1993, 5).

The Imperial Household Council formally approved the choice of Owada as the future crown princess January 19, setting off another media blitz. TBS ran the longest broadcast, eight hours and 40 minutes, while TV Tokyo had only three hours. Three TV stations began to sell 15-second congratulatory spots on and after that date, at ¥300,000 to ¥500,000.

The wedding on June 9 made international headlines. Japan's June bride even made the cover of *Newsweek* (May 24) in the United States, but some Japanese did not like the headline "Reluctant Princess." In fact, Owada had had serious reservations, having taken two months to answer "yes" to the prince's proposal. At earlier meetings between Owada and the prince in 1986–87, the media hounding bothered Owada so much that she took herself out of the running.

Indeed, Grand Steward Fujimori of the Imperial Household Agency told the press that without their help "the selection of the bride for the Crown Prince could not have progressed so smoothly" (Yamada 1993, 17). Even for journalists, the ban had some advantages. Said one reporter, "I myself was not so interested as to follow every woman . . . we did not have to waste our time or worry about the others getting a scoop." And since the ban did result in a new future empress, it "served the national interest . . . the media have the right not to report," said another ("Media disagree" 1993). In an editorial, the *Yomiuri* justified its adherence to the blackout as positive and necessary.

But not all journalists agreed. "The people's right to know ended up being empty talk," comments Chamoto (1993). "Why did the Japanese media abide by the embargo contract despite the fact of the engagement?" Professor Naoyuki Arai of Soka University has coined the term *sō-journalism-jōkyō* [total journalism], meaning that the unbridled praise of the engagement would brand anybody who was critical of it as unpatriotic (Chamoto 1993).

Very easily, the lack of criticism of the royals could lead to other types of controls. The press initially called the prince's mother, Michiko Shoda, "Mitchie", then "Michiko-sama," then *Hidenka* [wife of the crown prince] and finally by the elevated term *Kōgō Heika* [empress]. Columnist Yukichi Amano (1994, 15) worries that the "press has made the royals much more remote from the average person." At this writing the marriage has produced no heirs to the imperial throne.

1993–94: A Political Era Ends

The politically unconcerned, status quo–minded Japanese electorate had finally had enough. When LDP vice president Shin Kanemaru got a mere ¥200,000 fine for accepting a ¥500 million bribe, his "profit" of ¥500.8 million enraged the public. On March 6, 1993, he was arrested for tax evasion.

Eventually, Kanemaru gave up his seat in the House of Representatives and his presidency of the Takeshita faction, the LDP's largest subgroup. Without a leader, this faction, which had controlled

Japanese politics since the premiership of Kakuei Tanaka, split in two and lost its dominance.

In June 1993, when a no-confidence motion was introduced in the Lower House, various LDP members broke ranks to vote against their party. Eventually 36 of them formed a new party, the Shinsei, and 10 others formed the Sakigake party. Meanwhile, Morihiro Hosokawa, a member of the Upper House and former governor of a rural prefecture, formed the Nippon Shinto (Japan New Party, JNP).

On June 18, 1993, Prime Minister Kiichi Miyazawa dissolved the Lower House and called for an election. Political reform was the major issue of the campaign. Was the prediction that "Japan will eventually evolve from being a country with third-rate politics to being a country with second-rate politics" (Ito 1993b, 77) finally coming true?

Compared with the United States, campaigns in Japan do not last very long and do not involve TV advertising by candidates, which is prohibited by law. An equal-time provision allows candidates to voice their views for 10 minutes (*seiken hōsō*). The Lower House Election took place July 18.

Taro Kimura, a former NHK newscaster, called it "the most important election in Japan since World War II," in large part because "suddenly everyone discovered that television, which was rarely central to previous elections, was something they had to worry about" (Sanger 1993). The old parties, the LDP and the Socialists, waged a traditional campaign. The three new parties, having no existing election machine, had to use television.

In "one of the most epoch making events in Japanese postwar politics" (Takeshita and Mikami 1995, 27), the LDP lost its longtime majority in the Lower House, maintaining only 223 of the 511 seats. The biggest opposition party, the Social Democratic Party of Japan (SDPJ), likewise came out a big loser, declining from 137 to 70 seats. On the winning side, the Shinsei got 55 seats; the JNP, 35 seats; and the Sakigake, 13 seats. After two weeks of negotiating, these new parties combined with some of the old ones to form a seven-party coalition under Morihiro Hosokawa, leader of the JNP. The coalition drove the LDP out of power.

Two months after the election, in September 1993, the *Sankei Shimbun* reported a remark that Sadayoshi Tsubaki, news director of TV Asahi, had made to the National Association of Commercial Broadcasters in Japan; he said that TV Asahi's news programs, including those of influential newscaster Hiroshi Kume, consciously sought to oust the LDP from power. In the ensuing uproar, Tsubaki was summoned to the Diet to testify under oath, where he denied everything. The Tsubaki affair "raised protests about the not-so-subtle campaign by the Government to bring the media back under its control"; on the other hand, "opinionated newscasters like Mr. Kume" have "plenty of detractors," who doubt their ability to lead a nation's political debate (Sanger 1993). The public felt that "this scandal symbolized that media handling of the election was biased not only by TV Asahi but by the general news media as well" (Takeshita and Mikami 1995, 28).

Did the media sway voters away from the LDP? Even though the public thinks it did, scientific analysis says it did not. A nationwide sample of about 2,000 people found that "media influence, if any, is small compared to the interpersonal or group influences" (Ikeda 1994b, 8). Another survey of a random sample of 650 voters in Tokyo and an analysis of three weeks of TV and newspaper election reporting found only a weak media influence on voters (Takeshita and Mikami 1995, 39).

Under LDP rule, Diet members preferred to meet with newspaper reporters. About one-third of the Diet members regularly met with reporters of national newspapers; another third, with those from local and bloc newspapers; 21 percent, with television reporters; 14 percent, with wire service reporters; and only 0.2 percent, with radio reporters (Feldman 1993, 204). As Chapter 2 showed, newspaper reporters stayed in contact with Diet members throughout the day, whereas TV journalists covered only specific events. LDP power brokers such as Takeshita or Kanemaru "clearly came off very poorly on television. They did not speak clearly, they were extremely good at speaking a long time and saying nothing and they had no appeal to a broadcast audience" (Sun and Sterngold 1994, 55).

After the election, relations between politicians and reporters began to change. Ichiro Ozawa, secretary general of the JNP and architect of the Hosokawa coalition government, abolished the exclusive *kisha* club briefings and late-night chats. A *Mainichi Shimbun* columnist (Hiroto 1993, 5) describes the new approach:

> Monday is meet-the-press time for Ozawa. . . . The atmosphere is electric. In attendance are not only members of the exclusive parliamentary press club but also reporters from weekly magazines and foreign news organizations, another innovation.
>
> Reporters are free to ask anything, a no-no at meetings restricted to the press club regulars, who are usually too closely tied to their sources to risk an embarrassing query. . . . Unlike the many politicos who are dying for a sound bite on the evening news, Ozawa doesn't smile for the cameras or court the media.

Under the premierships of Hosokawa and his successor, Tsutomu Hata, key policy-makers spoke not to the *kisha* clubs but directly to the public through television. During periods of contention, after each meeting, the key politicians would often stand before a television camera. . . . As a result, the newspapers lost their monopoly on information and suddenly, everyone in Japan had an equal access, at least in some respects, to the information and an equal opportunity to draw their own conclusions. And of course there are still backroom deals being made and not everything was transparent but the role of TV has clearly changed political reporting a lot (Sun and Sterngold 1994, 53).

Thus the Japanese experienced in a short time "the arguments that Americans have made for decades about the mixed blessings of television" (Sanger 1993).

After Tsutomu Hata resigned, the strangest of bedfellows–the SDPJ, LDP and new Sakigake party–formed a coalition cabinet. Tomiichi Murayama, the second Socialist prime minister after World War II, came to power 47 years after the last Socialists left. In addition, an amendment of the election law changed the size of electoral districts. Furthermore, the new New Frontier Party became the first political party in 39 years with more than 200 Diet members.

Clearly, "Japanese voters have to wait yet another several years until they have a normalized political situation" (Sakata 1995, 13–15). Four prime ministers in 12 months testifies that the new status quo has not yet emerged. On January 11, 1996, yet another change occurred as the coalition government selected Ryutaro Hashimoto of the LDP to succeed Moriyama, who resigned.

1995: Aum Shinrikyo, Sarin Gas and Armageddon

After March 1995, when they allegedly killed 12 people with sarin gas in Tokyo's subway, the Aum Shinrikyo [Supreme Truth] cult ranked as Japan's top story. Before the attack, the cult had gained only passing media attention over the years.

The cult's leader, Shoko Asahara, who had studied Buddhism in Tibet, began dabbling in politics after he established his religious group in 1987. In 1990, after predicting he would handily win election to a seat in the Diet, Asahara and 24 followers made news only as losers. He had also predicted the end of the world, having moved all his group to a southern island for safety–but again, his prediction proved false. These public losses of face seem to have convinced him to manipulate future events so as to fulfill his prophecies.

The cult attracted some media attention in November 1989 when a lawyer, who represented worried parents of some cult members, disappeared, along with his wife and child. Later events implicated TBS-TV producers in the murder (see Chapter 12). Despite the resistance of parents and others, the cult, which grew to 10,000 adherents in Japan, also attracted followers in Russia, the United States, Germany, Australia and Sri Lanka.

While trying to control bad publicity in the mass media by eliminating critics and intimidating potential cult defectors, Aum actively used media to tell its own story. It spent $1.6 million in Russia on nationwide radio broadcasts and had a 30-minute weekly TV program in Moscow. Using its Moscow radio station, it also made broadcasts to Japan. The religious messages included the Christian concept of Armageddon, which Asahara predicted would occur in 1997.

In 1994, seven people in Matsumoto in central Japan were mysteriously poisoned. Then on March 20, 1995, in the Tokyo subway during the morning rush hour, nerve gas killed 12 people and injured about 5,500 others. After the Kyodo News Service reported that police had matched evidence from both sites with material found at one of Aum's properties, the media unleashed saturation coverage.

At the same time as the O. J. Simpson trial was fueling tabloid as well as mainstream U.S. coverage, in Japan the cult "became the top front-page story daily not only in the general newspapers but in the sports papers as well" ("In pursuit" 1995, 1). Beginning in late March, "Japanese [were] glued to the TV for weeks" ("Cult's broad reach" 1995). The NHK special "Aum Shinrikyo" garnered a rating of 33.1 percent. As the story took on international dimensions, Japan's overseas correspondents got involved. One based in the United States reported that an Aum believer tried to purchase U.S.-made computer software for handling chemicals.

Media criticism swirled around several aspects of the story. Since police served as the source for ongoing information about the investigation, whether stated officially or leaked to certain reporters, "there were few scoops" ("In pursuit" 1995, 1). Journalists acknowledged respect for freedom of religion as guaranteed in the Constitution but strongly emphasized the law enforcers' viewpoint that the cult posed a danger to society.

On the one hand, reporting slighted violations of civil rights; on the other, it failed to "criticize the investigative methods or forcible conduct of the police" ("In pursuit" 1995, 2). More than 100 Aum adherents were summarily arrested, most of them on minor and normally ignored charges, such as distributing leaflets or riding a stolen bicycle. Tetsu Yamazaki, a playwright and commentator, worried about "the authorities becoming too authoritarian because of a lack of media criticism" (Barr 1995, 6).

Coverage of the cult pitted newspapers against television. Although newspapers printed reams of stories, they also warned commercial TV networks against giving the group a prime-time forum that it could turn to its own advantage. Aum's lawyer, its public relations director and the chief of its scientific/technical unit often appeared on commercial television to criticize the police investigation and explain the group's doctrines. NHK, however, refused to give live, unedited airtime to any Aum leaders.

On television, "lengthy talk shows [were] punctuated by occasional reports of an actual event" (Barr 1995, 6). The commercial stations brought in academics and former prosecutors to question the cult's spokespersons, who gave answers that managed to satisfy many viewers. The interviews "took on a 'show' character" ("In pursuit" 1995, 2). Indeed, Fumihiro Joju, the group's PR director, became something of a media star, even inspiring some young girls to create a sort of fan club for him. Hideo Murai, the cult's science chief, met quite a different fate. In late April, in front of TV cameras and 10 policemen, a self-described rightist stabbed him to death.

Finally, 57 days after the subway gas attack, in a hidden chamber at the religious group's complex in Yamanashi Prefecture, police found Asahara. They had obtained arrest warrants for the partly blind guru and 40 other cult leaders on May 15. To cover the arrest, the five major dailies and the two news agencies pooled aerial photo coverage to avoid noise, extra expense and possible collisions. However, NHK and each major commercial network used separate helicopters. The newspapers issued "arrest extras" shortly after noon on the day of the arrest.

Newspapers, according to an NSK survey, bested television in reporting the Aum story, although the "younger generation is rather critical of both newspapers and TV concerning Aum reporting" (Katsumata 1996, 45). Survey questions and answers were:

1. Was there much reporting that pandered to popular taste?
    Newspapers: yes, 17.5 percent; no, 81.9 percent
    Television: yes, 68.3 percent; no, 31.5 percent
2. Was there much reporting on the core problem or its background?
    Newspapers: yes, 51.5 percent; no, 47.2 percent
    Television: yes, 60.6 percent; no, 39.1 percent
3. Did the media pay due consideration to privacy or human rights of those reported on?
    Newspapers: yes, 66.5 percent; no, 32.5 percent
    Television: yes, 41.9 percent; no, 57.8 percent
4. As a whole, was the reporting credible?
    Newspapers: yes, 77.1 percent; no, 21.6 percent
    Television: yes, 55.6 percent; no, 43.9 percent

Asahara went on trial in April 1996 for murder and attempted murder. Three judges heard the evidence against him (Japan has no system of jury trials). No cameras are allowed in Japanese courts.

In this chapter, we have taken a horizontal look at how the news media performed in five different situations–the formation of public opinion and coverage of natural disasters, activities of the imperial family, national party politics and a murder/manhunt frenzy. Now we will look vertically at segments of the communication industry, expanding upon news coverage to include entertainment and the related functions of advertising and public relations.

Part 2
Industry Profiles

4
Postwar Newspapers

Sumiko Suzuki, 35, who lives in Nagoya with her husband and two children, subscribes to both the *Chūnichi Shimbun*, a regional newspaper, and the *Yomiuri*, one of the Big Five national dailies. Taro Tanaka, 20, lives in Tokyo with his mother and father, who subscribe to the *Asahi Shimbun*—a paper that Taro seldom reads. Sumiko and Taro, who represent two of Japan's postwar baby boom population surges, will accompany us through the next chapters to put a human face on Japan's gargantuan mass media system.

Overview

On October 18, 1994, an *Asahi Shimbun* helicopter crashed in Osaka Prefecture, killing all those aboard. The *Asahi* helicopter, returning from covering a tanker collision, was grazed in midair by a *Mainichi* helicopter en route to the same site. This tragedy involving two newspaper aircraft blemished the *Asahi Shimbun*'s accident-free aviation history. Westerners may associate aircraft with TV accident coverage and radio traffic reports, but in Japan, all major newspapers use them extensively.

The *Asahi Shimbun* fleet—two light jets and five helicopters—in 1991 logged 2,519 hours. The fleet covers news, carries staff and equipment, takes part in ceremonial fly-bys, carries extra editions and provides VIP transportation and inspection flights. The *Asahi Shimbun* created Japan's first regular airmail delivery in 1923 and first regular passenger service between Tokyo and Osaka in 1928. In 1937, an *Asahi* plane made the Tokyo-to-London flight in a record 94 hours, 17 minutes and 56 seconds. After being disbanded at the end of the war, *Asahi*'s Aviation Department was re-established in 1952.

In 1968, the *Mainichi Shimbun* used a Beechcraft aircraft to get a photo of the Japanese flag replacing the Stars and Stripes on Iwo Jima. The ceremony ended just 15 minutes before the evening paper's deadline, but by combining several aircraft, on-board photo developing, radio transmission and undersea cable, the *Mainichi* scooped its competitors by picturing the historic territorial return. As a *Yomiuri* executive said at the time, "We never fly executives–only reporters and photographers" ("Japanese air" 1969).

These anecdotes about aircraft illustrate a number of traits that characterize Japanese newspapers. They eagerly use techniques and technologies that enhance news delivery. They lavishly expend personnel and resources to cover important stories. They compete furiously against each other. They sponsor public service projects and events. And they operate at a scale grand enough that they can afford to maintain their own aircraft fleets.

Circulation

Newspapers of the magnitude of the *Yomiuri*, *Mainichi* and *Asahi* dwarf any U.S. daily, even though Japan has about half the U.S. population. As Table 4.1 shows, *Asahi* has a combined daily morning/evening circulation of more than 12.6 million, whereas the *Yomiuri* boasts a staggering 14.5 million circulation. Even though the *Mainichi* has a combined circulation of "only" about 6 million, the largest U.S. papers–*USA Today*, the *Wall Street Journal*, the *New York Times* and the *Los Angeles Times*–with circulations between 1 and 2 million as of late 1994, pale in comparison. While Japan boasts four of the world's five largest dailies, none of the 1,570 U.S. dailies even makes the top 10 list (see Table 4.2).

As of October 1994, Japan had fewer (121) but larger daily newspapers than the United States, with a much larger absolute circulation of 71,924,000. With 1.2 copies per household, many families get one national paper and one non-national. For example, in central Japan, every day more than 4 million copies are published of the *Chūnichi Shimbun*, a major paper that happens to own one twin-engine airplane and four helicopters–yet no doubt few non-Japanese have ever heard of it.

Since the 1960s Japan has ranked at or very near the top of worldwide newspaper "saturation" figures, with 578 copies per 1,000 people in 1992 (the U.S. figure of 260 per 1,000 people puts it far down on the list). Of the factors that boost circulation, Japan has them all (Lewenstein 1987, 10): high literacy, relatively high per capita income, evenly distributed wealth, homogeneity, interest in world affairs, good educational system, efficient distribution techniques and heavily used public transportation. Moreover, the Japanese "tend to revere the printed word" (Whittenmore 1961, 7).

Table 4.1. Japan's leading daily newspapers, 1995*

Location	Circulation	Employees	Establishment
National (Tokyo office listed)			
Asahi Shimbun 5-3-2, Tsukiji Chuo-ku, Tokyo 104-11	8,258,739 a.m. 4,439,159 p.m.	7,972	1879 (Osaka)
Mainichi Shimbun 1-1-1, Hitotsubashi Chiyoda-ku, Tokyo 100-51	4,010,231 a.m. 1,937,102 p.m.	4,164	1882 (Osaka)
Nihon Keizai Shimbun 1-9-5, Otemachi Chiyoda-ku, Tokyo 100-66	2,882,479 a.m. 1,654,082 p.m.	4,483	1876 (Tokyo)
Sankei Shimbun 1-7-2, Otemachi Chiyoda-ku, Tokyo 100-77	1,916,412 a.m. 965,840 p.m.	3,318	1933 (Osaka)
Yomiuri Shimbun 1-7-1, Otemachi Chiyoda-ku, Tokyo 100-55	10,115,811 a.m. 4,458,177 p.m.	7,100	1874 (Tokyo)
Bloc			
Chūnichi Shimbun 1-6-1, Sannomaru Naka-ku, Nagoya 460	3,075,320 a.m. 1,247,822 p.m.	3,633 (includes *Tokyo Shimbun*)	1942 (Nagoya)
Tokyo Shimbun 2-3-13, Konan Minato-ku, Tokyo 108	700,586 a.m. 201,192 p.m.		1942 (Nagoya)
Nishi Nippon Shimbun 1-4-1, Tenjin Chuo-ku, Fukuoka 810	821,756 a.m. 201,192 p.m.	1,152	1877 (Fukuoka)
Prefectural			
Hokkaido Shimbun 3-6, Odori-Nishi Chuo-ku, Sapporo 060 (011) 221-2111	1,191,028 a.m. 773,746 p.m.	1,800	1942 (Sapporo)

Source: Nihon Shimbun Kyokai (NSK), *The Japanese Press '95.*

*Combined morning and evening circulation totaling 1 million or more.

Table 4.2. World's top 10 largest-circulation daily newspapers, 1995

Yomiuri Shimbun (Japan)	**14,573,988**
Asahi Shimbun (Japan)	**12,697,898**
Mainichi Shimbun (Japan)	**5,947,333**
Bild (Germany)	5,567,100
Nihon Keizai Shimbun (Japan)	**4,536,561**
Chūnichi Shimbun (Japan)	**4,323,142**
Sun (England)	4,023,548
Sankei Shimbun (Japan)	**2,882,252**
Renmin Ribao (China)	2,740,000
Daily Mirror (England)	2,568,957

Source: Editor & Publisher Co.

Geographical Reach

Japan has five national dailies and three types of non-national newspapers. In addition, both national and regional sports papers add spice to Japan's media menu.

Prefectural and community newspapers

All of Japan's 47 prefectures (political units somewhat like the U.S. states) have at least one newspaper, except for Shiga Prefecture. Many papers also have readers in neighboring prefectures, and some of the large prefectures, such as Fukushima, Fukui and Okinawa, have more than one.

Community papers, a supplement to the national and prefectural newspapers, concentrate on local topics and culture.

Bloc newspapers

Newspapers such as the *Chūnichi* and *Nishi-Nippon* span prefectural boundaries but do not circulate nationally. The *Tokyo Shimbun*, published by *Chūnichi* in and for the Tokyo area, is usually included in this group. The *Hokkaido Shimbun*, covering Japan's northernmost main island of Hokkaido (geographically vast, but a single prefecture), is often treated as a bloc rather than prefectural paper.

National newspapers

Based in Tokyo, the Japanese-language National Five dwarf the four nationally circulating English-language dailies (see Appendix 2) in both size and influence. Junichiro Suzuki, editor-in-chief of the independent *Japan Times*, sees the English press as "playing somewhat a mediating role" and giving "interpretive angles" to Japanese news (Vanden Heuvel and Dennis 1993, 81).

The readership of the English press includes the foreign diplomatic corps, employees of foreign companies and other foreign residents and tourists as well as Japanese businesspeople, government employees and students. The oldest, the *Japan Times* (a morning paper established in 1897) had a 1995 circulation of 65,596. More recently, all of the Japanese Big Three created English-language sister papers: the *Daily Yomiuri* (morning, 1955), with 51,498 circulation; the *Mainichi Daily News* (morning, 1922), 46,000; and the *Asahi Evening News* (evening, 1954), 38,800. (Figures for the daily *Shipping and Trade News* are not available.)

The *Asahi* ["Rising Sun"], *Mainichi* ["Each Day"], *Yomiuri* ["Read and Sell"], *Nihon Keizai* ["Japan Economic"] and *Sankei* ["Industrial Economic"] newspapers all have circulations of more than 3 million. Together, they count for more than 50 percent of Japan's total newspaper circulation. Their printing centers in Osaka, Nagoya, Hokkaido and elsewhere also publish local-interest editions. Within the National Five, the Big Three stand out as general-interest papers of more than 4 million circulation each.

Sports newspapers

Japan's 17 sports dailies have branched out from their original sports-only focus. General news coverage of elections, including tabulated results, competed directly with the mainstream press beginning in 1990. In 1990–91, the sports dailies' Gulf War reports and, in 1992, political scandal stories took a more compact, dramatic, storytelling approach than reports in the Big Three.

In April 1992, the month the pro baseball season opened, sports stories took up 40 percent of space (half of that was baseball stories); racing reports and leisure activities, 30 percent; popular entertainment, 8 to 10 percent; general news, 9 percent; and radio/TV coverage, 8 percent (Takabatake 1993, 43).

Sports papers have become Japan's popular press. They have banner headlines and big color photos to attract customers who pass by newsstands, but these factors also make them easy to read even if they are home delivered. On the one day a month when mainstream newspapers do not publish, to give the delivery personnel a holiday, sports papers publish double-sized editions for newsstand sales.

Sports papers derive less income from advertising (about 40 percent) and more from sales (about 60 percent) than the mainstream dailies. The 17 sports papers increased 3.2 percent in circulation to more than 6 million copies a day between 1991 and 1992, while the 104 mainstream dailies decreased 0.6 percent.

However, the Big Three need not worry unduly, as they own three of the main sports papers: *Nikkan Sports* (owned by *Asahi*), *Sports Nippon* (*Mainichi*) and *Hōchi Shimbun* (*Yomiuri*). In addition, the *Sankei*, *Chūnichi*, *Nishi Nippon* and *Hokkaido* dailies likewise have their own sports papers.

The Big Three

History

As Table 4.1 shows, the Big Three, two of which started in Osaka, have histories stretching back more than 100 years. After the Meiji Restoration, as a commercial rather than political center, Osaka "favored newspapers with less emphasis on party politics and more on general news reporting. The men destined to run Asahi and Mainichi had enterprising spirits" (Komatsubara 1971, 71). The descendants of *Asahi*'s two founders, Ryohei Murayama and Riichi Ueno, still jointly own the newspaper today.

The *Mainichi*'s early history is shakier than the *Asahi*'s. A savvy entrepreneur, Hikoichi Motoyama, rescued the dying *Mainichi* newspaper and put it on sound financial footing. Motoyama, along with Murayama of the *Asahi*, "is regarded as the greatest newspaperman in Japan" (Komatsubara 1971, 71).

The *Yomiuri*, originally a literary newspaper, changed radically when Matsutaro Shoriki took it over in 1924. He instituted sports pages, color comics, columns devoted to the game of *go*, science coverage, a hyped newswriting style and promotional gimmicks. Circulation zoomed from 50,000 in 1924 to 840,000 in 1937.

After a "relatively liberal period," by the late 1930s "the press became subservient to the militarists" (Whittenmore 1961, 11). By government policy, the 1,200 dailies published in 1937 dwindled to 104 in 1940 and a mere 54 in 1942. Then in 1945 B-29 air strikes destroyed or crippled many of those remaining. Reporters who had to describe all military retreats as "transfers" and write only patriotic-sounding copy "lost their reportorial sense" (Komatsubara 1971, 78).

During the postwar Occupation, the Supreme Commander, Allied Powers (SCAP) saw the press as a means to democratize the Japanese. SCAP repealed prewar censorship laws and allowed surviving newspapers to continue publication but purged their executives from office—including Matsutaro Shoriki of the *Yomiuri*. Later, as Cold War tensions heightened, SCAP instituted a different kind of purge, "the darkest page [in] the postwar history of the Japanese press" (Komatsubara 1971, 81). In all, 700 suspected Communists were dismissed from 47 newspapers, news agencies and the Japan Broadcasting Corp. (NHK), meaning that mass media lost a higher percentage of personnel than any other industry.

In an effort to prevent monopoly control, SCAP encouraged the founding of various new newspapers. But the press revival did not take hold until the 1950s. In May 1951, newsprint controls were lifted. In October 1951, all the major newspapers began to publish morning and evening editions, selling both editions as a package. In 1952, after the San Francisco peace treaty was signed, the major newspapers began to expand their overseas news-gathering networks.

Then, during May and June of 1960, "all unsettled postwar issues burst open" (Komatsubara 1971, 84) after the Kishi government rammed through the Diet ratification of a revised Japan-U.S. Security Treaty. Editorials criticized the government, while news stories treated the ensuing street demonstrations favorably.

At the time of the demonstrations, the *Asahi* staff included 242 members of the leftist Japan Congress of Journalists (JCJ), an affiliate of the International Organization of Journalists (IOJ)–twice the membership of the *Yomiuri* and *Mainichi* put together. (The IOJ, headquartered in Prague, drew most of its other members from the Communist bloc.) In 1960, with the Cold War raging, the IOJ officially opposed a Japan-U.S. military alliance and exhorted its members to "carry the voice of the people" who demonstrated against the treaty (Whittenmore 1961, 17). While all of the Big Three opposed the government, *Asahi*'s JCJ members seem to have omitted or slanted events more than the other two. Many Japanese today think that the anti-government, anti-superpower stance still affects *Asahi*'s interpretation of events.

After Kishi resigned, "a general apathy toward politics" ensued (Komatsubara 1971, 85), and instead, Japan threw its energies into a phenomenal growth and development effort. Newspapers, "engulfed by a wave of technologic innovations" (Haruhara and Hayashi 1990, 12), happily jumped on the development bandwagon. Newspaper production reforms included the *kanji* telex and facsimile printing. In 1959, *Asahi* established the world's first facsimile printing system when it opened its Hokkaido office. This writer remembers seeing her first fax machine in operation in 1967 when a correspondent in Hokkaido sent a handwritten bulletin in *kanji* characters about an earthquake to the *Asahi*'s English sister paper, the *Asahi Evening News*.

As a further benefit of Japan's economic expansion in the 1960s, advertising increased newspapers' revenues. Traditionally dependent on subscription revenue, newspapers began to depend more heavily on advertising beginning in the mid-1960s. The number of copies printed (with morning and evening editions counted separately) increased by 125 percent, swelling from 29,922,000 copies in 1951 to 68,300,000 in 1985.

Today the Big Three continue their prewar role as an integral part of national life, sponsoring everything from art exhibits to Arctic explorations. The newspapers' cultural centers offer classes in traditional arts, modern ballroom dancing and a myriad of other topics. The *Asahi Shimbun*'s showplace Hamarikyu Asahi Hall opened in 1992. Recently, the long-standing relation of newspapers and sports (see Chapter 2)–the Yomiuri Giants even carry a newspaper name on their jerseys–has expanded beyond baseball to such events as *Asahi*'s International Women's Marathon.

Content

Except for newspaper holidays, the national papers usually put out four morning editions, each with content tailored to a different distribution area, and three evening editions a day. Newspapers, which average 24 to 28 pages for their morning editions and 14 to 20 pages for their evening editions, may seem thin to Westerners used to separate news, sports, lifestyle and classified sections. The ratio of editorial content to advertising in Japanese newspapers averages about 56 to 44.

Domestic coverage

Editorially, the Big Three follow predictable patterns, according to van Wolferen (1993, 128): "The Asahi's editorial line is influenced by columnists and editorial advisers who tend to be anti-U.S. and were in some cases weaned on an old-fashioned Japanese version of Marxism.... The Mainichi still tends to follow the Asahi line on these matters as all the others used to do." But breaks in "post-war taboos on the discussion of military matters" have appeared; in the "most important press development in recent years," the *Yomiuri Shimbun* has defied "the conventional anti-US, anti-defence stance" (van Wolferen 1993, 128).

In November 1994, the conservative *Yomiuri* published its version of a revised Japanese Constitution that differs from the existing "peace" Constitution (see Chapter 3). *Yomiuri*'s proposed version would authorize "an organization for self-defense"–which in fact already exists in Japan– and sanction personnel support for U.N. peacekeeping missions–which in fact Japan already provides ("Yomiuri breaks" 1994).

Empirical content studies can convey in greater detail the world view that Japanese newspapers present to their readers. Researchers study the *Asahi*, "which has the most prestige" (van Wolferen 1993, 128), more closely than other papers; indeed, Merrill (1990) includes it as the lone

Japanese newspaper among the world's 20 great dailies. Mulcahy (1994), for example, found that domestic issues took precedence (72 percent) in *Asahi* editorials in both 1982 and 1992; editorials dealing with foreign countries or international issues totaled 28 percent.

Between July 1993 and June 1994, Japan's ruling Liberal Democratic Party (LDP) lost power after 38 years, and three prime ministers held office, including the first Socialist ever. Not surprisingly, the top theme of *Asahi Shimbun* editorials during this period was "change/reform"; the top topic, "domestic politics." The editorials concentrated heavily (70.6 percent) on domestic issues (Cooper-Chen 1997).

Another content study of editorial page opinion likewise found a concentration on domestic issues. Feldman (1995), who looked at editorial cartoons in the *Yomiuri* and *Asahi*, found a domestic focus in 68.1 percent. Feldman studied the first three months in office of six prime ministers: Zenko Suzuki, Yasuhiro Nakasone, Noboru Takeshita, Toshiki Kaifu, Kiichi Miyazawa and Morihiro Hosokawa. Prime ministers, pictured in 44 percent of the cartoons, were depicted as a sumo wrestler, truck driver, statue, hot dog in a bun, baseball team manager and (most frequently) a tired, old man. Like a baseball team manager, the prime minister must bind individuals together into a working unit by building consensus; he cannot act on his own priorities, but when anything goes wrong, he must take the blame (often by resigning).

International coverage

When the newspapers' agenda does turn to foreign countries, one clearly stands out: the United States. In a database of 800,000 news items in the *Asahi* in 1987, 1990 and 1993, the United States turned out to be far and away the most newsworthy country in the *Asahi*'s eyes (Ishii 1996b). Does the *Asahi* overcover the United States? Using statistical techniques, the author found that countries with a large population and high gross domestic product consistently (and logically) got more coverage. Thus the *Asahi* did not offer too much U.S. coverage.

Of all foreign countries, China and Russia (formerly the U.S.S.R.) also ranked high in prominence. China, the United Kingdom and Peru got more coverage than their intrinsic importance would suggest. Peruvian President Alberto Fujimori, whose parents came from Japan, gives Peru a strong "home news abroad" (Sreberny-Mohammadi 1984) connection for Japanese readers. The United Kingdom—like Japan, an island nation with a long history, a former empire and a royal family—has long fascinated the Japanese. China, with its economic potential and military might, has hosted correspondents from Japan since the 1970s.

Despite China's prominence, geographical distance was not related to coverage. Indeed, three of the five undercovered countries for 1993 were in Asia: Hong Kong, Taiwan and India (the others were Germany and Italy). Because of political pressure from Mainland China, the *Asahi* has no correspondent in Taiwan. The *Asahi* and other papers received early postings in China by promising the Chinese government "to write only positive reports about China under Mao Tse-tung," but the *Sankei Shimbun*, "which has a right-leaning reputation," refused to go along (van Wolferen 1993, 128). To date, no study has explored the Big Three's positive/negative reporting on China.

A recent study (Sasaki 1995) compared *Asahi's* and *Chūnichi Shimbun's* coverage for October–December 1994. All of *Asahi's* stories on its international page concerned foreign countries, but, quite naturally for a regional paper, 23 percent of the *Chūnichi's* international stories had a "home news abroad" angle (such as sales of Japanese cars in Hungary). The international section amounts to one or two pages out of 24.

Considering the front pages, "pure" foreign news (no Japan angle) had a harder time breaking in (*Asahi*, 13 percent; *Chūnichi*, 5 percent). Nearly three-quarters of stories in both papers had a "home news abroad" focus. Surprisingly, "pure" domestic stories accounted for less than 10 percent of stories in both papers; neither one was extremely provincial.

As the year 2000 approaches, Japan may be turning more toward Asia. In a study of *Asahi Shimbun* editorials in 1993, Cooper-Chen (1997) found that the United States lost its traditional place as Japan's main overseas focus to Korea, with Russia coming in a close third.

Distribution and Production

Home Delivery

With 93 percent of regular dailies home delivered, sports papers or evening-only papers account for most newsstand sales (only about 0.6 percent are delivered by mail).

The major newspapers print both morning and evening editions, the most common form of subscription being a package including delivery of both. Where twice-daily delivery is not feasible, readers can get special morning editions that include summaries of the previous day's evening paper at a slightly reduced rate. Some newspapers publish only a morning or only an evening edition.

For newspaper distribution, trucks have replaced trains as Japan's system of expressways and its trucking industry have improved. Distribution areas are clearly defined, and exclusive dealers usually handle only their main-client newspaper and its affiliated sports paper and other publications. Some semi-exclusive dealers do exist in remote regions with too few subscribers to support multiple dealers.

The leading newspapers sell 60 to 70 percent of their papers through exclusive dealers. Although dealerships operate independently, their parent papers impose considerable regulations regarding whose newspapers they handle. Some of the larger regional papers operate their own dealerships.

Although Japan's labor laws do not prohibit home newspaper delivery by youths, they are too busy studying for entrance exams to have paper routes. The proportion of adults delivering newspapers in 1994 continued to increase, surpassing 80 percent of all delivery personnel. Part-time females make up the largest category, at 37.6 percent ("Sales/distribution" 1995). Delivery personnel numbered 481,835 as of October 1, 1994.

Intense competition means newspapers try to avoid raising their prices. In 1980 the Fair Trade Commission decreed that the National Five constituted an oligopoly and required prior approval of any price hikes. Subsequently, the national newspapers kept their monthly subscription rates fairly constant throughout the 1980s. With the introduction of the consumption tax in April 1989, the standard newspaper subscription rate was raised to ¥3,190 a month (tax included). In the early 1990s, subscriptions went up again to ¥3,850 (morning and evening combined) to provide revenue during the recession.

Newsprint and Production

Newsprint represents 18.8 percent of newspapers' expenditures, making Japan second only to the United States in newsprint consumption. Total domestic consumption in 1992 was approximately 3,451,000 tons, and total domestic production was about 3,445,000 tons. This total domestic consumption included some 37,700 tons of imported newsprint—not a significant amount compared with Japan's dependence on timber imports to provide the pulp needed for papermaking.

Japan's lack of forestry resources has spurred a nationwide recycling drive. In 1983, 92.2 percent of Japanese newspapers were recycled, the highest recycling rate in the world. One can see stacks of papers awaiting pickup outside any high-rise apartment in Japan. Old newspapers are also imported from the United States for recycling.

The drop in advertising, pages and circulation in 1992 resulted in a decrease in domestic newsprint output, which had grown steadily in the 1980s. In 1993, the *Yomiuri* and *Asahi* adopted ultra light newsprint, which the *Nikkei* had adopted in 1989.

Journalists

Japanese newspapers maintain large rosters of reporters and other writers. In 1994, editorial staffers numbered more than 26,000 nationwide (41.1 percent of the total of all newspaper employees). National newspapers typically have about 1,500 to 2,000 writers, most of whom stay with the same paper until they reach retirement age. Recently, however, a number of young and middle-aged journalists have begun to switch employers or leave journalism entirely.

However, journalism remains a satisfying profession, according to nearly three-quarters of journalists at Japan's 51 leading newspapers and news agencies in a 1993 survey (1,735 replies, a response rate of 62 percent). Men constituted 91.6 percent of those polled; women, 8.4 percent. The average age of the pollees was 37.07 years. Almost half (48.2 percent) worked for national papers; 14.6 percent, bloc papers; 30.9 percent, regional papers; and 6 percent, news agencies (Akao 1995). Still, compared with 20 years ago, fewer reporters in 1993 (74.3 percent) than 1973 (83.5 percent) found satisfaction in their jobs, and fewer thought they were contributing to society. More than half of the reporters polled in 1993 thought that the influence of newspapers would decline in the future. Quite a number criticized the *kisha* club system (see Chapter 2).

Partly because final responsibility for articles lies with the newspaper rather than the individual reporter, Japanese newspaper articles seldom carry bylines. Commonly, reporters and columnists do get bylines, or at least their initials, on interviews, special columns and background analyses. Overseas correspondents are usually given bylines, as are the few outside contributors.

New technology will give reporters more individual control over their work and change their responsibility for what they write. In 1991, *Asahi* installed a communication network that enables reporters anywhere to dispatch their stories composed on word processors. Only in the 1990s have reporters joined the computer age. Previously, technical innovations affected largely transmission and production processes.

Technology

In 1980, when the *Asahi Shimbun* moved from Yurakucho to Tsukiji, it switched from conventional lead-cast letterpress printing to the computerized News Editing and Layout System of Newspapers (NELSON). With its own ground link for satellite communication, *Asahi Shimbun* began publishing internationally in 1986, first in London and later in New York, Los Angeles, Singapore and Heerlen.

In 1992, next to the Tsukiji headquarters, a state-of-the-art facility opened. Like the main building, the new facility has 16 stories above ground and four levels below ground, doubling available space. The new facility houses studio and transmission facilities for a satellite TV network that will provide *Asahi Shimbun* news to cable TV outlets throughout Japan.

Asahi is introducing newsroom changes more slowly. Traditionally, raw copy had to pass through an editor to the makeup department and finally to computer operators in the production division. Starting on April 1, 1995 (April 1 is the day of "new beginnings" in Japan), *Yomiuri Shimbun* reporters began to plan page layouts and make up pages using layout terminals.

Local newspapers such as the *Shinano Mainichi Shimbun* could introduce reporters to computer production some years earlier than the national dailies, which are burdened by the need to issue several editions daily. The *Yomiuri Shimbun*, for example, introduced the new procedures gradually, starting with the feature pages of the cultural news department, science news department and the public opinion survey office.

The *Asahi Shimbun* plans not only to shift composing to the reporters for its feature pages like *Yomiuri* but also to have the local bureaus lay out and make up the local pages by the spring of 1996. Thus local editions produced locally will more closely reflect each region and its readers.

Design and technological changes that swept U.S. newspapers in the 1970s have finally arrived in Japan. This writer returned to Japan after a 25-year absence only to find the *Asahi Evening News* looking almost exactly the same. Then on April 1, 1993, the paper switched to a new look, new production technology and new location in the *Asahi* Tsukiji building.

According to Self (1990, 19): "For a country as advanced in electronic technologies as Japan is, its newspaper industry has been surprisingly cautious about adopting some technologies already widespread in the United States and now sweeping national newspapers in England.

"The approaches to using new technologies in Japan seem rooted in the cultural environment of Japan itself and these cultural elements seems to twist the use of technology more than the technology shapes the cultural traditions."

Several reasons account for the slow change. First, the 1,940 Chinese characters that newspapers use meant developing software systems that use *kana,* the Japanese syllabic sound symbols, in conjunction with the *kanji* characters—a much more complex task than using an alphabet. Second, management works slowly, from the bottom up. Innovations, recommended by each division, come to top managers, most of whom have never used computer keyboards, for their approval (Self 1990). Third, consolidation of duties may not necessarily mean fewer personnel because of the lifetime employment system; thus a cost-saving incentive for installing labor-saving technology does not exist.

Readers

Japan's large mass media have, ironically, a reputation of disdain for the masses—whether mistreating victims of disaster in pursuit of a story (see Chapter 3) or disregarding the needs of readers. Newspapers routinely made assumptions about guilt by publishing photos and dropping honorific titles such as *san* in reports about suspects in criminal cases. In 1989, the *Mainichi Shimbun* began clarifying a person's status as a still-presumed-innocent suspect or not publishing names at all. Now most newspapers refrain from printing pictures of crime victims, "reflecting the trend to pay more attention to protection of human rights" (Tamura 1993, 33).

Also recently, "readers' opinions, complaints and queries are being treated more seriously, which are being reflected [in] the editorial policies of the newspapers" (Tamura 1993, 33). Telephone hot lines have been installed. A newspaper's "Letters to the Editor" column will now likely include criticism of the paper itself.

Moreover, newspapers now indulge in self-criticism. In 1989, when an *Asahi Shimbun* photographer faked a photo for a story on coral (see Chapter 12), the newspaper carried reports of its own investigations of the incident—"unprecedented measures [for] a newspaper company in Japan" (Tamura 1993, 33). *Asahi* also decided to take more seriously its publication of apologies and corrections, which most newspapers avoided altogether, wrote perfunctorily or buried. Even the taboo against criticizing other media has eroded. In 1991, *Asahi* created on its city page a daily (Tuesday through Saturday) media column, which in 1992 received a Japan Newspaper Editors and Publishers Association (NSK) editorial award (the equivalent of a Pulitzer Prize).

A grain of self-interest may have prompted the *Asahi* media column, which aimed to help readers understand the media and promote introspection by the media themselves. According to a 1993 telephone survey of 1,367 adults, "Newspaper credibility among people in their 30s it was conspicuously low" (Iwasaki 1994, 37). Whereas the average score for responses by men was 48 points, the average for men in their 30s was an anemic 26. The average for women was 49 but for those in their 30s, it was only 35.

Credibility recovered slightly in 1993, compared with results of a 1989 survey, and recovered again in 1995, the 11th such survey (Katsumata

1996). Overall evaluations in 1995 were 67 percent positive, 19 percent negative and the rest neutral. "Social responsibility" got 80 percent positive responses, followed by 74 percent for "accuracy" and 73 percent for "reliability." Low evaluations were given to "fairness" (52 percent) and "consideration for human rights" (57 percent).

In 1993 (Iwasaki 1994), one in every four people called newspapers "indispensable," with women rating them higher than men (31 percent of women called newspapers indispensable). Among the people polled, 75 percent said they read a newspaper "every day," but fewer than half of people in their 20s do so. Since 1989, about 10 percent of 20-somethings shifted from reading newspapers "every day" to "sometimes." Among men in their 30s, 82 percent read "every day"—still high, but a drop of nearly 10 points since 1989.

In addition to a drop in the frequency of newspaper reading, the average time people said they spent with newspapers per day also dropped—to 41.2 minutes (47.2 minutes for men and 35.5 minutes for women). Compared with 1989, in 1993 men in their 30s showed a sharp decline of seven minutes, whereas students and men in their 40s reported a drop of six minutes. Comparing that 41 minutes with the average time spent watching TV per day, 154.8 minutes, gives newspaper executives cause for concern.

Problems

Until the 1970s, radio, television and magazines played second fiddle to Japan's premiere mass medium—its newspapers. But in 1975, as the diffusion rate for color television reached more than 90 percent, newspapers lost their dominant share of the advertising dollar to television (see Chapter 8).

Revenue not available from advertising can hardly come from new customers in the already saturated newspaper market of Japan, where the low birth rate may result in negative population growth and even fewer future customers. The number of copies per household had remained virtually constant over the past 25 years, but in the early 1990s, copies per household declined from 1.3 to 1.2.

With a finite pool of subscribers, the national newspapers compete furiously among themselves and with the regional newspapers, often skirting the law by offering illegal premiums to new subscribers. Besides, the larger newspapers have side ventures from TV networks to baseball teams to sustain them (see Chapter 2). The market share of small newspapers can shrink drastically in the face of large newspapers' superior capital, technical know-how and sales organizations.

Closures

In 1991, Osaka's *Kansai Shimbun*, burdened by debt after borrowing heavily from the Ito-man trading firm, went out of business. Then in 1992, the *Fukunichi Daily* and *Fukunichi Sports*, published in Fukuoka City on the southernmost main island of Kyushu, as well as the *Tokyo Times*, shut down. Such a rash of closures had not occurred since the recession year of 1965, when 10 papers were suspended, merged with other newspapers or sold to other companies. In the 1970s and 1980s, only a handful of closures had occurred. The tremendous growth of many papers during the booming '80s, especially after 1986, masked financial difficulties of a number of smaller newspapers.

The *Fukunichi Shimbun* and *Tokyo Times*, which had not made a profit in any single fiscal year during the previous 19 years, fell victim not to the present severe recession but to long-standing problems. Both of these postwar publications met with initial success, but the appeal of their unique features disappeared as the years went by. Even a switch to morning publication and altered page size and format could not save them ("Newspaper closures" 1992).

Costs and Expenses

Sales constitute newspapers' largest source of income, 48.0 percent. But this revenue source dropped in the 1990s as dailies in general, except the sports papers, lost circulation. Many newspapers raised subscription rates by an average of ¥200 in late 1993 and early 1994 to increase revenue. The big papers raised the monthly charge for the morning-evening set by about 5.5 percent, from ¥3,650 to ¥3,850, or about $40 ("Newspaper price hikes" 1994).

Advertising constitutes newspapers' second largest source of income, 36.1 percent. In the recession of the early 1990s, newspaper ad spending decreased three straight years for all types of products. The share of newspaper ads in total advertising spending continued to decrease. The ad revenue drop (9.4 percent) in 1993 was the worst since the survey was started about 40 years ago ("Advertising spending down" 1994).

Newspaper publishers must also deal with the burden of interest payments on money borrowed to expand equipment and facilities during the late 1980s. Newspaper operating profits dropped for three years in a row during the 1990s. Newspapers with circulations of 600,000 or more and those up to 150,000 showed alarming profit drops of more than 70 percent.

Personnel constitutes the biggest expense (28.2 percent) after fixed business costs. To cut expenses, the big papers will try to reduce their work force by 10 percent in three to five years. New hiring will be stopped or curtailed, while retirement incentives will increase. As of April 1994, employees nearing retirement–those aged 45 to 59–made up the largest group. Decreases will affect regular pay, overtime pay and bonuses, given in the summer and at the year's end, which can equal four or five months' salary in good times.

Personnel problems in the opposite vein affect delivery. A shortage of delivery people, along with the problem of timely news presentation, has increased facsimile transmissions. Domestic fax papers proved useful to deliver current sporting results during the 1992 Winter Olympics in Albertville, France. Many newspapers have Japanese-language fax publications, which usually come out Monday through Friday mornings, for readers at home and abroad. The *Tokyo Times*, which died in July 1992, was reborn two months later as a fax-only publication ("Demand for faxed" 1992).

Future Directions

What other efforts using new technologies will newspapers make to stay financially healthy into the 21st century? A growing number of newspapers and news agencies provide text, sound and images over the Internet (see Table 4.3). Asahi Internet Service, which went on-line in August 1995, reports 500,000 hits daily, including those to its Asahi Job Network. In the future, ads may appear only electronically, instead of duplicating those that run in the printed classifieds. All newspapers are studying ways to use the Internet for advertising.

Other ways of diversifying and increasing revenue already exist. In a survey of 75 companies, NSK ("Newspapers confident" 1995) found that 57 were participating in new media ventures. Participation was defined as capital investment of more than 1 percent and assigning personnel for management purposes.

Databases

A total of 31 newspaper companies operate an article-retrieval database service (including internal use), and the *Mainichi Shimbun* also supplies a photo database. The database business had sales of approximately ¥211.6 billion in 1993, a decline from the peak figure of ¥215.9 billion in 1991, according to a survey conducted by the Ministry of International Trade and Industry. The decline resulted from the slow growth of corporate use caused by the 1990s recession.

Table 4.3. Internet addresses of leading Japanese newspapers

Asahi Shimbun Publishing Co. (Publication Division)*	http://www.asahi.com http://www.opendoors.eccosys.com/
Mainichi Newspapers†	http://www.mainichi.co.jp/
Yomiuri Shimbun‡	http://www.yomiuri.co.jp/
Nihon Keizai Shimbun	http://www.nikkei.co.jp/nikkei-x/
Tokyo Shimbun	http://www.tokyo-np.co.jp
Sankei Shimbun	http://www.sankei.co.jp
Hokkaido Shimbun Press	http://oroppas.sec.or.jp/news/news.html
Chūnichi Shimbun	http://www.chunichi.co.jp/
Nishi Nippon Shimbun	http://www.coara.or.jp/coara/ns-press/nishinippon.html

Source: Nihon Shimbun Kyokai (NSK).

*Affiliation with Knight-Ridder, Inc., with server at *San Jose Mercury News* (Calif.); provides articles in Japanese and in English (from the *Asahi Evening News*), as well as flash news, corporate press releases and job-hunting service.

†Provides articles in Japanese and English (from the *Mainichi Daily News*).

‡Provides articles in Japanese and English (from the *Daily Yomiuri* and the monthly magazine *This is Yomiuri*).

Cable Television

Forty-one newspaper companies and news agencies, up four from the previous survey, participated in the CATV business. Local newspapers especially have jumped on the cable bandwagon. The *Shinano Mainichi Shimbun*, for example, had interests in 10 CATV stations. Japan has more than 150 commercial large-scale, two-way cable TV stations, according to the Ministry of Posts and Telecommunications (MPT). As of December 1994, more than 9 million Japanese subscribed to cable.

Teletext news has been attracting more subscribers. Although the 100,000 subscribing households of Nihon Network Service in Kofu City west of Tokyo is an unusually high number, many stations have more than 10,000 subscribing households.

Videotex

Although more than 25 newspapers and news agencies still provide videotex, the venture has not met with success. Problems include user dissatisfaction, difficulty in maintaining the information supply and a low customer base. Many newspapers are pulling out of videotex operations.

Personal Computer Communication

Compared with the West, Internet use in Japan remains low (see Chapter 12). Only 33 newspapers and news agencies–including affiliated companies–communicate via personal computers. These provide flash news, article databases, information about their own events, electronic bulletin boards and E-mail feedback from their readers ("33 news firms" 1996).

Telecommunications

Local newspapers have eagerly adopted the pager. Participation in pager service ventures ranges from 1 percent capital investment to major shareholder. Six local newspapers have sent presidents to pager firms; 32 have invested capital in pager companies and nine in the cellular telephone business.

CD-ROM

Six newspapers now sell CD-ROM packages, supplied off-line in databases–four since the previous survey. Eleven companies provide broadcasting programs.

To face the leaner and meaner 21st century, many newspapers have created committees to re-examine management. It seems clear, though, that the 40-page paper, much talked about in the 1980s, will not appear any time soon.

5
Postwar News Agencies

Along with more than 3 million other Japanese, Sumiko Suzuki took a sightseeing tour of the United States in 1990; thus she can add a personal perspective to the U.S. news she reads. Taro Tanaka has never traveled outside of Japan, but like most other Japanese, he rates the United States as the country he likes the best (see Chapter 2)–possibly because the mass media have made it so familiar.

Overseas Coverage

Of all countries in the world that cover the United States, Japan dispatches the largest flotilla of correspondents: 181 (Germany runs a close second). As Table 5.1 shows, to the Japanese, the U.S. financial capital of New York (with 82 correspondents) rates as more newsworthy than the U.S. political capital of Washington, D.C. (with 65 correspondents). Conversely, no other country comes close to the United States as a news magnet for Japanese mass media (the United Kingdom draws only 59 Japanese correspondents; China, 45; and Russia/Commonwealth of Independent States, 40).

Kyodo News (called Kyodo News Service until January 1, 1996), which no single mass medium can match for breadth and depth of coverage, likewise sends more correspondents to the United States than to any other country. In an irony of history, the news agency for which Americans served as midwife grew up to turn against the United States but has now come full circle again.

History

The first news agencies were founded in Japan around 1890 to receive foreign news and distribute it to Japanese newspapers. In 1914,

Table 5.1. Japanese foreign correspondents, 1995

NORTH AMERICA 183

Canada   2
  Toronto •   2

United States   181
  Washington ••   65
  New York ••   82
  Houston   1
  San Francisco ▫• 4
  Los Angeles ••   14
  Chicago •   2
  Seattle   2
  Anchorage ▫   1
  Atlanta   7
  Kansas City   1
  Honolulu ▫   2

CENTRAL &
  SOUTH AMERICA 19

Argentina   3
  Buenos Aires ▫   3

Bolivia   1
  Santa Cruz   1

Brazil   9
  Sao Paulo •   6
  Rio De Janeiro ■   3

Mexico   4
  Mexico City ••   4

Peru   2
  Lima ▫   2

EUROPE   205

Austria   12
  Vienna ••   12

Belgium   10
  Brussels ••   10

Commonwealth of
  Independent States 40
  Moscow ••   33
  Khabarovsk   1
  Yuzno-Sakhalinsk   1
  Vladivostok ▫   5

Czech Republic   3
  Prague ■   3

France   31
  Paris ••   31

Germany   26
  Berlin ••   10
  Bonn ■   10
  Dusseldorf •   1
  Frankfurt ••   4
  Hamburg •   1

Hungary   1
  Budapest ■   1

Italy   7
  Rome ■   5
  Milan   2

Poland   3
  Warsaw ■   3

Spain   1
  Granada   1

Sweden   1
  Stockholm ▫   1

Switzerland   9
  Geneva ••   8
  Zurich   1

United Kingdom   59
  London ••   59

Yugoslavia   2
  Belgrade ■   2

AFRICA,
  MIDDLE EAST   33

Egypt   16
  Cairo ••   16

Kenya   2
  Nairobi ■   2

South Africa   3
  Johannesburg ■   3

Cyprus   1
  Nicosia ■   1

Iran   4
  Tehran ■   4

Iraq   1
  Baghdad   1

Israel   5
  Jerusalem ■▫   5

Lebanon   1
  Beirut ▫   1

ASIA   190

Cambodia   4
  Phnom Penh ■   4

People's Republic
  of China   45
  Beijing ••   36
  Shanghai ■   9

Taiwan   1
  Taipei   1

Hong Kong ••   27

India   8
  New Delhi ••   8

Indonesia   7
  Jakarta ••   7

Republic of Korea   27
  Seoul ••   27

Malaysia   1
  Kuala Lumpur ■   1

Mongolia   2
  Ulan Bator ■   2

Myanmar   1
  Yangon ▫   1

Nepal   2
  Katmandu ▫   2

Pakistan   1
  Islamabad ▫   1

Philippines   14
  Manila ••   14

Singapore ••   16

Thailand   28
  Bangkok ••   28

Vietnam   6
  Hanoi ■   6

OCEANIA   8

Australia   8
  Sydney ••   8

Total overseas correspon-
dents sent by all media:
638

■ = Kyodo bureau; ▫ = Kyodo stringer; • = Jiji bureau; ◦ = Jiji stringer.
Source: Nihon Shimbun Kyokai (NSK). *The Japanese Press '95.*

The Associated Press helped Japanese diplomats and businesspeople set up Japan's first true international news agency, Kokusai. An American, John R. Kennedy, served as general manager. Under subsequent Japanese management, Kokusai merged with the Toho agency in 1926 to form the Nippon Rengo News Agency, still a non-profit cooperative like the AP.

Its rival, the commercial Nippon Denpo agency, established in 1901 and supported by the United Press, engaged in both news and advertising services. (The advertising section later grew into today's Dentsu advertising agency.) The two American wire services proceeded to fight a proxy war via their Japanese protégés. Moreover, the agencies differed in that Nippon Denpo favored the militarists' viewpoint, whereas Nippon Rengo reflected the Foreign Ministry's.

In 1936, the final merger occurred: the two rivals formed the Domei News Agency, the de facto government mouthpiece that spread anti-U.S. propaganda during World War II. While the government subsidized and gave impetus to creating Domei, journalists and businesspeople had for years been pushing for a single, powerful agency, according to Purdy (1987).

After Japan's surrender, Domei President Inosuke Furuno dissolved the discredited agency in November 1945 in order to create two new wire services—Kyodo Tsushin and Jiji Tsushin. But prewar legacies and linkages remain even today. According to van Wolferen (1993, 235): "These links are reinforced by cross-shareholding. Dentsu is kept informed of the news that Kyodo handles, and especially with local newspapers can instantaneously intercede on behalf of its clients."

After the war, Kyodo had about 1,000 employees (a fifth the number Domei had at its peak), obsolete leased telephone lines and a wireless communications network built during the war. Jiji had only 260 employees, who together put up ¥100,000 in equity to restart the agency. To avoid a situation like the intense prewar rivalry between Nippon Rengo and Nippon Denpo, the struggling agencies made an agreement. Kyodo would operate as a cooperative (like the prewar Nippon Rengo and AP), supplying general news to newspapers and broadcasters, and Jiji would operate as a for-profit service (like the prewar Nippon Denpo and UPI), specializing in economic news for businesses and book publishers. This division of labor did not last long, however.

During the Allied Occupation, news about Japan was reported exclusively by foreign journalists because the Supreme Commander, Allied Powers (SCAP) banned Japanese news agencies from engaging in overseas services. When the peace treaty was signed in 1952, Kyodo resumed its English-language overseas service with Morse code transmission.

Kyodo faced several crises in the early postwar years. The Big Three national dailies—*Asahi, Mainichi* and *Yomiuri*—began to develop their own news-gathering systems. In 1952, they dropped out of the cooperative, thus avoiding Kyodo's heavy membership fees, which were based on newspaper price and circulation. Since the fees from the Big Three constituted a large part of Kyodo's budget, the loss hurt. Kyodo managed to survive the crisis with strong support from the other Japanese newspapers, which were involved in fierce circulation battles with the Big Three. In 1957, the Big Three resubscribed to Kyodo's foreign news service.

Faced with financial difficulties and feeling constrained by the postwar agreement with Kyodo, Jiji soon breached it. In 1951, Jiji established its own overseas service, first using Morse code to transmit romanized Japanese and then in 1952 switching to facsimile. In 1951, Jiji had acquired patent rights to the facsimile system developed by Hogan, a U.S. firm. This technology, a precursor of the fax era, dominated transmission for some time.

The Jiji English Service was established in 1952. Jiji started its own general news service for newspapers and broadcasters in 1964 after concluding agreements with various foreign wire services and improving its domestic and overseas operations. In 1982 Jiji established an English-language economic news service, JIJI-WIN, which became available worldwide as of 1988 under Reuter auspices.

Kyodo for its part concentrated on ways to transmit the *kanji* ideographs and *kana* syllables that make up the written Japanese language. The first breakthrough, the tape character transmission system, replaced voice transmission in 1949. Twelve years later, Kyodo developed a teletype system for *kanji* and *kana,* which also had applications for newspaper layout.

Kyodo began electronic transmission in 1961. In 1965 it instituted an English teleprinter news service called Kyodo World Service. Kyodo computerized its news gathering and transmission in 1975, vastly increasing transmission speed, which it replaced by a new system in 1982.

The Kyodo-Jiji rivalry further gained momentum when Kyodo started publishing business and non-media information services, which had been Jiji's domain. The competition and structure remind one of the AP-UPI rivalry of the 1950s and 1960s. UPI lost the battle when, in the late 1970s, it experienced severe financial problems (Scripps-Howard sold UPI in 1982). After filing for bankruptcy in 1991, "its future is uncertain" (Stevenson 1994, 289). By contrast, both Kyodo and Jiji remain viable. As of 1995, Jiji had 1,439 employees and 29 foreign locations to Kyodo's 1,972 employees and 50 foreign locations (see Table 5.2).

Table 5.2. Overseas bureaus of Japan's mass media

	Bureaus	Stringers	Total
Wire services			
Kyodo	40	10	50
Jiji	28	1	29
Newspapers			
Yomiuri	32		32
Asahi	30	1	31
Nihon Keizai	28		28
Mainichi	20	2	22
Chūnichi	16		16
Sankei	14		14
TV networks			
NHK	27		27
ANN	24	2	26
FNN	18		18
JNN	16		16
NNN	16		16

Source: Nihon Shimbun Kyokai (NSK), *The Japanese Press '95.*

Even though Kyodo and Jiji compete intensely, in 1995 they signed an agreement to help each other in the event of a disaster as calamitous as the 1995 Kobe earthquake. Operations to transmit domestic news would shift to Osaka if the Tokyo headquarters of either agency could not function.

Content

Few people have the need, chance or desire to read the daily 320,000-character Japanese output or 55,000-word English output of a wire service such as Kyodo. Instead, Sumiko Suzuki and Taro Tanaka read only what a newspaper, radio or TV news editor has selected for them from Kyodo. Sometimes, though, a researcher goes behind the scenes to examine the raw wire service "menu" from which the mass media select their news "diet."

Henningham (1979, 30) found "wide disparities" in content categories for five randomly selected days in 1977 between Kyodo's English service and the Japanese service from which the English service is drawn and translated. Both the Japanese and English services gave about the same attention to domestic economic, scientific, labor union and police stories.

However, the English service overemphasized stories with international angles; it underemphasized hard news stories about domestic Japanese politics, as well as soft news such as Japanese education and culture stories.

Every day the main Kyodo newsroom distributes vast amounts of Japanese copy to the English news desk. From hundreds of Japanese stories, a handful of news editors selects only about 25 percent of the items to translate into English. In response to a questionnaire, the editors at Kyodo's English service "maintained that they used objective criteria, rejecting suggestions that they were concerned to promote or defend Japan's foreign image" (Henningham 1979, 30). The editors did not attempt to duplicate the news emphases of the basic Japanese service; instead, they provided a greater proportion of items involving relations between Japan and the rest of the world. In sum, according to Henningham (1979, 23): "Kyodo plays an important role in determining the picture of Japan formed by the outside world, a role made all the more important by the language barrier which prevents all but Japanese specialists from reading newspapers and magazines which the Japanese themselves read."

Operations

Kyodo News

The Kyodo Tsushinsha [news agency], a non-profit cooperative organized by 63 major newspapers and the Japan Broadcasting Corp. (NHK), has its world headquarters near the Toranomon subway stop in Tokyo. Figure 5.1 shows how information flows into and out of the Tokyo nerve center. Funded entirely by membership dues and subscription revenues, Kyodo had a 1995 annual budget of ¥42.8 billion and employed nearly 2,000 people—about 1,200 of them editors, reporters and photographers. Of those, about 50 work for the Kyodo World Service.

Kyodo World Service

Kyodo plays such a monumental gatekeeping role because its English service, Kyodo World Service (KWS), is used by (1) nearly 100 national news agencies through direct and indirect exchange links, (2) overseas media that do not have their own Japan-based correspondent, (3) overseas media that do have bureaus in Japan but need a backup service to allow correspondents to work on major stories, (4) the Japan-based foreign correspondents themselves, (5) the five Tokyo-based English-language dailies, (6) foreign diplomatic missions in Tokyo and (7) hotels, trains and certain other organizations.

NEWS FLOW

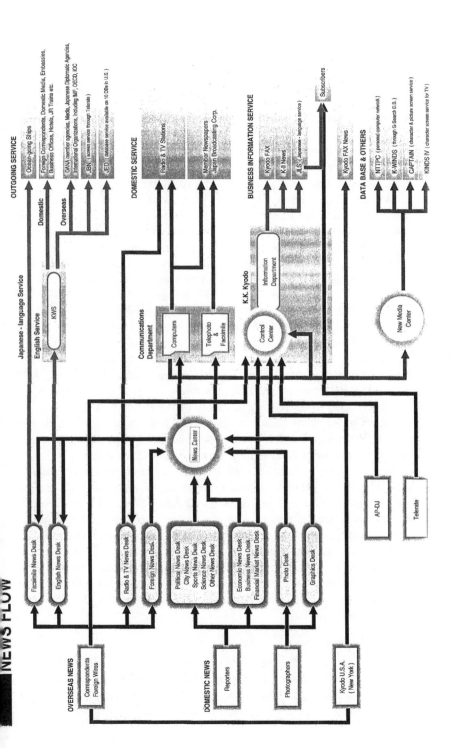

Figure 5.1. Operations at Kyodo News, Tokyo. (Graphic courtesy of Kyodo News.)

In addition to filing translated stories, KWS has its own correspondents at bureaus in Beijing, Kuala Lumpur and Washington, D.C., and in Tokyo at the Prime Minister's Office, the Ministry of International Trade and Industry, the Foreign Ministry, the Finance Ministry, the Bank of Japan, the Tokyo Stock Exchange and other places from which important breaking news must be moved quickly. KWS journalists write directly in English when they attend important trade talks, press conferences or sports events with colleagues who work for the Japanese domestic service. KWS journalists also produce enterprise stories.

William May, a bilingual journalist, worked from 1986 to 1989 at the KWS sports desk and then switched to the news desk. In April 1996 he switched back to the sports desk in preparation for the Summer Olympics, which he covered from Kyodo's news bureau in Atlanta, and for the Nagano Winter Olympics in 1998. While on the news desk, for a story on *kenbei* [U.S. hatred], May interviewed the originator of the phrase. Media such as the *New York Times* may get ideas from KWS and "write another story, slanted for their readers" (May, personal communication, June 21, 1993). "AP likes to cover events themselves, but if they can't, they may say 'Kyodo reported' and rewrite our stories."

The KWS output goes directly to certain large national news agencies, including Reuters, the Press Trust of India, Antara (Indonesia), AFP (France), DPA (France) and AP–Dow Jones. Selected stories from KWS go to 21 other OANA (Organization of Asia-Pacific News Agencies) members through the Bernama news agency of Malaysia, which houses the OANA computer. KWS is also translated into Spanish and distributed to 60 media in Latin America by Italy's ANSA Agency.

In May 1995, a potential competitor to KWS began full operations: the AFX-Asia English-language news service, headquartered in Singapore. Staffed by 35 journalists in 13 Asian cities, AFX-Asia reports financial and political news that relates to Asian economic trends. Capital comes from the French AFP news service (25 percent), the Australian AAP Information Services (25 percent), the *Nihon Keizai Shimbun* (15 percent) and AFP-Extel News, a service based in London (10 percent). *Nihon Keizai* has exclusive rights to translate the AFX-Asia texts into Japanese, but such news would merely supplement the services of the dominant Kyodo network.

Japanese-language domestic service

Fewer than 100 people work for KWS. Most of Kyodo's employees collect domestic and international news for its 62 Japanese members. Kyodo also sells news to the non-member Big Three dailies (*Asahi, Mainichi* and *Yomiuri*), a few other non-member dailies and more than 100 radio and television companies, which receive broadcast versions of stories. In effect, Kyodo serves almost all newspapers and radio and television stations in Japan.

Entry-level employees, usually hired in their early 20s, serve first at one of Kyodo's 54 domestic bureaus. News gathered at these bureaus and the Tokyo headquarters is edited in Tokyo and Osaka. Overseas news flows in from correspondents in 40 cities and stringers in 11 other locations throughout the world (see Table 5.1). Although numbers of Kyodo stringers fluctuate, Kyodo consistently maintains its 40 permanent bureaus.

Table 5.1 demonstrates the agency's emphasis on Asia. Including stringers, local hires and regular staff, about 40 of Kyodo's 100 overseas journalists work throughout Asia. Kyodo has the sole Japanese bureaus in Malaysia (Kuala Lumpur) and Mongolia (Ulan Bator)—but no bureau at all in Taiwan. Kyodo and all other Japanese media have to abide by certain rules to keep their bureaus in Beijing and Shanghai (see Chapter 4). (The *Sankei Shimbun* chafed at the restrictions, opted out of the agreement with the Chinese government, left China and set up the sole Japanese bureau on Taiwan.)

Kyodo times the sending of its news and feature menus to its clients' production and broadcast schedules. It distributes the menus after each of four daily editorial meetings, held at 9 a.m., 3 p.m. and twice in the evening. On average, Kyodo files 495,000 characters of Japanese-language news and 170 photographs (including color photos) daily over its computer-controlled optical-cable digital circuits. The system delivers sports and election results with great speed. Its communications network now extends 6,200 kilometers.

Jiji Press

Jiji Press is currently capitalized at ¥495 million, with all of its 9.9 million shares held by its 1,400 employees. In addition to its head office in Tokyo, Jiji has 82 branch offices in Japan and 28 offices overseas (see Table 5.1). In North America, it has a main office in New York and branch offices in Washington, D.C., Chicago, San Francisco, Los Angeles and Toronto. Offices in other areas of the world are shown in Table 5.1, with the larger ones having numerous correspondents. Jiji has contracts or joint agreements with Reuters, AFP, UPI, DPA, Xinhua and Tass. The Reuters arrangement lets Jiji use Reuters' worldwide network to broadcast its English-language economic news service (JIJI-WIN) for access through Reuters monitors.

Jiji has almost 70 different services. Of these, the media service and business information service, supplied to industry and government agencies, are the most important. The media service goes out to about 120 newspapers and broadcasters.

Jiji offers news not only in English but also Chinese and Spanish. JIJI-WIN was begun in 1982 and has since gone electronic. Articles from JIJI-WIN are entered in the Mead Data Central, Newsnet and the British Finsbury databases. Jiji set up JETS (Jiji Press Editing System) and JACS (Jiji Press Advanced Communication and Processing System) in 1982. JACS, for example, incorporates article functions to enable searching by personal computer. Jiji's overseas Japanese-language service, started in 1953, is available in most major cities worldwide by facsimile, called the JOIN service, or in print.

Jiji, also a publisher, puts out *Shukan Jiji*, a general magazine of political, economic, social and cultural news; *Sekai Shūhō*, a weekly focusing on international affairs; and the *Jiji Nenkan* almanac, published annually since 1945. In addition to these periodicals, Jiji publishes 40 to 50 books each year.

Like Reuters, Jiji has found a niche delivering financial information, as Japan's increasing effect on the financial markets has made information from Japan more important for other traders as well. The arrival of the computer has changed the delivery methods of this information.

Technology

Jiji Press

Subscribers can have real-time access to information from their own computers. Jiji has offered electronic news services for finance and securities since 1986 and for commodities since 1989. MAIN–an on-line, real-time database of general news and economic information on currency exchange rates as well as stocks and bonds started in 1986–includes banks, securities companies, trading houses and manufacturers among its subscribers. For Jiji, MAIN's introduction just as the yen was appreciating contributed to its rapid diffusion. Since 1988, MAIN has been available in Hong Kong and Singapore, where most of the users are Japanese affiliates.

In 1989, Jiji initiated two new electronic media services: J-COM1000 and J-COM3000. J-COM1000 gives users, mainly commodities trading houses, on-line, real-time prices, trading volumes and other information for all listed commodities (gold, grains, rubber, etc.) from the 16 commodities markets nationwide.

Business information in print includes the *Kancho Sokuho* with news developments at government offices from the national government to local village councils. There are also specialized services focusing on education, finance, taxes, welfare, agriculture and forestry.

In 1990, Jiji switched to a digital network linking Tokyo, New York and London to give the company the ability to transmit information worldwide at very high speeds and large volumes. It has signed a contract with Reuters to mutually distribute financial data.

Kyodo News

Kyodo News also uses electronic media to distribute news. The New Media Center offers a video-screen news service (called KINDS IV) to help television networks and non-media clients and operates a database (called KWINDS). The center also provides the CAPTAIN videotex information service and serves as an information provider for E-mail. Personal computer users can access host computers in Tokyo or New York via the News Machine through local phone networks.

KWS is rewritten into a news summary for database use, called JED, and fed to six databases in the United States, including Dow Jones News Retrieval and two European databases–Datastar and Minitel.

Kyodo's Japanese-language overseas service is transmitted in the form of a facsimile newspaper, published twice a day, for some 3,000 ocean-going ships, nine Japanese-language newspapers and radio or television stations in the United States and Latin America as well as other Japanese media overseas.

In addition to its non-profit operations, Kyodo has a business subsidiary, K.K. Kyodo, established in 1972. It is a rare phenomenon–a news agency that also sells services to the general public and non-media organizations. Its Japanese Language Service (JLS) is transmitted via the Dow Jones Telerate network to clients, mainly Japanese businesspeople, in Tokyo, New York, London, Hong Kong, Singapore, Seoul, Manila and Sydney. This subsidiary also serves as the sole sales agent for Telerate in Japan. K.K. Kyodo publishes books and magazines, plans and promotes events, runs a speaker's bureau and sells financial information, specialized information and photographs.

6
Postwar Magazines and Manga

Taro Tanaka, a *rōnin* [high school graduate who failed college entrance exams and plans to take them again], stops at a 7-11 store in Tokyo to pick up a ready-made box lunch on his way from his part-time job to classes at a cram school. Sumiko Suzuki stops at a 7-11 in Nagoya to pick up some medicine on her way home from work. Taro also buys a *manga* comic; Sumiko buys a copy of *Josei Seven* magazine.

Sales and Distribution

In 1992, the 24-hour 7-11 convenience store chain pushed past the Kinokuniya bookstore chain to rank as Japan's largest book and magazine retailer. That year, 7-11 sold magazines and paperbacks worth more than ¥100 billion, nosing out Kinokuniya's ¥93 billion in sales. Kinokuniya does not feel threatened by 7-11, however, because books constitute 90 percent of Kinokuniya's sales, whereas 7-11 caters to the magazine and comic buyer. Instead, the U.S. convenience store invasion has affected small, independent bookstores that rely on magazines for 70 percent of their sales; in the early 1990s, about 1,000 per year of the mom-and-pop stores went out of business.

In 1982, convenience stores accounted for only 2.8 percent of printed matter sales, but 10 years later, the figure stood at 16 percent. Magazines reach consumers by many routes, so 16 percent represents a large chunk. In 1992, besides 7-11, the Lawson chain sold printed matter worth ¥67 billion, and Family Mart sold ¥35 billion worth. Point-of-sale data let the central management of the chains know immediately which printed items do and do not sell well so they can act accordingly.

Impulse buyers like Taro and Sumiko prompt publishers to design eye-catching covers and keep prices low. Indeed, virtually all magazines in Japan are purchased individually, whether at convenience stores, railway kiosks or bookstores. Mail subscriptions form a negligible mode of delivery. Thus hyped-up Publishers Clearinghouse–style subscription blitzes do not exist in Japan.

Neither do mega-selling magazines such as the 22-million-circulation *Modern Maturity* or 16-million *Reader's Digest.* As Table 6.1 shows, Japan has relatively few periodicals with a circulation of more than 1 million. By contrast, 81 U.S. magazines had circulations of more than 1 million, according to the Audit Bureau of Circulation (1992). In 1995, for the first time in history, more than 4,000 magazines were being published in the United States; the 1995 figure included 838 new titles. The staggering number of U.S. quarterlies, most of them specialized and academic journals with smaller circulations, overwhelms the few in Japan.

Over the past 20 years, Japan has evolved from a nation of book buyers to a nation of magazine buyers. As Table 6.2 shows, in 1970 books held a slight edge, at 52 books for every 48 magazines sold. The ratio of book to magazine sales reversed in 1976, tipping in favor of magazines. By the early 1990s, magazines were outselling books three to two.

The shift simply meant a reallocation of resources within certain companies, such as Kodansha, Shogakukan and Shueisha, which publish comics and books. Indeed, these three publishing giants control more than three-quarters of the lucrative men's comics market. The top 10 publishing companies account for more than half of all printed materials. Most (80 percent) of Japan's publishing companies are headquartered in Tokyo, with only 5 percent in Osaka, making it a heavily centralized, as well as an oligopolistic, industry.

Distribution also tends to be concentrated. A wholesaler delivers books and magazines to retailers, picks up and disposes of unsold inventory, collects money from the retailer and pays the publisher. Retailers, who decide how long to display a magazine, often return unsold copies within a week. Of 100 wholesale agents, two–Tokyo Shuppan Hanbai and Nippon Shuppan Hanbai–together control 80 percent of all publication distribution.

The habit of buying individual copies of magazines serves the publishers well. As Table 6.2 shows, today Japan produces enough magazines for every man, woman and child to have more than 16 monthlies and nearly 13 weeklies a year.

History

Prewar Magazines

Modern printing, begun during the Meiji period (1868–1912), was initially used as a tool for education. Japan's first modern magazine,

Table 6.1. Japan's leading magazines, 1993 (circulation 1+ million)*

	Circulation*	Publishing frequency
Comics for males		

Gekkan Shōnen Jump   1,400,000   Monthly
Shūkan Shōnen Jump   6,200,000   Weekly
    Publisher: Shueisha. This magazine pair is mainly read by college students and young businessmen. It has a unique editorial policy and uses tie-ins creatively. The weekly ranks as the largest-circulating magazine in Japan.

Ribbon   2,400,000   Monthly
    Publisher: Shueisha. Publication aimed at a younger audience than the *Jump* series.

Big Comic   1,000,000   Semimonthly
Big Comic Original   1,600,000   Semimonthly
Big Comic Spirits   1,200,000   Weekly
    Publisher: Shogakukan. Comic magazines for adults. Noted for cartoons featuring the themes of "escaping" from the home, society and Japan.

Shūkan Shōnen Sunday   1,300,000   Weekly
    Publisher: Shogakukan. Comics for a younger age range than the series above. "Shonen" means "young."

Comic Morning   1,000,000   Weekly
    Publisher: Kodansha. This comic magazine is intended for young adults from age 20 to younger than 40, the so-called comic generation. It aims to make readers happy with dreamy, pleasant, well-plotted stories.

Shūkan Shōnen Magazine   3,500,000   Weekly
Gekkan Shōnen Magazine   1,750,000   Weekly
Young Magazine   1,550,000   Weekly
    Publisher: Kodansha. These magazines are published for young men aged 17 to 22 and deal with romance, sports and contemporary topics.

Nakayoshi   2,000,000   Monthly
    Publisher: Kodansha. Meaning "bosom buddies," this publication aims at a young teen audience.

General
Friday   1,000,000†   Weekly
    Publisher: Kodansha. A pictorial magazine featuring everyday happenings in all fields, from politics to sports and news of international interest.

Magazines for women
Ie no Hikari   1,070,000   Monthly
    Publisher: Ie no Hikari Association (11, Ichigaya Funagawara-cho, Shinjuku-ku, Tokyo 162). Magazine for farming people meaning "light of the home." Carries articles to improve the quality of life of rural communities.

Orange Page   1,100,000   Semimonthly
    Publisher: Orange Page K.K. (6-2-1, Ginza, Chuo-ku Tokyo 104). Published by the supermarket chain Daiei for housewives, sold at the chain's outlets.

non • no   1,200,000   Semimonthly
    Publisher: Shueisha. Resembles *Seventeen* and *Glamour*. Topics range from fashion and cosmetics to travel, cooking and movies.

Table 6.1. *Continued*

	Circulation*	Publishing frequency

Cooking

NHK Kyo-no-Ryori   1,100,000†   Monthly
  Publisher: Nippon Hoso Shuppan Kyokai (41-1, Udagawa-cho, Shibuya-ku, Tokyo
  150). Textbook to go with NHK's TV cooking program.

TV and entertainment

Myōjō   1,800,000†   Monthly
  Publisher: Shueisha. Entertainment magazine with stress on leisure information and
  articles about popular performers.

The Television   1,200,000   Weekly
  Publisher: Kadokawa Shoten Publishing Co. (5-24-5, Hongo, Bunkyo-ku, Tokyo 113).
  Youth-oriented magazine with detailed TV information.

TV Cosmos   1,500,000†   Monthly
  Publisher: Kadokawa Shoten Publishing Co. (5-24-5, Hongo, Bunkyo-ku, Tokyo 113).
  A TV-information magazine with special attention to satellite transmissions. Features
  monthly schedules, summaries of major programs and essays.

Source: Fujitake and Yamamoto (1994, 167).

Note: Major magazine publishers are Shogakukan Inc. (2-3-1, Hitotsubashi, Chiyoda-ku,
Tokyo 101-01), Kodansha, Ltd. (2-12-21, Otowa, Bunkyo-ku, Tokyo 112-01), and Shueisha
Publishing Co., Ltd. (2-5-10, Hitotsubashi, Chiyoda-ku, Tokyo 101).

*All circulations are estimates (not verified by Japan Audit Bureau of Circulation).

†1990 estimated circulation figures from Dentsu (1991), *Japan 1992 Marketing and
Advertising Yearbook.*

Seiyō Zasshi [Journal of the West], launched by scholar Yanagawa
Shunsan in 1867, featured translations of articles from a Dutch magazine.
The first commercially successful magazine, the *Reader's Digest*–like *Nihon
Taika Ronshu* [Collected Essays of Japanese Luminaries], included articles
from other newspapers and magazines. From then on, publishers realized
that popular periodicals could make a tidy profit.

  During the Taisho years (1912–26), mass publishing began in earnest.
In 1922, two national newspapers had enough resources to create the
popular weeklies *Shūkan Asahi* and *Sunday Mainichi*, both modeled after
the meaty Sunday editions of Western newspapers. More so than
monthly magazines, weeklies demanded a large editorial staff and large
numbers of writers. They included serialized fiction as well as commentary on current affairs. *Chūō Kōron* [Public Debate], founded in 1899, still
ranks as one of Japan's leading opinion journals; *Kaizō* [Reform], founded
in 1919, carried articles of Marxist and Socialist debate (it ceased publication in 1955). "Known for their vigorous spirit of social and political

Table 6.2. Changes in Japan's magazine market, 1970–90

	1970	1980	1990
Monthly magazines			
Actual sales (¥100 million)	1,363	5,670	9,069
% Previous year's sales	116	113	106
Monthly index	(1970=100)	(416)	(665.4)
Circulation (10,000 copies)	84,113	181,759	260,116
No. of titles	1,319	1,836	2,246
No. of copies purchased per capita per year	6.6	12.0	16.5
Weekly magazines			
Actual sales (¥100 million)	739	2,129	3,569
% Previous year's sales	121	112	106
Monthly index	(1970=100)	(288)	(482.9)
Circulation (10,000 copies)	110,077	134,490	182,928
No. of titles	48	55	78
No. of copies purchased per capita per year	8.5	9.4	12.7
Magazine total			
Actual sales (¥100 million)	2,102	7,799	12,638
% Previous year's sales	118	112	106
Monthly index	(1970=100)	(371)	(601.2)
Circulation (10,000 copies)	194,210	316,241	443,044
No. of titles	1,365	1,891	2,324
No. of copies purchased per capita per year	15.1	21.4	29.4
Books: magazines (%)	52:48	46:54	41:59

Source: Dentsu (1991), *Japan 1992 Marketing and Advertising Yearbook.*

Note: Monthly magazine figures for 1980 and 1990 include comic books, which were counted as books before 1975.

criticism" (Ueda 1994), they were both closed down by military authorities in 1944.

During the war, many journals either merged, shrank in size or ceased publication altogether. The July 1945 issue of the women's monthly *Shufunotomo* [Housewife's Friend], for example, had only 32 pages. Because of wartime restrictions and shortages, the publishing industry was down to about 300 companies by August 1945.

Postwar Opinion Journals

After the war, with the Occupation guaranteeing and encouraging freedom of speech, many new titles appeared–the majority of them *sōgō zasshi*, magazines aimed at educated readers that carried commentary, light essays and some fiction. In 1945, new titles included *Shinsei* [New Life], *Hikari* [Light], *Ondori Tsūshin* [Ondori News], *Jinmin Hyōron*

[The People's Review] and *Minshu Hyōron* [Democratic Review]. In 1946, new intellectual journals included *Tembo* [Prospect], which ceased publication in 1951, was revived in 1964 and closed for good in 1978; *Sekai* [The World]; *Sekai Hyōron* [The World Review]; and *Asahi Hyōron* [Asahi Review], published by the *Asahi Shimbun.* New literary journals of 1946 included *Ningen* [Humanity], *Sekai Bunka* [World Culture] and *Liberal.* Meanwhile, *Chūō Kōron* and *Kaizō* resumed publication. Many of the new titles looked hopefully toward the future by incorporating words such as "democracy" and "freedom."

Yasuo Ueda (1994, 1), a professor of journalism at Sophia University, explains the role of the rather bland and staid large newspapers vis-à-vis opinion journals, which "lead the way in the kind of opinion journalism that is found in the West in the quality papers like The New York Times and The Times (of London). Despite the inevitable time-lag resulting from monthly as opposed to daily publication, they have effectively made up for Japan's lack of newspapers with national circulation willing to print partisan opinion." Ueda (1994, 1) cites three incidents that underscore the journals' catalyst/advocacy/investigative roles:

1951: *Sekai* published a series of essays criticizing the San Francisco Peace Treaty in order to highlight issues that the mass-circulation press did not address.

1950s: *Chūō Kōron* published novelist Kazuo Hirotsu's reports on the 1951–53 trials involving 20 Japanese arrested on charges of sabotage and murder, some of whom were sentenced to death. Hirotsu's prolific writing on the case during the height of the Cold War, when the Supreme Commander, Allied Powers (SCAP) moved to suppress leftist activism, played a key role in winning acquittals.

1974: *Bungei Shunjū* published an article by commentator Takashi Tachibana exposing Prime Minister Kakuei Tanaka's corrupt political and financial dealings, which led directly to the toppling of the *kinken naikaku* [money-politics cabinet].

Postwar Weeklies

After the war, in the early 1950s, the already-established *Shūkan Asahi* and *Sunday Mainichi* rebounded with such vigor that the *Shūkan Asahi* sold more than 1 million copies in 1955. As Japan got back on its feet, only large newspapers could muster the staff and distribution networks that publication of a weekly magazine demanded. Three more newspapers joined *Asahi* and *Mainichi* in creating weeklies that carried their names: the *Shūkan Yomiuri, Shūkan Sankei* and *Shūkan Tōkyo* (published by the *Tōkyo Shimbun*).

With the popular combination of "insider" cover stories, light reading and fiction in these new publications, advertisers flocked to them. The strong sales and healthy advertising revenues of weeklies soon encouraged start-ups that had no newspaper backing, beginning in 1956 with the *Shūkan Shinchō*.

Other weeklies followed: *Shūkan Josei* for women (1957), which was later taken over by the publisher of *Shufu-to-Seikatsu* [Housewife and Life], a magazine that had debuted in 1946; Shueisha's entertainment-world gossip magazine *Shūkan Myōjō* (1958); and Kobunsha's *Josei Jishin* for women (1958). In 1959, debuts included *Shūkan Bunshun, Shūkan Gendai* (Kodansha), *Shūkan Kōron* and *Shūkan Heibon*, as well as comic magazines (*manga*) for youngsters, such as *Shōnen Magazine* (Kodansha) and *Shōnen Sunday* (Shogakukan) (see below).

Magazines grew steadily in the 1960s, with 61 new titles and a circulation of 500.3 million monthlies and 700.1 million weeklies in 1965. New weeklies included Shogakukan's *Josei Seven* for women (1963); the humor magazine *Heibon Punch* (1964); Shueisha's *Shūkan Playboy* (1965), a sports/music/fashion publication for young men (distinct from the Japanese edition of *Playboy*, a monthly also published by Shueisha); and Shogakukan's *Shūkan Post* (1968).

Magazine industry concentration, which had begun with newspaper-magazine publishers (such as the *Asahi Shimbun*) and book-magazine publishers (such as Kodansha), expanded to include multititle magazine publishers. Leading companies include Shogakukan, Shueisha, Kobunsha, Bungei Shunju and Magazine House.

Table 6.3 shows continued growth in the 1970s, with 133 new titles in 1970 and 175 in 1975. In the mid-1970s, at about the same time as magazine sales edged out that of books (see above), the number of copies published of monthlies surpassed the number of copies published of weeklies, with the gap continuing to widen every year (2.8 billion monthlies

Table 6.3. Start-ups and closures of Japanese magazines, 1970–90

	1970	1975	1980	1985	1990
No. inaugurated (revised)	133	175	235	245	155
No. suspended (discontinued)	63	69	107	151	81

Source: Fujitake and Yamamoto (1994, 169).

Note: In addition to 1980 and 1985, start-ups topped 200 in 1983 (244) and 1984 (238); closures topped 100 every year from 1980 to 1987.

vs. 1.9 billion weeklies in 1992). Also in the mid-1970s, the Japanese made television their medium of choice (TV ad expenditures surpassed newspaper ad expenditures in 1975).

What do couch potatoes read when they do read? TV magazines, of course. Previously, only *TV Guide* and *Shūkan Terebi Bangumi* [Weekly TV Programs] had this market niche to themselves. But with the success of *The Television*, launched in 1982, more publishers jumped on the bandwagon. Currently, about 10 TV magazines vie for readers. Moreover, general magazines now cover TV as a topic and contain TV schedules. *Chou Chou*, aimed at women in their early 20s, has two weeks' worth of TV listings as well as 19 pages of stories on TV stars and shows. Like TV magazines, many other specialized publications proliferated in the 1980s.

Magazines Today

The Volatile 1980s

As Table 6.3 shows, a magazine explosion occurred in the 1980s unlike anything Japan had previously seen. True, closures marred the picture, but the number of closures was nothing like the staggering number of start-ups: more than 200 new titles per year in 1980, 1983, 1984 and 1985.

A new trend began in 1981 with the debut of *Focus*, a weekly heavy on sensational photographs and light on descriptive text. *Focus*, which survived early publishing difficulties, eventually hit a circulation high of 2 million copies each week. This success touched off a spate of rivals by the major publishers: Kodansha published *Friday*; Shogakukan, *Touch*; Bungei Shunju, *Emma*; and Kobunsha, *Flash*. *Touch* and *Emma* later folded, today leaving as photo weeklies only the "3 F's" (*Focus*, *Friday* and *Flash*). Now, *Friday* (1 million circulation) outsells both *Flash* (600,000) and the original *Focus* (700,000).

Started in 1987, the magazine *Hanako* has taken Tokyo by storm. Its readers–young, unmarried, working women in the Tokyo area (who usually live at home with their parents)–can spend their salary on whatever *Hanako* deems *torendi* [trendy]: "Today the magazine is so influential that any shop or restaurant it praises enjoys a massive, instant boom in business. *Hanako* is defining a generation of Japanese working women; marketers are talking about *Hanako-san*–the perfect *Hanako* girl. She is in her 20s, single, independent and affluent" (Whipple 1991, 47).

Kanai (1996, 1) sees *Hanako* as providing a role model that young women do not experience in real life–someone unlike both the *ryōsai kembo* [good wife, wise mother] and "the tight-lipped career woman willing to give up both marriage and children to capture a place in the corporate world on a par with white-collar men." The magazine asserts that "women ought to be freer and more aggressive"–not only while single but also after marrying and having children (Kanai 1996, 1). Now, a decade after *Hanako*'s debut, its original 20-something readers, who call themselves "trente ans Hanakos" ("30-something Hanakos") "are starting to declare that 'Mother is just as important as child'" (Kanai 1996, 2).

Other women's weeklies–*Josei Jishin, Josei Seven* and *Shūkan Josei*–which offer gossip about television and film stars, have circulations larger than *Hanako*'s 350,000 because they are sold nationwide. Indeed, *Josei Jishin* and *Josei Seven* have circulations of close to 1 million.

The 1980s saw the first American-style, all-news weeklies, which differ markedly from the typical Japanese weekly's mix of fiction, features and cartoon serials, alongside current news. *AERA*, with a circulation of about 450,000 (started in 1988 by the *Asahi Shimbun*), has caught on more quickly than the Japanese edition of *Newsweek*, with a circulation of about 150,000 (started in January 1986 by TBS Britannica). However, neither one has taken its place as Japan's premiere print medium for current news.

In the United States, *Time* (4+ million copies) and *Newsweek* (3+ million copies) hold that exalted position, but in Japan, the nationally circulating newspapers feed the national hunger for print news. Magazines will not usurp that role unless they change, believes Ueda (1994, 2): "Unlike the news weeklies of the West, which have research and reporting staff networks capable of covering international topics on a par with the major newspapers, none of Japan's weeklies have correspondents stationed overseas."

Although having a longer time horizon, some young men's investigative/opinion monthlies of the 1980s had tie-ups with overseas journals and featured international news. One, Shueisha's *Bart* (circulation 250,000), still publishes in the 1990s. Another, Bungei Shunju's *Marco Polo*, folded in 1995, when it printed an article claiming that the Holocaust of World War II did not happen (see below).

Trends of the 1990s

The year 1990 saw only 155 start-ups, a disastrous plunge from the 245 of five years earlier (see Table 6.3). Yet in November 1993, Japan still published 2,435 monthly magazines (total circulation, 259,570,000) and 79 weekly magazines (total circulation, 163,440,000), according to the Research Institute for Publications of the National Publishers Association. As economic and social conditions changed from the 1980s, an inevitable shakeout occurred.

Closures

The February 1995 issue of *Marco Polo* contained an article by Masanori Nishioka, M.D., titled "The biggest taboo in postwar history: there were no Nazi gas chambers," which claimed that the Polish government had constructed the concentration camp at Auschwitz after the war and opened it to the public. Condemning the article, the U.S.-based Simon Wiesenthal Center asked that the Japanese government criticize *Marco Polo* and that major firms pull their ads. Many major advertisers did so.

In response, *Marco Polo*'s editor offered space to the Israeli embassy in Tokyo to reply to the article. The embassy refused the offer. Then on February 2, 1995, the president of Bungei Shunju publications and Rabbi Abraham Cooper of the Wiesenthal Center held a press conference to announce that *Marco Polo* would cease publication. President Kengo Tanaka not only apologized but resigned as well, following the Japanese tradition of the person at the top taking responsibility for subordinates' actions ("Monthly folds" 1995).

Heibon Punch, once a pacesetter among men's weeklies, died for different reasons. Even a one-year break in 1988 and re-entry in 1989 under the title *New Punchsauras* could not revive interest in its brand of humor. Similarly, the monthly *Gekkan Asahi* (published by *Asahi Shimbun*) tried to survive by reducing its format to A5 size (148×210 mm), but with sales still dropping, it ceased publication with the March 1994 issue. Opinion monthlies such as *Gekkan Asahi* have a hard time staying current in the era of broadcasting and news weeklies.

Certain well-known women's magazines ceased publication as well. The venerable *Shufu-to-Seikatsu* hit a circulation peak of 800,000 in 1970 but fell to 75,000 by 1990; it published its last issue in April 1993. Another two of the "Big Four" women's magazines, *Fujin no Tomo* and *Katei Gaho*, had died in the late 1980s. The fourth, *Shufunotomo*, changed its content markedly in 1993. The Big Four once held a position similar to the "Seven Sisters" magazines in the United States, but no longer.

Changing women's markets

All of the Big Four promoted the image of the "good wife, wise mother." Explaining the demise of *Shufu-to-Seikatsu*, the director of its parent company said that "the needs of readers have become too diversified to be satisfied by a general interest magazine." In response, *Shufu* tried to change and narrow its content, but readers still viewed it as "the one that mother used to read" ("Women want" 1993).

Seeing the handwriting on the wall, in 1990 *Shufu-to-Seikatsu*'s parent company launched an entirely new publication, *Suteki na Okusan*

[Wonderful Wife], with the motto "life fulfillment for the energetic woman." With a 1993 circulation of about 800,000 (up from 300,000 in 1990), its focus on reader letters has caught on. The company CEO attributes the success to the "perception that the source of information and receiver are on equal footing" ("Women want" 1993). It contains very little celebrity lifestyle copy.

Instead of focusing on the "good wife, wise mother," the service publishers now aim to help the harried housewife with practical information and downplay the lifestyle of conspicuous consumption. When *Shufunotomo* surveyed married women 35 to 45 years old, it found that 70 percent worked, typically at part-time jobs. That 70 percent spent about half the time on housework that full-time homemakers did. The magazine's revamping in 1993 included ideas on how to save both time and money. For starters, it lowered its own cover price from ¥750 to ¥500.

The dozen or so service publications increased their circulations in the late 1980s and early 1990s. *Lettuce Club* claims 800,000 biweekly, and the Queen of Practicality, the biweekly *Orange Page*, sells 1.1 million copies. It reviews products and provides recipes that require common ingredients and little time. Originally sold only at Daiei Supermarkets, it has since gone independent. About 1,500 to 3,000 people send in the mailback comment forms that appear in each issue ("Cooking up" 1993).

Although Japanese women's magazines help women cope at home, some critics (Shinoda 1990) say that they do not help them cope at work. *Nikkei Woman* (240,000 monthly) probably comes closest to the U.S. *Working Woman* magazine, but it stands nearly alone in a vast array of 70 women's publications. Those few that have intellectual content emphasize culture rather than politics. Women's magazines have treated public affairs poorly, assuming that women still care most about fashion and food, love and marriage (Inoue 1989).

The numbers tend to confirm that assumption. *Fujin Kōron* [Women's Public Opinion], published by *Chūō Kōron*'s parent company, sells fewer than 200,000 copies; it started out with discussions of the women's movement and women's role in society, but over the last 15 years grew less serious in an effort to attract younger readers. On the other hand, *non•no*, with 300 pages devoted biweekly to fashion, makeup and travel, sells 1.2 million.

Although enough support may not exist for a Japanese equivalent of *Ms.*, changing women's roles have affected Japan's parenting magazines, such as *Pand*, which now purposefully address fathers as well as mothers. *Kodomo Angle* [Children's Angle], launched by the Shufu to Seikatsu Co. in 1992, sports the motto "the parent-child out-and-about magazine." In the frenetic 1980s, fathers in their 20s and 30s hardly ever saw their children, but the recession and changing roles of women created a need for family activities. "Play centered only on children is not popular. It must be play which children can enjoy together with their parents," stated the publication's editor ("Magazines" 1993, 5). *Kodomo Pia* [Children's Pia], which debuted as a monthly in 1991, switched to a semimonthly publication in 1992. Targeted specifically at Tokyo, it carries the motto, "For kids and parents." Since parents feel comfortable with the *Pia* format, spin-offs have a good chance of success.

Special interests

The *Pia* publications target specific cities with detailed, annotated listings of TV programs, activities, movies, sports, concerts, live shows and restaurants. Listings include maps, subway directions, hours, ticket prices and qualitative reviews. The word "Pia" has no meaning; the publishers simply wanted an easy-to-pronounce, distinctive name. The largest city edition, *Pia* for Tokyo, sells about 500,000 copies a week. A similar publication, *Tokyo Walker*, has about half of *Pia*'s circulation.

Topics of special-interest magazines in the 1990s, an era of narrowcasting in print, range from television programming (see above) to travel to singles looking for mates. Many of the special-interest publications target men. For example, a plethora of magazines serves Japan's huge video game audience. Two brothers are duking it out for market dominance with similar titles and content, five at each of their rival companies. The younger Sato brother resigned in 1992 from Kadokawa Publishing to start his own firm, Media Works, taking most of the 71 employees with him. Such magazines also rely heavily on free-lancers ("New twist" 1992).

The more traditional spectator and participant sports, such as golf and pro wrestling, have their own publications, while sports that are growing more popular in Japan, such as soccer and basketball, have created a spin-off industry of new magazines. Japan's 100 or so sports magazines had a 1993 circulation of about 70 million.

According to Toshiharu Sasaki of the Publications Research Institute, the market can support only about three magazines per sport. A shakeout will occur in soccer, for example, as 10 entries compete for survival. Attrition has already occurred in some older sports. The monthly *Asahi Golf*, for example, ceased publication when the economic recession decreased golf club memberships. Remaining golf magazines must focus on people who patronize urban driving ranges ("Sports magazines" 1993). A new entry, *Vert*, targets women golfers.

Formula 1 racing has likewise passed its 1980s peak, with Honda engines no longer in competition and the retirement of racer Satoru Nakajima. *F-1 Grand Prix Special* has seen circulation decline from its

1991 high of 230,000. Interest in car owners' magazines, however, supports 12 publications; all but one sport titles in English, including the popular semimonthly *Driver*, which claims to sell 400,000 copies.

Speakers of English, considered as a special-interest group, can choose from magazines that keep them in touch with the world, such as the Asian editions of *Time* and *Newsweek*, to others that keep them in touch with Japan. They can also buy magazines imported from home (in 1988, Japan exported ¥4,203.18 million worth of magazines but imported more—¥10,206.38 million worth).

Appendix 2 includes English-language magazines that circulate nationally or focus on Tokyo. In addition, every large city has a local English-language periodical. If one were to include newsletters, the list would grow exponentially. Nagoya, for example, a city of 2.1 million, boasts two glossy monthlies: *Nagoya Avenues* and *Eyes*. *Kyoto Journal*, although published in Kyoto, reaches beyond that city's limits to carry "thought-provoking articles on Japan and Asia."

CD-ROM publications

Even though relatively few consumers have personal computers in their homes (see Chapter 12), "CDs are generally included inside regular magazines to allow distribution through bookstores and other magazine outlets" (Kilburn 1994). Another problem is the murky area of intellectual property rights regarding software.

Media Direct, a quarterly, provides previews of games and even some pornography on a disk included with the purchase price; it claimed some 30,000 copies sold of the first issue's publication in November 1993. A special issue of *Popeye* with a disk included did even better, selling all 200,000 copies in two weeks.

Still, the up-to-date and ephemeral nature of periodicals is at odds with the somewhat costly CD-ROMs, which are best suited for long-term use. But since magazine publishers are also book publishers, they can work both sides of the fence. For example, more than 100,000 copies of the *Kojien*, "the Japanese equivalent of an Oxford or Webster's dictionary" ("Japanese readers" 1996), have been sold since 1987.

Sensational Muckraking

In 1995, after *Marco Polo* published a story that denied the existence of the Holocaust, the *Asahi Shimbun* called the article "shallow and sensational," and the *Mainichi Shimbun* faulted the magazine for "giving priority to sell with a sensational approach." Television programs criticized *Marco Polo*'s obsession with scoops. When the president of Bungei

Shunju publications resigned over the incident, he admitted the need for more care "through, for example, an ombudsman system, and double-check and triple-check" ("Monthly folds" 1995).

The *Yomiuri* agreed that "the company should have carefully verified its substance." However, it contended that once the article was published, the parent company too quickly abandoned and killed the publication. Would Bungei Shunju or another publisher capitulate to the next threatened ad boycott? Would the next complaint result in a further silencing of voices?

The *Marco Polo* saga illustrates the dual role played by Japanese magazines, which at their best "reveal behind-the-scenes, in-depth stories that the mainstream media can't or don't want to provide. When they are bad, they can be very bad indeed" (Morikawa 1993a). Table 6.4 shows the range of topics and approaches magazines can take.

As Chapter 2 noted, magazine journalists cannot join *kisha* clubs. Thus as outsiders, they need not fear opprobrium about breaking codes of silence. Their investigative, risk-taking journalism has acted as a catalyst in bringing down several prime ministers and exposing political corruption (see Chapter 3). The political section of the U.S. Embassy in Tokyo deems two monthly magazines—*Bungei Shunjū* and *Chūō Kōron*—so important that it translates the title and summarizes the content of every article in every issue. For five other monthlies—*Sekai, Seiron, Kankai, Shokun* and *Sekai Orai*—the embassy translates the entire table of contents for every issue. These influential monthlies do not appear in Table 6.1 because, except for *Bungei Shunjū* with a circulation of 700,000, they do not sell as well as the irreverent and lively general-interest weeklies.

The flip side of investigation—the sensationalism of magazines—often entails sloppy reporting, lack of verification, half truths, fabrication and violations of privacy. Such practices, which nearly scuttled the Crown Prince's search for a bride, prompted the Imperial Household Agency to request a press embargo (see Chapter 3). Magazines agreed to abide by it. However, once the bride search ended and the prince married Masako Owada in June 1993, not even the royal family could escape the magazines' irreverence. In August 1993 *Takarajima 30* published an article allegedly by an Imperial Household Agency official titled "The Imperial Family Crisis." This article, later repudiated by the palace authorities, sparked a running debate that filled the weeklies for some time.

Monthlies can and do engage in scandal; for example, *Uwasa no Shinsō* [The Facts About Rumor] specializes in exposés about entertainment personalities. However, weeklies trade more on sensationalism, although in varying degrees. Some weeklies, such as the *Asahi Journal*, take the high road. Others, such as *Shūkan Shinchō* and *Shūkan Bunshun*, sometimes

Table 6.4. Magazine headlines, spring/summer 1993

Weeklies

Who is Myojin Shigeru, a salaried employee alleged to have earned 700 million yen last year? (*Shūkan Bunshun 5/27*).

Is the bloodied PKO Operation a "living body experiment" by the Miyazawa cabinet? (*Shūkan Post 6/4*).

Focus (5/28) says a Khmer Rouge messenger was in Japan on a secret mission.

A "book war" is raging between two media-minded religious cult leaders, Okawa Ryuho of Kofukuno Kagaku and Asahara Shoko of Aum Shinrikyo (*Sunday Mainichi 6/6*).

A former Unification Church executive who master-minded a fraudulent sales scheme confesses his crime to *Shūkan Gendai* (6/5).

Rie-Mama puts the cat among the pigeons again by announcing: "Rie is a virgin" (*Josei Jishin 6/8*).

Friday (6/4) persuades "foreign beauties" to undress and talk about their life in Tokyo in their humble four-and-a-half mat rooms.

Monthlies and semimonthlies

Can you really eat true "ethnic food"? (*Playboy* July).

Do you have trouble making decisions by yourself? Maybe you're an "advice junkie" (*Cosmopolitan 6/20*).

To its male readers, *Cadet* (June) says: "Let's get married to a nice one!" and provides a photographic guide to 100 young women in search of a husband.

Bishō (6/12) claims that not only has New York–based singer-songwriter Yano Akiko been abandoned by her Oscar-winning husband, Sakamoto Ryuichi, she's also an active Jehovah's Witness.

Bart (No. 11) reports on the true state of sexism in the men's heaven called South Korea.

Source: Ito, T. (1993).

pander but often do conduct valuable investigations. Those at the low end, such as *Shūkan Hōseki*, contain pages of titillating nudes and *manga* comics (see below).

As a case in point, three weeklies took different approaches to the story of six Japanese college women who were raped by a Japanese-speaking Iranian in Rome in 1993. The Japan Newspaper Editors and Publishers Association (NSK) has a policy that newspapers do not reveal rape victims' names, but the 76-member Japan Magazine Publishers Association policy leaves the decision up to the individual publication. The February 18, 1993, *Shūkan Bunshun* revealed the name of the students' college and their department, making the victims easily identifiable; it also included criticism of young women travelers and the travel agencies they use. The February 26 *Shūkan Post*, which carries nudes and *manga* comics, did not identify the university. *Bishō* [Smile], a women's weekly, "provided the most responsible coverage . . . [it] focused on how the Iranian had been able to win their confidence . . . and finishes up with a list of ways female travellers can protect themselves while overseas" (Morikawa 1993a).

By and large, legal guarantees of free speech protect the weeklies (see Chapter 10). A few months before the *Marco Polo* suspension, another Bungei Shunju publication came under fire, but this time, the company put up a fight. In June 1994, the East Japan Railway Co. suspended the sale of *Shūkan Bunshun*, a "clean" weekly suitable for family reading, because an article in the June 16 issue alleged that JR East's management and the company's labor union head had close ties. The magazine's absence at railway station stores in eastern Japan could have deprived the weekly of 110,000 in potential sales of its total circulation of 900,000. The Tokyo District Court said July 22 that the railway had no right to violate its agreement to sell the weekly. After the ruling, the railway put *Shūkan Bunshun* back on its station stores' shelves ("JR rejects" 1994).

Manga

Japan stands alone in its appetite for comics, or *manga*. Comics are "the defining characteristic of Japan's publishing culture" (Fujitake and Yamamoto 1994, 168), accounting for more than one-third of all periodicals published. Comics' share of total periodicals increased steadily from 29.1 percent in 1986 to 35.6 percent in 1992.

The earliest "professional" cartooning in Japan, as practiced by Buddhist artist-monks, dates back at least to the seventh century (see Appendix 1). In 1814, the wood-block artist Hokusai coined the term *manga* by combining the Chinese characters *man* ("involuntary," but with a secondary meaning of "morally corrupt") and *ga* ("picture"). The resulting combination carries the dual meaning of "whimsical (and slightly risqué) sketches" (Schodt 1986, 18).

Ranging from saddle-stitched anthologies of about 350 pages to perfect-bound tomes of more than 1,000 pages, modern *manga* carry from 15 to 35 thirty-page stories. Printed on cheap, recycled stock in black and white (sometimes with a page or two of color at the beginning), they cost ¥230 to ¥500.

Table 6.1 shows the dominant place of comics in the magazine world. Of Japan's 17 "million sellers" in 1993, 13 were *manga*, including the top 10. The warhorse *Shūkan Shōnen Jump*, which claims to sell 6.2 million copies a week, ranks as Japan's most popular magazine. It set a single-issue record of 6.5 million copies with its final 1993 issue. Sales of all types of *manga* magazines brought in almost ¥5.4 billion in 1992. Because of *mawashiyomi* [pass-along readership], sales do not reflect the true astronomically high circulations of the comics.

Although overall sales of *manga* have almost doubled from the early 1980s to the early 1990s, sales of adult comics have almost tripled (from

311 million to more than 815 million). This increase in adult comics sales and relative decrease in children's comics "is probably a function of the aging of the Japanese population in general" (Smith 1993, 1). These older buyers probably account for an upsurge in the republished *manga* collections, which have more than doubled their sales since 1982 (to almost 500 million units) and tripled their total cash sales to more than ¥2 trillion.

Cartoonist/author Osamu Tezuka (1929–89), "the god of *manga*," wrote of foreigners' amazement "when they discover just how big the boom in Japanese comics is"; they can't believe that a "Japanese businessman on his way to work sits in a train with his nose buried in a children's comic book" (Schodt 1986, 11). Tezuka embued his *manga* heroes, including Tetsuwan Atom (called "Astro Boy" overseas) and Buddha, with philosophical overtones quite different from run-of-the-mill, one-dimensional comic personalities.

Magazine or Book?

Magazines, books and *manga* together constitute the output of the publishing industry–which, if *manga* were omitted, would look dismal indeed. In 1992, of all books and magazines published in Japan, 40 percent were *manga* comics. In 1993, the industry as a whole saw a 5.7 percent increase in revenue, attributed largely to *manga*, "virtually the sole sustenance for the otherwise languishing publishing trade" ("Overview" 1994). Counting books alone, paperbacks showed strong growth–again largely because of *manga* published in book form. Manga books saw an 8.8 percent increase, or an unprecedented 10 percent rise in monetary value. In 1994, with a 3.4 percent rise in revenue over 1993, once again "what sustained the industry was the boom in manga comic books" ("Publishing" 1995).

In Japan, "the publishing industry tends to oligopoly" (Ueda 1990, 76). Thus firms such as Kodansha and Shogakukan publish both books and *manga* (as well as conventional magazines that contain *manga*), so they can easily repackage popular stories as paperback books. These 200- to 300-page books (*tankobon*), printed on a better grade of paper, retail for ¥400 to ¥500. For the connoisseur, more expensive hard-bound editions are available.

Japan's book best-seller lists do not include *manga* books, but "genre is the only reason they are not there" (Ueda 1990, 75). Indeed, the term "best seller" applies more aptly to *manga* paperbacks than to conventional hardbacks. Examples of mega-million seller paperbacks include Fujio-Fujiko's comedy tale of the robot cat Doraemon, which began serialization in a Shogakukan magazine in 1970; Kazuhiro Kyuichi's *Be-Bop High School* (Kodansha); the *Oishinbo* series (Shogakkan) by Tetsu Kariya and Akira Hanasaki, which appears five times a year; Rumiko Takahashi's comedy soap opera *Maison Ikkoku*, aimed at women and girls; and volume 7 of *Chibi Maruko-chan*, which registered a first printing of 2.4 million copies.

Even with *manga* banished from best-seller lists, the biggest-selling conventional book of 1993 traded on the popularity of *manga*: *Isono-ke no nazo* [Riddles of the Isono Family] sold 1.86 million copies. A cross between Trivial Pursuit question cards and "Star Trek" fanzines, it presents details of a fantasy world created for the TV cartoon series "Sazae-san," named after Sazae, the mother of the Isono clan.

The Appeal of *Manga*

Osamu Tezuka (Schodt 1986, 10) sees television as *manga*'s international "entry port, not just in the West but in the Middle East and Africa, in South America, in Southeast Asia and even in China. . . . In France the children love watching *Goldorak*. *Doraemon* is a huge hit in Southeast Asia and Hong Kong. Chinese youngsters all sing the theme to *Astro Boy*." The TV versions of *manga* overcome language problems through dubbing and the difficulty of "backwards reading" (right to left) by universally understood animation. Printed Japanese comics, "designed for Japanese readers who share particular attitudes and customs," in many cases "simply cannot be understood unless the reader is Japanese" (Schodt 1986, 10).

An exception is Taiwan, which shares enough cultural heritage to make *manga* a big hit. Beginning around 1980, pirated *manga*, identical to the Japanese originals except for word balloons translated into Chinese, flooded Taiwan. However, under the provisions of a June 1992 copyright law, many legal *manga* now carry copyright transfer contracts. A typical legal comic, with about one-third the pages of a Japanese *manga*, might have up to 10 Japanese stories and a few by Taiwanese cartoonists. Printed on better-quality paper, the Taiwan editions appear four or five days later than the Japanese originals.

Both Chinese and Japanese use characters that originated from pictures. Studies of brain activity have shown that readers of alphabetic scripts process writing and pictures in opposite hemispheres, whereas readers of ideographic scripts process language and images such as *manga* in the same brain hemisphere. *Manga* expert Frederik Schodt (1986, 25) explains that Western comics demand more attentiveness, but *manga* are simply absorbed by the reader's eye, moving "forward and back, absorbing the information the drawings contain and augmenting it with the printed word. Taking in the page as an integrated whole is an acquired skill, like slurping a bowl of piping hot Japanese noodles, in seconds, without chewing." Sergei Eisenstein, the Russian filmmaker, saw Japanese culture as inherently "cinematic"–a process of combining pictures into a montage to express complex thoughts (Schodt 1986, 20).

Beyond the visual affinity for *manga,* Japanese find them "faster and easier to read than a novel, more portable than a television set" (Schodt 1986, 25). *Manga* are perfectly fitted to a crowded, urbanized, workaholic society that depends heavily on public transportation and has little space outdoors for children to engage in physical activity. Besides, the thrills they offer cost very little.

Japan's educational system is set up so that young people must devote almost all their time to studying for examinations. *Manga* permit escape, letting the harried teenager go farther away in 10 minutes of reading *manga* than he or she could in 10 minutes of watching television. Moreover, theorizes Schodt (1986, 27), "reading comics is a silent activity that can be carried on alone. The Japanese . . . of necessity place a premium on space and on not bothering others."

Genres and Themes

The *manga* market splits neatly down the middle, with children's *manga* accounting for about half of sales and adults' the other half. The market in 1992 broke down as follows: boys' comics (*shonen manga,* usually weeklies), 39 percent; girls' comics (*shojo manga,* usually biweeklies, monthlies), 8.8 percent; young adults (sitcoms, sports, action/adventure), 35.8 percent; ladies', 7.9 percent; and miscellaneous others (four-panel *yon-koma,* pachinko, golf, erotica), 8.5 percent (Smith 1993, 1).

Erotic *manga,* which combine sex and violence against women (see Chapter 12), have a mainly male audience. Through the efforts of mothers' groups, they now "voluntarily" carry warning labels (see Chapter 10). One called *Rape-Man* finally closed under pressure from consumers "because it glorified rape" (Kristof 1995, 5).

Another male comic depicting women stereotypically coined a word and a concept. In 1986, artist Katsuhiko Hotta introduced a new comic, *O-batalian,* about the adventures of a "dumpy, 40ish battle-ax" (Ranard 1990). The title, which won a contest for the most creative new word in 1989, derives from *oba-san* [a middle-aged woman] and Batalian, the creature-star of the horror film "Night of the Living Dead." Professor Senko Maynard of Princeton decries the word as "a sarcastic admission that women are in fact very capable and powerful" (Kambara 1990). She

points to a parallel phrase, *sōdai gomi* [giant garbage], which refers to retired men who hang around the house. It did not win a prize in the contest; the concept of the *Hanako* girl came in second.

Until 1980, women had to read *manga* designed for teen-age girls, boys
or men, but in that year two monthlies, *Be Love* and *Big Comic for Lady*,
debuted. By 1985, women had their choice of 18. Then in the late 1980s,
a counter-romantic genre of submission fantasy comics drew a solid audience. The December 1995 issue of *Amour*, a sexually explicit comic for
women that claims a circulation of 400,000, had rape scenes in 90 of its
316 pages. Like the violence depicted in men's comics, these rape scenes
do not mean that women necessarily wish to be raped, but "there remains the paradox that the growing independence of Japanese women is
reflected not in stories of assertive women" (Kristof 1995, 5).

Even with clear gender/age targeting, considerable crossover readership occurs. In a 1980 survey, four children's *manga* appeared among university students' 10 favorite magazines. Many of the comics aimed at
young adults, which appeal to both sexes, contain work by a mix of men
and women *mangaka* [manga creators]. Most women work on comics
aimed at females, just as most men work on comics aimed at males. The
manga field also offers enormous opportunities for women. According to
Schodt (1986, 13): "New experiments throughout the comic industry are
constantly being made. . . . The only thing most magazines have in common is an English word in the title, an unstated requirement for success."

Boys' comic magazines, the largest single market segment, contain stories about samurai warriors, sumo wrestlers, *yakuza* gangsters, sports heroes, science fiction creatures or students. Whatever the setting, they often graphically depict Freudian fixations. Oral themes include "constant
eating, references to food, plots which are structured within a universe of
oral delights, oral aggression and oral eroticism" (Adams and Hill 1991,
105). Anal themes include portrayals of mooning, farting and defecation.
Phallic symbols and graphic depictions are rife, sometimes for fun, but
often to "strive for shock value" (Adams and Hill 1991, 122).

Girls' *manga*, which emphasize idealized love, make use of lavender
and pink on covers or pages with color. The stylized characters' faces
may all look the same, but the elaborate clothes differ greatly. The artists
include many Caucasian-looking heroes and heroines whose unnaturally
large eyes often glisten with stars and tears. Japanese comics, especially
those for women and girls, "are very 'wet' as opposed to 'dry'; that is,
they are unashamedly human and sentimental" (Schodt 1986, 16).

Varied *manga* plots of universal appeal include Osamu Tezuka's life of
Buddha, Reiji Matsumoto's tales of student *ronin*, and Kazuo Kamimura's
chronicles of young people, *Dōsei Jidai* [The Age of Cohabitation]. In
sum, "comics have as much to say about life as novels or films" (Schodt

1986, 16). Smith (1993, 1) adds, "As long as artists meet a minimum standard of competency (and have an appealing style), they'll be accepted–as long as their stories are good." Indeed, a simple artistic style can be an asset.

Artistic Conventions

From the naive but expressive *haniwa* burial figurines (fifth century) to spare, understated architecture, Japanese art conveys the ideal of less as more. Stark black-and-white *manga* use visual effects to pull the reader along at a clip of about 3.75 seconds per page; "with no coloring, and with shading at a minimum, the mere curve of a character's eyebrow takes on added significance" (Schodt 1986, 22).

Stories often continue for pages with pictures only. A simple symbol, such as a leafless tree, can speak volumes about life and death. Since the typical story runs for about 30 pages, Japanese comic artists have the luxury of showing a scene from a variety of "camera angles." They have learned to make the page flow by breaking it up creatively in odd-angle slices–or not breaking it up at all and instead using the whole page as a montage.

Artists can use Japan's four separate writing systems to good effect by, for example, using Chinese ideograms arranged vertically in the dialogue balloon when a Chinese person appears in a story. If a Westerner is speaking, those balloons may be written horizontally in *katakana*–the syllabic script used for foreign words.

Katakana also appear in a special category of "foreign" sounds: onomatopoeic sound effects. The Japanese–especially *mangaka*–take pride in creating new sound words, even if the concept they want to express has no actual sound. The lexicon includes the following: SURU–*suru* noodles being slurped; ZA, BOTSUN BOTSUN and PARA PARA–subtly different types of rain; SHUBO–the sudden flame from a cigarette lighter; FU–the vanishing of a ninja warrior-assassin in midair; HIRA HIRA–leaves falling from a tree; BIIN–a penis suddenly standing erect; PO–someone's face reddening in embarrassment; DOSUN–someone falling down with a thud; SURON–milk being added to coffee; and SHI-IIN–the sound of silence (Schodt 1986, 23).

In sum, many *manga* "are poorly executed. Many are trash. Yet all are an integral part of Japan's popular culture and as such reveal legacies from the past, ideals of love and a basic love of fantasy" (Schodt 1986, 16). According to Smith (1993, 1), "Perhaps the easiest way to perceive the place of manga within Japan's culture and publishing industry is to consider it a true, separate media–not unlike television." We turn next to that postwar phenomenon.

7
Postwar
Broadcasting

Taro Tanaka manages to watch television for 2.5 hours each weekday, often using a VCR to record his favorite shows on the TV set in his bedroom. Yet his heavy TV habit does not by any stretch match that of his grandmother, Megumi, who watches more than 6.5 hours a day. As Table 7.1 shows, women older than 50 rank as Japan's champion TV watchers. By contrast, Sumiko Suzuki, like other women in their 30s, watches less than she did a few years ago because of her new part-time job but still manages about four hours of viewing time.

Overview

Each Japanese spends more than three hours each day watching television, including more than one hour with the Japan Broadcasting Corp. (Nippon Hoso Kyokai, NHK) and more than 2.5 hours with commercial stations (NHK survey in June 1993). In the United States, the average person watches less: two hours, 26 minutes a day (Nielsen survey in May 1993).

In Japan, the world's most enthusiastic TV culture, almost all citizens consider themselves middle class and shun holier-than-thou attitudes (Kato 1988, 315). The "subject of conversation in Japan among high school students is . . . often about television and radio programs," whereas U.S. teenagers would probably talk instead about the opposite sex (Sata 1991, 214).

The average household has its TV set turned on for an incredible eight hours and eight minutes a day (see Table 7.1). The period from 7:30 to 10 p.m., called the "golden hours" in Japan, represents the highest viewing segment, but other peaks occur in the morning and at lunch time. About 21 to 22 percent of the population watches morning programs, while

Table 7.1. Daily hours spent watching television

	Weekdays	Saturday	Sunday
Per person			
Average	3 hr, 57 min	4 hr, 17 min	4 hr, 49 min
4–12 years old	2 hr, 57 min	2 hr, 51 min	3 hr, 03 min
13–19 years old	2 hr, 32 min	2 hr, 48 min	3 hr, 26 min
20–34 years old (men)	2 hr, 17 min	2 hr, 58 min	3 hr, 50 min
35–49 years old (men)	2 hr, 29 min	3 hr, 35 min	4 hr, 45 min
50+ years old (men)	4 hr, 48 min	5 hr, 47 min	7 hr, 14 min
20–34 years old (women)	4 hr, 06 min	4 hr, 08 min	4 hr, 05 min
35–49 years old (women)	4 hr, 42 min	4 hr, 55 min	4 hr, 48 min
50+ years old (women)	6 hr, 35 min	6 hr, 15 min	6 hr, 17 min
Per household			
Annual Average	8 hr, 08 min	8 hr, 20 min	8 hr, 54 min
January to March	8 hr, 21 min	8 hr, 33 min	9 hr, 01 min
April to June	7 hr, 52 min	8 hr, 12 min	8 hr, 44 min
July to September	8 hr, 12 min	8 hr, 17 min	8 hr, 56 min
October to December	8 hr, 08 min	8 hr, 17 min	8 hr, 51 min

Source: Video Research Ltd.

Note: Information is for Tokyo and its surrounding area, 1992.

keeping an eagle eye on the figures showing the time in one corner of the screen.

The visual orientation of the Japanese helped make television Japan's medium of choice. Moreover, given the dichotomy between *uchi* [home, with the nuance of relaxation, safety and security] and *soto* [outside, with the nuance of formality, insecurity and discomfort], television meant that Japanese could stay comfortably inside while looking out (Kitamura 1987, 144-45).

Commercial broadcasting companies in operation as of October 1993 numbered 186 (see Table 7.2). A typical TV viewer in the Kanto (Tokyo metropolitan) area has a choice of two NHK channels (educational and entertainment), five commercial channels (Nihon TV [NTV], Tokyo Broadcasting System [TBS], Fuji TV, TV Asahi and TV Tokyo), UHF channels with in-school programs and local news, two NHK satellite channels (requiring purchase of a small dish) and WOWOW, a pay-TV channel.

Until 1994, Fuji had captured the largest audience share, but in 1994, NTV (21.2 percent share) pulled out ahead of Fuji (19.5 percent) and TBS (17.7 percent). NHK does not command as large an audience (16.5 percent) as these top three commercial networks. NHK broadcasts 18 hours a day; TBS, Fuji, NTV and TV Asahi have had round-the-clock programming since the late 1980s. However, NHK's radio coverage far exceeds that of commercial broadcasters; in that broadcasting field it got an early start.

History

Radio

Radio broadcasting was begun in Japan on March 22, 1925, by the semigovernment Tokyo Broadcasting Station. The Tokyo radio station was merged with similar semigovernment radio stations in Osaka and Nagoya in August the following year to form the predecessor for today's NHK. The NHK radio service, unabashedly modeled on the BBC when it was established in 1926, became a military propaganda tool during World War II.

Early postwar years

After the war, NHK was reorganized to become a public corporation under the Broadcast Law and the Radio Law enacted on June 1, 1950. The new laws, formulated during the Allied Occupation, also

Table 7.2. Broadcasting facts and figures, 1993

Commercial broadcasting companies: 186
  Radio companies: 60 (11 AM, 1 shortwave, 43 FM, 1 PCM-BS, 4 PCM-CS)
  TV companies: 90 (14 VHF, 69 UHF, 1 broadcast satellite, 6 cable satellite)
  Radio and television companies: 36 (34 AM/VHF, 2 AM/UHF)
  Multiplex teletext companies: 10
  Satellite channels: Three public service direct broadcast satellite (DBS) (2 NHK, University of the Air); 1 private subscription (WOWOW);14 other satellite-to-cable; 6 PCM audio broadcasting companies (each with three channels)(two closed down in July 1993)

TV networks: NHK (public)–two nationwide networks; Commercial–five nationwide networks with Tokyo lead stations (NTV, TBS, Fuji TV, TV Asahi, TV Tokyo); independent local stations

TV households: 38.7 million (est.), 33.7 million (NHK contracted)

TV sets: 77 million; TV sets per household: 2+

VCR penetration: 83.4%

Cable penetration: 25.0%; no. of subscribers: 10+ million (1994); no. of subscribers to any of 26 cable pay TV channels: 2 million

NHK DBS penetration: 18.6%; no. of subscribers: 5.5 million (1995)

Technical standard: NTSC (same as U.S.)

Regulatory body: Ministry of Posts and Telecommunications (MPT)

---

paved the way for the establishment of private (commercial) broadcasting companies, giving Japan the mixed system it has today.

The first two commercial radio companies, one in Nagoya and the other in Osaka, started operation in September 1950. Since then, commercial broadcasting in Japan has experienced many stages of development. FM Aichi Broadcasting in Nagoya began commercial FM radio broadcasting on December 24, 1969. Six AM radio broadcasting companies in 1951 increased in number to 40 in 1957, thus enabling radio broadcasts to cover virtually all of Japan. With Japan's economic growth, radio advertising expenditures soared from ¥300 million in 1951 to ¥15 billion in 1957. This period is called the "golden era" of radio broadcasting.

However, this rapid growth of radio broadcasting came to a halt in 1958 with the advent of VHF television throughout Japan. Advertising expenditures began to decline after having reached a peak of ¥17.8 billion in 1960 and continued to decline through 1965. But the situation stabilized in 1967, when AM radio broadcasters created new program formats especially for portable radios and car radios. Following experimental AM stereo broadcasts conducted in April 1991, Motorola's C-QUAM system for stereo broadcasts was adopted. As of October 1993, 14 companies carried AM stereo broadcasts.

FM and shortwave

FM radio broadcasting reached a full-fledged stage in December 1969 when service began in major cities such as Tokyo, Osaka, Nagoya and Fukuoka following more than 10 years of experimental broadcasts. These ad-supported FM stations have been financially successful by answering a need for high-quality music in stereo. The Ministry of Posts and Telecommunications (MPT) has a goal of at least one FM radio station in every prefecture, with two or more in major cities.

On August 27, 1954, Nihon Short-Wave Broadcasting of Tokyo was established as Japan's first domestically beamed shortwave radio station. Its programs, broadcast nationwide, offer program fare different in many ways from that offered by AM or FM stations.

The first community radio station, FM Iruka [dolphin] in Hokkaido, started transmitting in 1992. Supported by commercials, it programs 70 percent music and 30 percent talk, including some programs in English. As of January 1994, five other community radio stations existed in Japan to address the need for local, as opposed to national or regional, information.

Leasing satellite time is expensive. Before the infamous religious group Aum Shinrikyo became involved in murder and conspiracies (see

Chapter 3), it demonstrated one way that special-interest groups can reach a wide audience at relatively low cost: It leased shortwave radio airtime from Russian authorities to beam programs back to Japan.

By the mid-1970s, mini-FM stations, with a radius of up to 1,000 meters (thousands of potential listeners in densely populated urban Japan) began to broadcast. The "idea of 'free radio' reached Japan from Europe at the end of 1980 through an interview with French radio activist Felix Guattari" (Sonnenberg 1994, 12). In 1982, KIDS radio, broadcasting U.S.-style rock programs on weekends in Tokyo's Aoyama area, attracted hordes of young people, who listened on car and portable radios. Other mini-FM stations of various types quickly sprang up. But in 1985, radio activist Mitsuru Yamagita was arrested, held in isolation for 10 days and fined ¥200,000 for interfering with legally licensed stations. Many ministations disappeared, so "it is hard to say, how many mini FMs there are in Japan at the moment" (Sonnenberg 1994, 14).

Television

Through the efforts of inventors Kenjiro Takayanagi (1899-1990) and Hidetsugu Yagi (1886-1976), TV engineering got a head start in Japan in the 1920s and 1930s (see Appendix 1). During the Occupation, American authorities shaped and directed broadcasting in Japan. They often placed stringent controls on Japanese broadcasters despite the fact that Occupation officials had an initial charge from Washington to give guidance without overt control. This situation may have made post-Occupation broadcasting in Japan vulnerable to governmental authority (Luther and Boyd 1995).

Early postwar years

On February 1, 1953, after the Occupation ended, NHK went on the air as a public service broadcaster—even though only 866 TV sets existed in the Tokyo area at the time (the cost of a set imported from the United States equaled the annual salary of an urban white-collar worker). Looking at this situation from the advertiser's point of view, Matsutaro Shoriki, president of the *Yomiuri Shimbun,* saw the need for large numbers of viewers rather than large numbers of TV sets. After receiving a TV license, he put NTV on the air August 28 of that same year.

Shoriki had ordered a number of large-screen receivers that he placed on street corners, in parks and at train stations. A newspaper article from October 27, 1953, described the live broadcast of a wrestling match that 20,000 people gathered to watch (Kato 1993, 7): "Because of the crowd, tram cars had to make long stops. Automobiles could not move at all.

Taxi drivers left their cars on the street to watch the match. Several people who were on trees nearby to get a better view fell down and were injured."

Commercial television had galvanized Japan. Soon, sets appeared in restaurants, bars and barber shops. By the late 1950s, domestic manufacturers dramatically lowered the price of a set. At the same time, salaries started going up.

The marriage of the present emperor to commoner Michiko Shoda, whom he had met at a tennis court, turned Japan into a nation of TV watchers. The lead time between the couple's engagement in 1958 and the royal wedding on April 10, 1959, gave manufacturers time to campaign for TV purchases: "Let's all watch the wedding parade live!" The love match, not an arranged marriage as in the old days, symbolized the new Japan. People rushed to buy more than 2 million sets, creating an audience of about 15 million for the 50-minute parade.

Only a month after the wedding, the International Olympic Committee announced the choice of Tokyo as the site for the 1964 Summer Games. This second symbol of postwar recovery (Japan was supposed to host the canceled 1945 games) likewise had a long lead time and telegenic potential. The Olympics stimulated not only more TV sales but the construction boom that truly began Japan's postwar economic miracle.

Two TV networks grew out of radio networks: TBS from Radio Tokyo and Fuji TV from Nippon Hoso radio, Bunka Hoso radio and movie companies. TV Asahi, formerly called Japan Educational Television, was created mainly by the publisher Ohbunsha. TV Tokyo was created by the Foundation for Science and Technology.

NTV and the Yomiuri company represent the earliest example whereby a national newspaper obtained TV station licenses. In the 1970s, other national newspapers got interested in television; in 1975, the financial connections were solidified. Later, local newspapers and broadcasters formed similar alliances. Thus the "happy coexistence" of information conglomerates that characterizes Japan today became a fact of life (Kato 1993, 21). TV stations often called on respected journalists from their "sister" newspapers to provide news and commentaries.

Colorful years

By 1963, a black-and-white set cost exactly one month's average salary—but with some scrimping and saving, a "salaryman" (white-collar worker) could purchase that prized possession, a color set, with his twice-yearly bonuses. On September 10, 1960, four firms in Tokyo and Osaka had initiated color TV service. By May 1968, color television was universally adopted by all broadcasters in Japan.

Japan exported its first black-and-white TV sets in 1962 and its first color TV sets in 1966. Through the 1970s, this robust Japanese industry virtually ended domestic U.S. TV manufacturing. But by the 1990s, exports of TV sets and VCRs plummeted because of the rise in manufacturing in other Asian countries. Japanese firms themselves set up overseas factories, such as Toshiba's subsidiary in Dalian, China, established in 1991.

For more than 7 million Japanese households, direct broadcast satellite (DBS) parabolic antennas–looking like turkey platters–that one often sees outside Japanese homes and apartments bring in two 24-hour NHK pay channels (Table 7.3). Chapter 12 will discuss further BS-NHK, as well as BS-WOWOW, a pay service that shows mainly movies.

Underway since August 1989, an innovation called Clearvision offers improved picture quality for wide-screen sets. The "Hi-Vision" high-definition (HDTV) system went on the air on NHK as an experimental broadcast in June 1989, and since 1991 test broadcasting has been conducted for eight hours daily by the Hi-Vision Promotion Association established jointly by NHK, commercial broadcasters and manufacturers. Digital technology has superseded Japan's analog technology, but pro-

Table 7.3. Weekday prime-time TV programs on satellite (Wednesday, April 3, 1996)

NHKS-1	NHKS-2	WOWOW
6:00 (B) CNN News	6:00 Cartoon Theater	6:00 Disney Cartoon
6:20 Weather	7:00 (B) News 7	6:30 Cartoon: Tetsuwan
6:25 (B) ABC World	7:40 Drama: Reiko no	Atom
News Now	Haisha-san	7:00 U.S. Movie:
6:50 News	8:00 Japan's Old Families	Solomon and Sheba
7:00 J. League Soccer:	8:50 Wild Birds	(subtitled in
Red Diamonds vs.	9:00 U.S. Movie:	Japanese)
Gamba	Cocoon–The Return	9:25 French Movie: Vivre
9:00 News	(subtitled in	Sa Vie (subtitled in
9:10 (B) Sports News	Japanese)	Japanese)
9:30 (B) Business Line	10:55 Movie Theaters	10:55 U.S. Movie: Tekwar-
9:50 Weather	11:00 "The Greatest	Teklords (subtitled in
10:00 Prime Time News	Performance on	Japanese)
10:50 Extinction of	TV" (Michael	
Species This	Jackson, Frank	
Century	Sinatra, Diana Ross	
11:00 Asia's Who's Who	and others appear)	
11:20 (B) World Report	11:50 European Music	
11:50 English Lesson	Travelogue	

Notes: (B) indicates bilingual; sets equipped for multiplex broadcasts can receive foreign TV shows and feature movies dubbed in Japanese or in the original language. To receive broadcast satellite programs from NHK, TV households must purchase a small receiving dish. To receive programs from WOWOW on their dish, customers must pay an additional subscription fee.

ducers' experience can be transferred if Japan opts to switch to digital technology. Despite protests from broadcasters, the MPT seemed to be leaning toward a switch to digital technology ("Digitalization" 1996) (see Chapter 12).

Cable

Japan has about 25 percent cable penetration, with more than 10 million households as subscribers (see Table 7.2). By contrast, in Taiwan more than 50 percent and in the United States (1992) 61.5 percent of households have cable service (more than 57 million subscribers). Japan's 25 percent figure, low as it is, belies the fact that most cable families receive terrestrial services simply because they live in the mountains or on remote islands.

Japan's use of cable for retransmission explains why most cable systems have fewer than 500 terminals and why Tokyoites, with seven readily available channels, do not want to pay for cable. Only 2 million households take "extra" pay cable services, partly because of "high costs resulting from restrictive regulation of CATV by the government" (Ishii 1996a, 24). The official granting of permission in 1996 for STAR-TV and other foreign cable services to enter Japan's closed market bears watching (see Chapter 10).

For all these reasons, "the multi-media, multi-channel era is slow coming in Japan" (Nishino 1994, 116). Whereas "Americans want to be able to choose by themselves what they will watch" (Stronach 1992, 64), the Japanese prefer *broad*casted programs of general appeal. According to Sawa (1994, 18): "They prefer to be on the receiving or passive end of information. . . . most people tend to watch the same programs with high viewer ratings. . . . It's a case of 'me-tooism.' And these programs become the topics of conversation and gossip over drinks the following day. That's Japan." The U.S. choice in number of cable channels, an average of 32, and topics, from local access to country music to Black Entertainment Television, gives it a *narrow*casted diversity unknown in Japan.

But one can also find in Japan "a number of truly local and non-commercial e.g. not profit-oriented [programs] in different shapes and sizes" (Sonnenberg 1994, 5). In contrast to the restrictions on bringing in foreign cable shows, the homegrown cable system can operate freely. Some of Tokyo's 23 wards have their own cable channels. Tama Cable Network, the first to open (in 1987), now has been joined by 17 similar local stations. Usually, taxpayer money supports them, which makes appearances by local officials controversial. A local Diet member who gives a New Year's address not only gets free airtime but violates the spirit of

Japan's campaign laws ("Politician-owned cable" 1993).

According to Sonnenberg (1994, 6), "Supervision of the program or broadcast operation through the MPT is practically non-existent, the only sensitive area being pornography." The operator does not, as is U.S. practice, have to offer cable access to the public for shows like "Wayne's World." Thus the channel in Sakaide, Kagawa Prefecture, on the island of Shikoku, stands out as an unusual community access example. A group of citizens began broadcasting in 1987 after the president of the KBN commercial cable system offered them the channel. They broadcast 60 to 90 minutes a day, from 7 to 8 or 8:30 p.m. The group of nine men and one woman works without pay and may hold discussions on topics such as the Gulf War. The topics, quite different from those covered on mainstream TV programming, are listed in a newsletter with a circulation of 6,000.

TV Programming

A fee collected from TV set owners funds the operation of NHK's commercial-free national network. Technically, the law (see Chapter 10) prohibits commercial stations from forming networks. However, in practice, cooperative arrangements between Tokyo "head stations" and local affiliates have created networks in all but name. Moreover, the law officially promotes diversity and forbids cross-media ownership, but newspapers have financial links to television that amount to ownership.

NTV (allied with the *Yomiuri* newspaper) and its 27 local affiliates form the NNN network; TBS (with *Mainichi*) and its 25 affiliates form JNN; Fuji (with *Sankei*) and its 27 affiliates form FNN; ABC (with *Asahi*) and its 20 affiliates form ANN; and the smallest, TV Tokyo (with *Nihon Keizai*), has affiliates in only Nagoya, Osaka, Sapporo, Fukuoka and Okayama. Networks provide 70 to 90 percent of local stations' programs; the local content includes local news to complement the national news broadcasts.

News

Various reasons account for a lack of investigation and critical reporting on television, including the *kisha* clubs (see Chapter 2) to which TV reporters belong. In pursuit of the value of harmony, Japan uses television to project "a picture of what society should be," while "America uses television like a microscope under which every flaw and problem is closely examined" (Stronach 1992, 56-57).

Japan boasts a strong dual TV system. TV Asahi's "News Station" with

Hiroshi Kume at 10 p.m. ranks as Japan's most popular news program, but NHK's news programs at 7 p.m. and 9 p.m. pull in respectable ratings as well. Imagine the "News Hour" on non-commercial PBS ranking anywhere nearly as high in the ratings as ABC's evening news with Peter Jennings. As Table 7.4 shows, daily news shows air at various times during the evening in direct competition with prime-time entertainment.

News/current affairs accounted for 17.5 percent of TBS's and 41.8 percent of NHK's all-day content, in a study covering March 2-8, 1992 (Ishikawa and Kambara 1993). Also in 1992, Miller (1994) analyzed 157 stories on NHK's and the commercial network NTV's 30-minute evening newscasts for a composite week in May and June. Both networks had the same top four categories (politics and government; economics, business, finance; disaster/accident; and crime), but the rank order differed because of NTV's greater emphasis on crime reporting. In sum, concludes Miller (1994, 83) "the national news reports at the two Japanese networks, NHK and NTV, offer a distinct difference in coverage."

In studying internationalization, Miller (1994, 95) states: "Despite the subtle differences in foreign reporting at NHK and NTV, in general, both networks report relatively few international stories. In a nation that produces much of the world's electronic news gathering equipment and has many foreign correspondents, international reporting is low."

However, an internationalization push seems to have had some effect in changing the near absence of the outside world on Japanese TV to at least an acknowledgment of its existence. The percentage of foreign coverage for NHK was 5.2 percent in 1974 (Shiramizu 1987), 9.2 percent in 1984, 14.1 percent in 1992 (Miller 1994) and 14.5 percent in 1993 (Cooper-Chen 1995). By way of comparison, figures for the three U.S. networks' foreign news abroad coverage were higher (Gonzenbach, Arant and Stevenson 1992): 20 percent in 1972, 22 percent in 1982 and 24 percent in 1989. Considering Japan's trade-based economy and ranking as the world's No. 2 industrial power, the figures for the amount of foreign news for both networks seem low. Its insularity (see Chapter 2) strongly affects TV content.

Analyzing newscasts from the United States, Japan and three other nations for September 1-5, 1986, Cooper-Chen (1992) found that Japan's NHK paid the least attention to foreign news (22.6 percent of total stories reported). Only violent international events made their way past NHK gatekeepers: a ship collision, a plane crash and a war. NHK did not even mention the two biggest stories of that week: the non-aligned summit and protests in South Africa.

Commercial networks, which air about five minutes of commercials per newscast, average 12 to 13 stories, while NHK can fit in 17 to 18 sto-

Table 7.4. Weekday prime-time TV programs (Wednesday, April 3, 1996)

1. Commerical stations

NTV	TBS	Fuji
6:00 News: Plus One	6:00 (B) News Forest	6:00 News: Super Time
7:00 Former Celebrities Today	7:00 Pro Baseball: Fine Plays and Bloopers	7:00 Special: Trip to the Spiritual World
8:54 News, Weather	8:54 News	8:54 News, Weather
9:00 Drama: Tata-kau Oyomesama Special	9:00 Documentary: Actresses' Checkered Lives	9:00 Night Hit Studio Special
10:54 Today's Events	10:54 Sports	11:09 Gourmet
11:25 Sports & Variety Show	11:00 News 23	11:15 News Japan

TV Asahi	TV Tokyo
6:00 News: Station eye	6:00 Cartoon: Choko Senshi Shanzerion
7:00 Special Report: 24 Hours with Emergency Services	6:30 Cartoon: VS Knight Ramune
9:48 Kyoto	7:00 J. League Soccer: Verdy vs. Marinos
9:54 See the World by Train	8:54 Living Information
10:00 News Station	9:00 Info Variety: Chasing the Unbelievable
11:20 The Hotel	10:00 Documentary: Human Theater
11:25 Variety: Challenging Funny Games	11:00 World Business Satellite
11:55 Tonight	11:55 Sports Today

2. NHK Networks

General	Education
6:00 News	6:00 Genius TV
6:07 NHK Network News	6:25 (B) TV Series: Full House
6:30 Evening Network	6:50 The World on a Plate
6:53 Weather	7:15 Topics
7:00 (B) News 7	7:20 Care for the Elderly
7:40 Drama: Reiko no Haisha-san	7:50 News
8:00 Science Variety: Trial & Success	8:00 ETV Special
	8:45 Health
8:45 Metropolitan News	9:00 Cooking
9:00 (B) News 9	9:25 Hobby Lecture: Pottery
9:30 Close-up	9:55 Japanese Verse
10:00 Drama: Sonzai no Fukaki Nemuri	10:00 Dress-up Factory
	10:25 English Conversation
10:45 Topics	10:30 Commentary
10:55 News, Weather	10:40 NHK Community College
11:00 News 11	
11:35 Commentary	11:10 English Conversation
11:45 Human Map	11:30 German Conversation
	11:50 Citizen's Seminar

Note: (B) indicates bilingual; sets equipped for multiplex broadcasts can receive foreign TV shows and feature movies dubbed in Japanese or in the original language.

ries (Cooper-Chen 1995; Miller 1994). In 1993 (Cooper-Chen 1995), Europe and North America combined accounted for a larger proportion of those stories (NHK, 10 percent; TBS, 9.6 percent) than South/Southeast/East Asia combined (NHK, 6.8 percent; TBS, 6.7 percent).

Remarkably absent from the TV "map" were Latin America, Africa and the Middle East; television excludes Third World countries except some in Japan's own Asian region. Thus Japanese newscasts present an even more clouded window than the distorted U.S. TV view, which virtually ignores Africa but acknowledges Latin America and the Middle East.

NHK's freedom from commercial pressures lets it tackle stories involving economists rather than criminals. NHK could also be free to educate viewers about the world beyond the archipelago and challenge the status quo. But it does not. NHK's low emphasis on international news and high attention to domestic minutiae point to a mission of Japanifying its viewers rather than pulling them out of their cultural comfort zones. In other programming, NHK likewise emphasizes tradition; it takes pride in its shows on Kabuki, *noh* drama and flower arranging (Stronach 1992, 74). Moreover, NHK has a much more traditional attitude toward women reporters than TBS (see Chapter 12).

In the late 1980s, various stations began increasing their news programs at the expense of TV dramas. In 1987, TBS, once known for quality TV drama, turned over a slot previously reserved for drama to a program called "News 22, Prime Time" with popular anchor Takero Morimoto, who was lured away from NHK. Although some say that TV drama in the 1990s has fallen on hard times, the genre still has legions of long-time fans.

Entertainment

In entertainment TV programming, Japan imports major movies but few regular TV series, meaning that it must shoulder its production burden alone (about 150 hours a week). Because of their "group-oriented nature" (Stronach 1992, 61), "The Cosby Show" and "Little House on the Prairie" did well in Japan. Conversely, in 1981, "Dallas" failed miserably (Katz, Liebes and Iwao 1991). It attracted only 4 percent of the audience, far short of the 15 percent needed for a respectable showing, so it lasted only six months. The partial nudity seemed "too prim to shock" by Japanese standards, whereas the evil that often triumphed over good was "too morally ambiguous" (Edelhart 1983, 22).

The growth of TV set ownership by rural audiences contributed to the demise of foreign drama series beginning in the mid-1960s, as Japan began producing its own fare. Rural residents "clearly tended to prefer domestic programs, often complaining that Western dramas were complicated and confusing" (Hagiwara 1995, 6).

Overall, NHK's general channel had 23.3 percent entertainment programming, while the 108 commercial channels had much more—43.0 percent (1990). However, the rather loose definition of cultural programming (commercial television and NHK, both 24.8 percent) makes it hard to distinguish entertaining culture from entertainment.

Drama programming

Home drama "is an expression derived from English but coined in Japan. It is a genre that developed in Japan under the influence of American soap operas and situation comedies" (Sata 1991, 207). The first postwar, experimental broadcast of TV drama was in 1952 with "Shinkon Arubamu" [Honeymoon Album]. Japanese home drama mirrors the home life of ordinary people, providing a documentary account of social changes. Home drama of 1955-64 centered around the events of the 1960 U.S.-Japan Security Treaty; the drama of 1965-74 reflected the concerns of the nation during the era of rapid economic expansion.

Home dramas by Taichi Yamada, So Kuramoto and other authors have received new lives as books. Yamada's 1981 *Kita no Kuni kara* [From the North Country] had been reprinted 22 times as of 1986, as viewers sought to relive scenes that they remembered from the televised versions.

In line with a penchant for choosing foreign elements and ideas and then adapting them, early Japanese TV dramas felt the influence of Reginald Rose and Paddy Chayevsky, playwrights prominent during the 1950s Golden Age of U.S. TV drama. Teruhiko Egami, author of "Aru Machi no aru Dekigoto" [A Certain Incident in a Certain Town] (NHK, 1959), adapted Rose's "The Remarkable Incident at Carson Corners," such that the janitor spoke with a Kyushu dialect instead of a U.S. ethnic accent. Likewise, technical methods and formats owe much to foreign countries, especially the United States.

But East-West differences abound. Japanese audiences enjoy sensitive, emotional TV dramas, as BBC staffers discovered when they were called in to re-edit for Western viewers "Asu wo Tsukame, Takashi-kun" [Take Tomorrow, Little Takashi], a documentary about a thalidomide baby (the first Japanese production to receive an Emmy Award). In one scene, Takashi's first day at school, his parents tearfully watch him struggling to put on his new school uniform, under orders from the child's doctor to allow the boy to take care of himself. This scene, which the British staff found too sentimental to leave in, moved the Japanese deeply.

According to Sata (1991, 216), expressing emotion "is the central goal of all traditional Japanese forms of art." In *noh* drama, a lover's passion may take the form of an elegant dance. The "Shakespeare of Japan," dramatist Monzaemon Chikamatsu (1653-1725), expresses passion with beautiful lyrics and heart-wrenching plots, such as *michi-yuki* [setting-foot-on-path] scenes, whereby "thwarted lovers run away to find a place to die together in hopes that their passion will be fulfilled in another world" (Sata 1991, 216).

The long-running series story has its roots in Japanese cultural preferences. Both NHK and the commercial networks cater to this taste for continuity, which derives from the traditions of humorous *emaki-mono* [picture scrolls] and *renga* [linked poetry], a game in which participants compose a poem by successively adding lines.

NHK's "Television Novel" series has aired six days a week, from 8:15 to 8:30 a.m., since 1961. Each "novel" in the series lasts for six months or one year. With women as the leading characters since 1966, this series has made the careers of many actresses. The morning show produced the most popular series in Japan's TV history, "Oshin," which at the height of its popularity, in November 1983, reached 65 percent of Japanese viewers. The average episode attracted 55 percent of viewers.

In 1968, the "TBS Television Novel Series" inaugurated its half-year series. This program and others, such as NHK's "Television Novel" and evening "Ginga (Galaxy) Television Novel," draw on the "tradition of serialized newspaper novels, but are characterized by the element of a narrator, which takes after the traditional method of story-telling" (Sata 1991, 218).

Since television dramas on commercial stations are aimed at a female audience, sponsors include manufacturers of cosmetics, appliances and food products. However, more women are taking jobs and decreasing their TV viewing, thereby changing their viewing preferences. They "seem to prefer detective and suspense drama, just as they also prefer newscasts to musical variety shows" (Sata 1991, 217).

Men "tend to watch television drama in order to relax from tension and enjoy themselves. Thus they prefer the action portrayed in historical and detective drama" (Sata 1991, 217). Historical drama has seen an evolution from *jōruri* [puppet theater] and Kabuki through motion pictures and television. One still-popular series, NHK's "Television Saga," broadcast since 1961 each Sunday from 8 to 8:45 p.m., depicts historical incidents (see Table 7.5).

Starting in about 1975, journalists began to speak of a decline in television drama. According to Sata (1991, 218), TV dramas on both NHK and the commercial networks have become "stereotypical and are now works produced by technicians rather than artists." Without doubt, genres of various kinds tend to fall into comfortable patterns, while view-

Table 7.5. NHK historical dramas

Year	Title	Historical period
1963	Hana no Shogai (The Life of a Great Senior Statesman)	Late Edo (c. 1860)
1964	Ako Roshi (The Forty-Seven Ronin)	Edo (c. 1840)
1965	Taiko-ki (Annals of the Grand Duke Toyotomi Hideyoshi)	Momoyama (c. 1573–1602)
1966	Minamoto no Yoshitsune (A Tragic Prince of the House of Genji)	Genpei (c. 1150–85)
1967	San Shimai (Three Sisters)	Edo
1968	Ryoma ga Yuku (There Goes Ryoma)	Late Edo
1969	Ten to Chi to (Of Heaven and Earth)	Sengoku (c. 1500–1600)
1970	Momi no Ki wa Nokotta (A Pine Tree Remains)	Edo
1971	Haru no Sakamichi (A Hill-Road in Spring)	Edo
1972	Shin-Heike Monogatari (The New Story of the Heike Clan)	Heian (c. 782–1185)
1973	Kunitori Monogatari (Battles among the Feudal Lords)	Sengoku (c. 1573–1602)
1974	Katsu Kaishu (The Life of Admiral Kaishu)	Late Edo
1975	Genroku Taihei-Ki (Genroku The Era of Peace)	Edo (1688–1703)
1976	Kaze to Kumo to Niji to (Wind, Clouds and Rainbows)	Heian
1977	Kashin (The Spirit of a Flower)	Late Edo
1978	Ogon no Hibi (Golden Days)	Sengoku
1979	Kusa Moeru (The Grass is Burning)	Genpei
1980	Shishi no Jidai (The Age of Lions)	Late Edo
1981	On'na Taiko-Ki (The Annals of Grand Duchess Toyotomi)	Sengoku
1982	Toge no Gunzo (War Parties at the Pass)	Edo
1983	Tokugawa Ieyasu	Sengoku
1984	Sanga Moyu (The Rivers and Mountains are Burning)	Mid-20th century
1985	Haru no Hato (Spring Swells)	Meiji (1868–1912)
1986	Inochi (Life)	Contemporary
1987	Dokuganryu Masamune (Masamune, the One-Eyed Hero)	Sengoku
1988	Takeda Shingen	Sengoku
1989	Kasuga no Tusbone (Mistress of the Inner Palace)	Early Edo
1990	Tobu ga Gotoku (The Young Lions)	Late Edo/Meiji
1991	Taiheiki (Military Story)	Nanbakucho (1300s)
1992	Nobunaga	Sengoku
1993	Ryukyu no Kaze (Okinawan Wind)	Edo
	Homura Tatsu (Blowing Fire)	Nara to early Heian
1994	Hana no Ran (A Shogun's Wife)	Muromachi
1995	Tokugawa Yoshimune	Edo

ers move on, even in traditional Japan. However, one recent series on TBS-TV touched a contemporary nerve so successfully that ratings reached as high as 40 percent. "Zutto anata ga suki datta" [I Always Loved You] featured a mother-fixated character, Fuyuhiko, who was "such a repellent but instantly recognizable character that the expression 'Fuyuhiko syndrome' has become the buzzword of the moment" ("Success" 1992).

Quiz/variety programming

In the 1960s and 1970s, song variety shows filled in around the costume and modern-dress dramas, documentaries and sports programs in prime time. The variety show, which often has several hosts and many entertainers on stage at the same time, "creates the feeling of a group—a group into which the audience is constantly invited" (Stronach 1992, 62).

A variety genre that has endured in Japan but disappeared elsewhere, the amateur talent show, proves that "the sharing of one's fun and embarrassment" ranks above "the actual quality of the performance" (Stronach 1992, 62). The prime example, the 45-minute NHK singing contest "Nodojiman" [Proud of Good Singing], began after World War II on radio and continued as a simulcast every Sunday afternoon since the early days of television.

In the 1980s, the variety show genre began to fade somewhat, replaced by more and more quiz programs. As of 1992, viewers had a choice of 32 domestically produced weekly game shows, making Japan more game-crazy than even the United States, which has twice Japan's population. Called in Japan by the English word "quiz," the shows differ markedly from game or quiz shows anywhere else in the world (Cooper-Chen 1994, 220-38).

The "Red Whale Tribe" (Fuji), which often rates among Japan's most-watched shows, features the comedy duo Tunnels playing matchmaker to young adults in their 20s and early 30s with an aura of innocence that "Love Connection" viewers would find childish. "TV Champion" (Tokyo) features civilians who demonstrate rather than just answer questions about their talents, from Chinese cooking to sweating. This author will never forget a compelling/repelling 30 minutes she spent watching three men eat hot noodles in front of a gas stove as the camera focused on bottles filling up with their perspiration—ending as the curtain drew across so they could wring a few last drops of sweat from their drenched bathing suits.

Since testing is a way of life for the Japanese, they feel comfortable with the Q-and-A format. With a few exceptions, the shows have interactive formats whereby viewers can guess the answers along with the panelists. Indeed, one quiz, "TV School," poses actual questions from high school entrance exams to its panel of celebrities, who sit at stylized school desks. Before its popular co-host Itsumi Masataka died of cancer in 1994, it ranked as one of Japan's top shows. Beat Takeshi (see below), the other co-host, suffered serious injuries in an auto accident but has returned to the small screen.

In contrast to Western shows that aim for low costs and high profits,

Japan's quizzes spare no expense as they compete in the fierce prime-time hours. A desire to break out of the studio (and the Japanese archi-pelago) characterizes quizzes in Japan as in no other country. The Japanese can travel vicariously on the wings of their travel quizzes. In 1992, "Discovering the World's Mysteries" (TBS), "World Professionals" (NTV), "Let's Go! the World" (Fuji) and "Round-the-World Gourmet Quiz" (Tokyo) featured on-location scenes from exotic overseas destina-tions—or unusual Japanese sites, in the case of "Changing Locales Quiz" (Tokyo) and "Look Out for Doubt" (TBS). The shows present travelogue videos, into which a question is woven for a panel of celebrities to dis-cuss. The answer is then shown by the on-location host or hostess.

If these shows bring the outside world into the TV studio, the peri-patetic "Trans-America Ultra Quiz" brings the studio (hosts, contestants, desks with buzzers—everything) to the outside world. A grandiose mix-ture of luck, skill, physical endurance and wanderlust, the "Trans-America Ultra Quiz" thinks big in every aspect of its conception and pro-duction. It begins with thousands of contestants gathering in a sports stadium in Tokyo to answer "yes" or "no" questions by moving to desig-nated sections of the playing field. This group is winnowed down to about 100 finalists, who must quickly pack their suitcases and face more questions on a flight to California, during which all but about 25 players are eliminated. At each stop, more quick-fire questions omit players, who must perform exhausting, bizarre and humiliating feats in the "*batsu* [loser's] game." In the end, only two of them make it to Oz/Utopia/Shangri-la (read the Statue of Liberty, New York), one of whom emerges as the "ultra" champion.

But quizzes that feature civilian players are atypical. Because celebrity panelists dominate the Japanese quiz scene, prizes do not inject a rags-to-riches dramatic element as they do in Western shows such as "The Price Is Right" or "Let's Make a Deal." Some celebrities capitalize on their in-ability to win, bantering and joking with hosts and other celebrities in a style reminiscent of the quiz/talk show "What's My Line."

TV Personalities

Entertainers

Most quiz shows feature celebrity panelists drawn from a finite stable of singers, comedians and personalities (including a few Japanese-speaking Caucasians). They appear so regularly that they nearly compete against themselves, hopping from one brightly lit set to another on dif-ferent channels. A host on one show commonly acts as a panelist on another, and vice versa. Meanwhile, a stand-up comedian on a variety special may appear the next day as a talk show host on another network.

The stable of *tarento* [talent] has clearly defined comers and goers, as NHK diligently does public surveys to determine who's moving up and who's moving down. Although most of the stars originally had a defined niche, such as singing or comedy, they endure as public figures who are famous for being famous. Masataka Itsumi, for example, started out as a newscaster.

Beat Takeshi, the top male in the NHK poll, whose weekly TV time can add up to 20 hours, has jumped around as a comedian, actor, talk show interviewer, variety show emcee and game show host for more than 15 years. He even appeared in David Bowie's 1983 movie, "Merry Christmas, Mr. Lawrence."

A 5-foot-4-inch entertainment machine, Takeshi Kitano, was born in 1946 in one of Tokyo's poorest neighborhoods. He dropped out of engineering school to perform *manzai* [comic dialogue] in night clubs before moving his comedy to television. Subsequently, he began to develop concepts for bizarre TV shows in which he himself starred. All this activity brings him a yearly income equal to many millions of dollars, which he flaunts by driving imported sports cars, keeping various mistresses and wearing flamboyant, un-Japanese outfits. Takeshi thinks Japan, where "making people laugh is of lower value than making people cry" (Meyer 1989, 29), takes itself too seriously.

Three comedy duos, considered together as one "personality," often make the NHK top 10 list: Downtown, Tunnels and Uchan/Nanchan. By the mid-1990s, the Matsumoto/Hanada duo (Downtown) each wrote books of their own and developed separate identities. Several times named the No. 1 female talent, Kuniko Yamada first appeared in the top 10 in 1984. Popular since the 1950s, Mitsuko Mori, who usually wears a *kimono* rather than Western dress, has had unusual staying power among female personalities.

News Anchors

Because of the tyranny of ratings, anchors at news shows with sagging viewer interest may not last long. Called *kyastahs* ['casters], the anchors commonly appear in male-female pairs. However, in 1990, NTV bucked the tide to go with a solo anchor; when they fired the man and kept the woman, Yoshiko Sakurai, ratings soared.

As Japan's politics go through a stage of upheaval, TV anchors and commentators have gained unprecedented power (see Chapter 2). Some credit Hiroshi Kume with changing the face of Japan after 40 years of Liberal Democratic Party (LDP) rule. The leading anchors include many, such as Hiroshi Sekiguchi, Taro Kimura and Soichiro Tawara, besides the five profiled below.

Hiroshi Kume: TV Asahi "News Station"

Born in 1944 in Saitama, Hiroshi Kume studied politics and economics at Waseda University from 1963 to 1967 but put his heart into a theater group as a director and actor. In his college years, as the Vietnam conflict escalated, he saw lone activists foster a mass anti-war movement and gained respect for individual initiative.

Kume was hired out of Waseda by TBS. After a two-year leave because of medical problems, he came back as host of "Doyo Waido" [Saturday Wide], where he honed his skills as a commentator. Later, as a free-lancer, he hosted four programs, including "Pittashi Kan Kan" and "The Best Ten," a popular music program on which Kume and co-host Tetsuko Kuroyanagi often bantered about current news. By then, Kume's presence on a show virtually guaranteed high ratings.

At age 41, he embarked on a new career as the anchor of TV Asahi's 10-11 p.m. "News Station," an iconoclastic news show that debuted on October 7, 1985. The top-rated program mixes well-researched information with user-friendly props (he once used a model of an exploding volcano to explain a story) and Kume's own forthright opinions, questions and reactions. Eschewing a TelePrompTer, he often laughs out loud and grimaces. Backed by TV Asahi executive Kyuemon Oda, Kume's contract stipulated the hiring of 40 staffers from his own production company as fact checkers and researchers.

"Journalists should not think of the national interest," says the influential Kume (Konaka 1988, 27-60). "This caused the tragedy of World War II. Their duty is to report on facts." Instead, Kume, who combines the "down-home appeal of Tom Brokaw, the earnest look of Dan Rather and the magnetism of Peter Jennings" (Sherman 1995, 11), feels a duty to represent citizen concerns not usually aired on straight news programs. In addition to "News Station," every year since 1983 he has moderated a TV special on cancer.

In October 1992, Kume began a diatribe against LDP power broker Shin Kanemaru, who had taken $4 million in bribes from a trucking company linked to Japan's mafia. His "on-air campaign was not the only reason, but Kanemaru did resign his seat in disgrace" (Sherman 1995, 11). In 1995, the French weekly *Le Nouvel Observateur* named Kume as one of the world's 50 most influential people.

Yoshiko Sakurai: NTV

Yoshiko Sakurai, whose father had business dealings in Southeast Asia, was born in Hanoi, Vietnam, in 1945. She graduated from the University of Hawaii, making plans to work as a high school English teacher. But her bilingual abilities landed her a job with Elizabeth Pond, Tokyo bureau chief of the *Christian Science Monitor.*

In 1980 she signed on as co-anchor of NTV's "Kyo no Dekigoto" [Today's Events]. In one coup, Sakurai nabbed an exclusive interview with Philippine President Corazon Aquino. In 1990, because of her international experience, NTV chose her over veteran journalist Yuichi Aoyama when the 11 p.m. newscast's ratings sagged to a mere 4 percent.

In 1994, her investigative series on HIV-tainted blood imports put the blame on a Ministry of Health official and named him. In 1995, her book on AIDS victims won the Soichi Oya non-fiction award. Also in 1995, when Aum Shinrikyo dominated the news (see Chapter 3), Sakurai's "all-news style and commanding presence made her the nation's broadcaster of choice" (Reid 1995b, B10). Ratings soared to 20 percent.

Sakurai has paved the way for other women anchors in a field where men used to dominate. In 1996, she left her anchor post to pursue projects related to the environment.

Yuko Ando: From TV Asahi to Fuji

Yuko Ando, born in Chiba in 1958, went to Michigan while in high school on an exchange program. After attending a junior college in Oakland, Calif., she enrolled in Sophia University's Foreign Language Department. In 1979 while still a college student, she applied for and landed a TV job.

Ando has served as announcer for "TV Scoop" (TV Asahi), anchor of "CNN Day Watch" (TV Asahi), anchor of Fuji's "Supertime" (6–7 p.m.) and, since 1994, anchor of Fuji's main newscast, "News Japan." Taro Kimura, once a leading anchor, lends authority and credibility to the program by contributing commentaries.

With her fluency in English, Ando remains one of few Japanese women to do overseas reporting (Cooper-Chen 1992). She has covered stories in Poland, Cambodia, the Philippines, Russia, Brazil and China, as well as many in the United States. In November 1987, she was doing a live stand-up in front of the White House during the Reagan-Gorbachev summit when a U.S. TV crew asked if they could interview her–whereupon she thought to herself, "I've made it!" Ando admires Japanese-American reporter Linda Taira, while she in turn serves as a role model for young Japanese women.

Takero Morimoto: From NHK to TBS

Takero Morimoto, born in 1939, the youngest brother of well-known critic Tetsuro Morimoto, graduated from Keio University's

English Literature Department and went to work for NHK. In 1980, when NHK changed its 15-year-old morning program "Studio 102" to "News Wide," it tapped Morimoto for the anchor slot. (The generic term "wide show" refers to a mixed news/feature/interview program like "The Today Show.") However, as a news reader, Morimoto did not participate in decision making and felt like a second-class citizen.

When TBS approached him in 1984, he resigned from NHK. Assigned to a gossipy entertainment show called "Morning EYE," Morimoto abruptly confronted the differences in personnel, prestige, wealth and power between NHK and the leaner commercial stations.

Morimoto later moved to TBS's night news program "Prime Time" but failed to bring in double-digit ratings. As producers were discussing changes to make the program more lively, the photo weekly *Friday* carried pictures of him coming out of a female director's apartment one morning. After taking a month off, Morimoto, a married man, apologized and was reassigned to a noontime show, "Super Wide" (Konaka 1988, 61-93).

Tetsuya Chikushi: From print to TV anchor

In 1989, after the Morimoto episode, TBS chose Tetsuya Chikushi, former editor of the *Asahi Shimbun*, as its news voice of authority. Born in 1935 in the city of Oita on Kyushu, he graduated from Waseda University in 1959 with majors in political science and economics. Immediately he went to work as a reporter for the *Asahi Shimbun*. After becoming a special correspondent stationed in Washington in 1971, he covered Nixon's visit to China and the Watergate affair.

In 1987 he assumed editorship of the prestigious *Asahi Journal*, often appearing on his company's affiliated TV network, TV Asahi. At this writing, as anchor of "News 23" on TBS at 11 p.m., he is regarded as one of Japan's most trustworthy journalists. He is noted for his liberal viewpoints and gentle demeanor. Intensely curious, he has many interests, ranging from ceramics and jazz to wine and mahjong. Chikushi has written or edited two books: *How the World Views the Japanese, Comments on Varied Issues* and *The God of the Living Room*.

Issues and Effects

In both news and entertainment programs, NHK (and the commercial stations as well) has a Japanifying effect (see above). In addition, the head of Japan's University of the Air, media sociologist Hidetoshi Kato (1993, 16-20), sees other negative effects of television on people.

Negative Effects

Narcotizing the populace

In a 1958 essay, popular writer and columnist Soichi Oya casti-gated TV watching for its "peanuts effect": Once you start consuming peanuts (television), you just can't stop, even though you're not really tasting them. In another essay putting down game shows, he criticized television for creating "100 million idiots"–a phrase widely quoted even today.

Loss of sleep

According to an NHK survey, people in 1970 slept on average seven hours and 57 minutes, whereas in 1990 they slept seven hours and 39 minutes. The survey concluded that television had drawn off 18 min-utes of sleep from the average person, which many make up by dozing on public transportation.

Decline of reading

Oya's "100 million idiots" theory predicted that television would destroy Japan's love of reading, which has occurred to some extent in the case of newspapers (see Chapter 4) and books and magazines (see Chapter 6). However, the most immediate effect was on two other mass media: movies and radio (Kato 1993, 19-21).

Death of the movie industry

Japan's per capita film attendance stands at an anemic 1.1 per year, one of the lowest rates in the world. Movie attendance grew steadily after the war, hitting a peak of 1.127 billion customers in 1958, while the peak of film production came in 1960, when six busy studios produced 547 films for 7,457 theaters.

As television captivated Japan, domestic film production fell precipi-tously. In 1991, Japanese companies produced only 230 films, most of them low-budget, soft-core pornography. That year, of 467 films released, more than half (246) came from overseas–primarily from the United States. Beginning in about 1960, the major studios, seeing the handwrit-ing on the wall, began to produce TV dramas and commercials.

Changes in radio

People used to listen to radio three hours a day in 1950, but the figure declined to 90 minutes in 1960, then to 30 minutes in 1965. The only remaining heavy listeners seem to be taxi drivers. By focusing on specific narrow audiences, radio in Japan, as in the United States, has managed to survive. Another group of likely users, women at home, have tapes and CDs and the sound of television to keep them company.

Other Effects

Other effects of TV include some positive changes and some with neither positive nor negative implications, just qualitative differences in life before and after television (Kato 1993, 13-16).

Care of the aged

While much criticism explores television's effects on children, the most devoted TV fans lie at the other end of the age spectrum. As Table 7.1 shows, older women watch so much (6.5 hours a day) that time spent with television assumes the proportions of a job. Men in their 50s do not watch as much as women, but those in their 60s watch nearly four hours and those in their 70s watch nearly five hours. Television provides social welfare services in the absence of other activities for the elderly.

Antidote to rural isolation

As early as the 1950s, visitors to rural villages discovered to their surprise old farm houses with brand-new television sets. Agrarian reform, coupled with the protective price of rice, have brought prosperity to the countryside but few options for entertainment after a hard day's labor, especially on chilly nights. Television has bridged the traditional gap between the urban and rural populations.

Homogenized speech patterns

Although Japan is a small, crowded country, each region used to have a distinct dialect with unique accents and vocabulary—to the extent that people from Kagoshima, on the southern tip of Kyushu, could hardly understand people from Aomori, at the northernmost point of Honshu. But now a version of the Tokyo dialect, called the "NHK dialect," has standardized the language. Television accelerated the process already begun by radio.

Family togetherness

In the era of one TV set per household, the whole family used to sit together every evening to watch their favorite programs. In response to this new habit, producers created a new genre of programs called home drama (see above). In the 1990s, each home has more than two sets; moreover, the average household size has declined to fewer than three people (in 1990, the figure dipped below three for the first time in history).

Encouraging domestic innovations

Home drama brought important peripheral information, beyond the story line, to masses of people. For example, a new kitchen used as a TV locale might serve as an impetus for viewers' kitchen renovations. Unlike movie stars, with whom viewers could not identify, the characters in home dramas seemed like neighbors and friends who regularly visited viewers in their living rooms.

Education

Hidetoshi Kato's own University of the Air, conceived in 1968 by the Ministry of Education and opened in 1985 as an alternate route to a college education, graduated its first class in 1989. As of 1995, nearly 58,000 students were enrolled, more than half in degree programs. The institute also airs general culture programs for people who do not wish to earn a degree and conducts research on education. Broadcasting only in the Tokyo area, it does not have the reach of NHK-e, the nationwide educational channel. The training of adults will increase in importance as the pool of 18-year-olds shrinks. Japan's population will peak around 2020 and thereafter probably decline.

TV Exports

In the 1970s, Japan shifted its status from importer to exporter of information (Ito 1990a). Specifically, the flow of TV programs tipped in Japan's favor in 1971. According to Professor Kazuo Kawatake at Komazawa Women's College ("Sekai ni" 1994), a dramatic change occurred over 20 years: In 1971, Japan imported 2,000 hours of TV programming and exported 2,200 hours; whereas in 1992, although imports did not differ much at 2,843 hours, exports shot up to 19,546 hours. The 737 shows exported in 1992 fell into the categories of animated cartoons, at 58.3 percent; drama and movies, 15.5 percent; and quiz/variety, 14.8 percent. Imports came from the United States primarily (2,300 hours) as well as Spain, Hong Kong, Thailand, South Korea and Taiwan.

Starting in 1984, "Oshin," the story of a woman's perseverance despite adversity as she ages from 7 to 83, captured hearts overseas, just as it had in Japan (see Table 7.6). Embued with "ambiguous messages and cultural archetypes" (Svenkerud, Rahoi and Singhal 1995, 147), it had a strong appeal in both Asian and non-Asian societies. In China, viewership soared as high as 90 percent in some regions. In Iran in 1987, ratings hit a remarkable high of 70 percent. The national TV system broadcast the program because government policy called for a spirit of self-sacrifice such as exemplified by Oshin, who finally reached prosperity in her later life

Table 7.6. Countries outside Japan airing "Oshin"

Country	Year	Episodes	Language (dubbed or subtitled)
Australia	1984	297	English
Thailand	1984	297	Thai
Singapore	1984	297	Mandarin
United States*	1984	297	English
Belgium	1985	297	Flemish
Brazil	1985	297	Portuguese
Canada*	1985	48	Japanese
China	1985	297	Chinese
Hong Kong	1985	297	Cantonese
Macau	1985	48	Portuguese
Poland	1985	48	Polish
Indonesia	1986	297	Bahasa
Iran	1986	297	Persian
Malaysia	1986	297	Malay
Saudi Arabia	1987	297	English
Sri Lanka	1987	297	English
Brunei	1988	297	Malay
Mexico	1988	297	Spanish
Bahrain	1989	48	English
Syria	1989	48	English
Qatar	1989	48	English
Bangladesh	1990	96	English
Dominican Republic	1990	48	Spanish
Pakistan	1990	48	English
Peru	1990	48	Spanish
Philippines	1990	48	Tagalog
India	1992	48	English
Vietnam	1994	NA	Vietnamese

Source: Nihon Shimbun Kyokai (NHK).

*Broadcast in Japanese (in the United States, with English subtitles) over Japanese-language stations in California, New York, Honolulu, Toronto and Vancouver.

(Mowlana and Rad 1992, 53). In Belgium, where many more programs competed in a crowded TV market, viewership still reached more than 17 percent. Groups of nuns rescheduled their prayer time in order to avoid missing "Oshin." The interest in women's lives and the similarity between Belgian and Japanese experiences 100 years ago made the program compelling (Svenkerud, Rahoi and Singhal 1995).

"Oshin" stands out as an exception to the rule; generally, Japanese dramas do not sell well in Europe and the United States. In Asia, however, dramas such as "100 First Proposals" (Fuji) and "Don't Tell Anybody" (TBS) have such appeal that within days of their first broadcast, pirate editions come out. In Taiwan, the ruling party initially forbade Japanese shows because of lingering resentment over Japanese rule before 1945, but the ban was lifted in 1993 after viewers protested. (Korea, also a former Japanese colony, still forbids TV imports.)

According to Yokoda Yasumasa of Fuji Sankei Communication International, "The boom in Japanese shows in Asia started two years ago when those shows were broadcast at saturation levels on STAR-TV. Fellow Asians aspire to Japanese fashion and leisure activities, but in Europe, Japanese faces are not well accepted" ("*Sekai ni*" 1994).

Shows with universal appeal include cartoons and, more recently, game shows. "An-pan Man" (NTV), "Dragon Ball" (Fuji) and other kids' cartoons blanket small screens throughout the world. Fuji Sankei's international subsidiary has contracts in 46 countries for an English-language version (minus its Japanese hosts) of "Naru hodo the world," the travel-locale show that has enthralled the Japanese since 1981. Fuji's Yokoda Yasumasa explains that the Q-and-A format is "easy to understand. Also, many places around the world appear in the program. Thus everyone, national boundaries notwithstanding, can accept the show" ("*Sekai ni*" 1994).

The TV trade imbalance in Japan's favor may benefit Japanese coffers, but it worries Shin Mizukoshi of Tokyo University's Social Information Research Center: "The import into Japan of few shows results from closing out cultures different from our own. If we don't accept more from overseas cultures, broadcasting will not enlighten us" ("*Sekai ni*" 1994).

New uses for television and new markets, such as those overseas via satellite (see Chapter 12), are crucial for the medium's future; the already-existing TV saturation (one set per 1.8 people) has several implications. NHK cannot expect increased revenues from new customers. Nor can TV advertisers expect much more attention paid to their messages since the average Japanese set already stays on about eight hours a day. As the next chapter will show, television takes the lion's share of the Japanese advertising dollar.

8
Postwar
Advertising

As Sumiko Suzuki leafs through her copy of *Josei Jishin,* she sees page after page of ads for Shiseido cosmetics, the largest purchaser of magazine ads in Japan. As Taro Tanaka tapes an episode of his favorite TV show, he finds his finger constantly on the pause button as he zaps out the numerous CMs (commercial messages).

Overview

Each year in Japan, advertisers spend more than $300 per person to reach consumers like Sumiko and Taro. Kao Corp. (which handles many products in addition to soap), House Shokuhin (food products) and Suntory (food products in addition to whiskey) spend the most on advertising (see Table 8.1).

Japan's changing demographics affect these advertisers' strategies. Even though respect for the aged is a tenet of the culture, readers and viewers find few older Japanese pictured in advertisements. For example, in 1990, one-tenth of 1 percent of female magazine models were older than 50; older men, at 8 percent of male models, are a more vibrant part of the magazine advertising scene (Cooper-Chen, Leung and Cho 1995).

The 10.37 million over-65 women and 7.2 million over-65 men–totaling 14.1 percent of the population–make Japan one of the "grayest" countries in the world. In the year 2025, Japan is expected to rank as the world's first nation to reach 25 percent senior citizens. (The United Nations defines a nation as "senior" when people over 65 make up 7 percent of the population.) But the average household headed by a person over 60 has a relatively low annual income, 80 percent of it from social security. So advertisers target other groups.

In 1984, the mammoth Dentsu agency formed a subsidiary aimed at targeting young female consumers. After school and before marriage,

131

Table 8.1. Top 10 firms in advertising expenditures, 1993

Firms	Lines	Ad spending (in thousands of $)
1. Kao Corp.	Chemicals	$385,801
2. House Shokuhin	Foods	342,459
3. Suntory	Foods	313,906
4. Lion Corp.	Chemicals	249,457
5. Shiseido Co.	Cosmetics	223,963
6. Procter & Gamble Co.	Chemicals	218,998
7. Matsushita Electric	Electrical equipment	215,389
8. Toyota Motor Corp.	Automobiles	213,553
9. Mitsubishi Motor Co.	Automobiles	200,504
10. Nippon Chokyhan	Direct sales	188,679

Source: McCann Erickson, as cited in *Advertising Age,* February 20, 1995: I9.

most young OLs ("office ladies") live with their parents, leaving their incomes 100 percent disposable and influencing their parents' purchasing decisions as well. Since the average age for a woman's first marriage is nearly 26 (nearly 29 for men), that period lasts many years.

Advertisers must woo both single men and women, who cannot be counted on to follow traditional Japanese consumer habits. The advertisers often use such a soft-sell approach, emphasizing the company rather than the particular product, that Westerners may wonder how any commerce occurs at all. Yet Japan, with half the U.S. population, ranks second only to the United States as the world's biggest spender on advertising–$128.64 billion in the United States and $38.43 billion in Japan for 1990. This advertising mega-industry had unlikely beginnings.

History

Consistently in Japan, "things sacred were transformed rapidly into artistic and commercial advertising media" (Tada 1978, 44). For instance, on votive towels, originally offered to spirits at shrines, stores began printing their names as advertisements. At other shrines, *tanzaku* [strips of fancy paper] tied to the branches of cherry trees bore the names of *oiran* [courtesans]. Even the name of the Canon camera comes from Kannon, the goddess of mercy. Among many media milestones (see Appendix 1), a Kabuki play performed around 1700 told of a peddler who advertised the benefits of moxa salve (Yamaki 1996).

Around 1820, when urban life flourished in Edo (Tokyo), restaurants and other businesses used eye-catching objects outside their shops–such as large fish or glamorous wigs–to advertise their wares. The object-as-ad survives today in the models of meals one sees in front of Japanese restaurants, detailed down to plastic sprigs of parsley atop wax omelets.

In 1901, when the news agency Nippon Denpo was founded, the agency also provided an advertising space service (see Chapter 5). In 1936, the pro-military Nippon Denpo merged with Nippon Rengo to form the Domei Agency, with separate news (propaganda) and advertising divisions. In 1945, two news agencies and one ad agency, Dentsu, emerged from the dissolution of Domei.

The evolution of ad contents followed Japan's postwar reconstruction (Fujitake and Yamamoto 1994, 218). The dominant forms of address used in ad texts changed from "everybody" (late 1940s) to "you" (1950s and 1960s) and then to "I" (1970s and 1980s), while themes showed similar shifts of priorities (see Table 8.2).

Following virtually uninterrupted expansion of advertising since World War II, the year 1992 was sobering for advertisers. Overall, ad expenditures dropped 4.6 percent from 1991–the first decline since a slight (1.5 percent) dip in 1965, which had occurred as a natural reaction against the heated-up ad frenzy that accompanied the 1964 Tokyo Olympics. Real estate ad outlays dropped the most after the boom market of the 1980s went bust.

For the first time since 1947, when Dentsu started compiling figures on ad expenditures by companies and local governments, TV advertising dropped. Experts "attributed the decline to the unpopularity of professional baseball programs and moderate advertising outlays for the Barcelona Olympics" ("Ad expenses" 1993). Advertising dropped again in 1993 but rebounded in 1994. Newspapers were up 1.1 percent over 1993; television, up 3.4 percent; and magazines, up 1.6 percent (radio advertising declined). Table 8.3 shows that television took in more revenues than any other medium–31.8 percent of the total in 1994.

Table 8.2. Themes of ad messages

Decade	Themes
1940s	Reconstruction, peace, life, birth control, radio
1950s	America, electrify, clean, beauty, domesticity
1960s	"My home," exports, overseas travel, speech, fashion
1970s	Nature, feeling, Japan, private life, woman
1980s	Self, health, bubble, earth, aging

Source: Hakuhodo, as cited in Fujitake and Yamamoto (1994, 218).

Table 8.3. Advertising expenditures by medium

Medium	Advertising expenditures (billion yen)			Component ratio (%)		
	1992	1993	1994	1992	1993	1994
Newspapers	1,217.2	1,108.1	1,121.1	22.3	21.6	21.7
Magazines	369.2	341.7	347.3	6.7	6.1	6.7
Radio	235.0	211.3	202.9	4.3	4.1	3.9
Television	1,652.6	1,589.1	1,643.5	30.3	31.0	31.8
Subtotals	3,474.0	3,250.8	3,314.8	63.6	63.4	64.1
Other*	1,975.7	1,864.6	1,840.9	36.2	36.4	35.6
New media	11.4	11.9	12.5	0.2	0.2	0.3
Totals	5,461.1	5,127.3	5,168.2	100	100	100

Source: "Advertising spending" (1996).

*Direct mail, fliers, outdoor, transit, point of purchase, directories.

Approaches to Selling

The "softness" of Japanese advertising sometimes surprises Westerners. For example, a 90-second TV commercial in 1992 for Nippon Telephone and Telegraph (NTT) showed close-ups of a baby for 45 seconds; subsequently a voice-over stated: "A long time ago, the earth belonged to the dinosaurs. Although the dinosaurs lived for a long time, they disappeared without understanding the universe or their own existence. But we humans can know these things. We can choose the future." Only at the end did the initials "NTT" appear briefly. The commercial sold no services or products.

The baby ad not only lacked hard information about prices, features and advantages of NTT services, its message—the nature of humanity—had no direct relation to NTT. Earlier, in the 1970s, an ad for a fountain pen consisted of nonsense phrases (akin to Lewis Carroll's "'Twas brillig and the slithy toves ... "). According to Tada (1978, 46), commercials like these, which aim to attract attention precisely because of their quirky non-relatedness, are "forming a new culture. In their greetings, gestures and conversation, young men and women use fragments of TV commercials. By so doing, they seem to want to be regarded as 'now.'"

As part of a homogeneous, high-context culture (see Chapter 1), Japanese audiences do not need specific, hard-hitting messages that say, "Buy this pen." They intuitively understand the indirect message and appreciate the conveyance of unstated sentiments. According to one copywriter, Japanese advertising "is like haiku," a short, meaning-laden poem (Shinohara 1992). In a study of 1987 TV commercials, three out of four used an emotional rather than informational appeal. Commercials for all types of products appealed to the heart rather than the intellect (Ramaprasad and Hasegawa 1990).

By the same token, indirectness has meant until recently a lack of comparative messages; one need not mention a competitor's name if everyone understands that Toyota competes with Nissan and Kirin beer with Asahi. Furthermore, belting out the name of one's competitors constitutes a brash, aggressive act that does not fit the Japanese values of *kenkyo* [modesty] or *omoiyari* [being considerate] (Hasegawa 1995, 11–12). Comparative ads are problematic "in a culture where it is rude to say I'm better than the other person" (Shinohara 1992). According to another theory, comparative ads are rare in Japan because of the influence of the giant advertising firm Dentsu, which represents a number of competing advertisers who would become upset if their products were attacked (Blustein 1991).

Not surprisingly, the first, and still main, users of comparative advertising in Japan were U.S. firms. In 1992, General Motors listed specifications of its Cadillac Seville against those of Nissan's Infiniti in a newspaper ad, but discreetly, in small type. Also, Honeywell cited Minolta cameras in another ad after winning a patent infringement case in U.S. courts.

In 1991, Pepsi established a Japanese precedent by running a TV commercial featuring M.C. Hammer that contrasted Pepsi with Coke. The rap singer, on stage sipping a Coke during a concert, dismays his hip audience by crooning a sentimental ballad. After he is handed a Pepsi, Hammer reverts to rap and brings the crowd back to life. Cans of Pepsi and Coke appeared in close-up.

TV stations pulled the spot when Coca-Cola of Japan filed a complaint of copyright infringement with the Japan Fair Trade Commission (FTC), but the FTC ruled the ad legal in July 1991. Pepsi for its part placed a print ad offering a video of the offending TV spot in return for viewers' opinions; 88,000 people responded, 95 percent of them favorably, and Pepsi Japan's sales jumped 16 percent in 1991. Coca-Cola's Japan unit had held a 57 percent share of the carbonated beverage market, and Pepsi, only about 7 percent. A survey conducted by Pepsi indicated that the ad quickly became the eighth most popular among Tokyo residents and the second most popular among youth (Blustein 1991).

Pepsi's hiring of M.C. Hammer points to the perception of foreign personalities and models as lending trendiness to Japanese advertising. Stars who do not deign to sell out for ad dollars at home—such as Jodie Foster,

Leonard Nimoy, and Bruce Springsteen–hawk products on TV commercial messages in Japan. And Western models appear frequently in print ads (Nakazawa 1993), as we discuss below.

Advertising in the Mass Media

Television/Radio

Broadcast regulations in Japan allow a maximum of six commercial minutes per 60-minute TV program. However, by airing many short programs, networks can boost TV commercial time (a program as short as five minutes can have a one-minute commercial). Thus in actuality, an average of more than 10 minutes of commercials can air per hour. In short, TV viewers are bombarded with advertising.

Most TV stations divide their airtime into four segments: A, or prime time (7 to 11 p.m. weekdays; 6 to 11 p.m. Sundays and holidays); Special B (the hours immediately before and after prime time, plus noon to 2 p.m.); B (the rest of the daytime); and C (early mornings and late nights). Special B costs about 70 percent of the charge for A; B, about 40 percent; and C, about 30 percent.

The base prime-time rate varies with each TV market. For example, in 1991 NTV in Tokyo charged ¥1,050,000 for a 15-second spot, while Okinawa TV charged only ¥200,000. Most radio stations charge a uniform amount for all time periods except early morning and late night. TBS radio in Tokyo charged ¥100,000 for a 20-second spot, while Radio Okinawa charged only ¥15,000.

In 1990, the food/beverage/tobacco category accounted for the lion's share–31.3 percent–of TV spot commercials, with service/leisure a distant second at 13.0 percent, followed by pharmaceuticals (9.2 percent), cosmetics/toiletries (7.7 percent) and home electronics/AV equipment (5.9 percent). Americans, who have not viewed cigarette commercials for many years, can see the Marlboro man ride again and vaguely familiar Salem couples happily puffing away late at night on Japanese television.

Of all commercials, about two-thirds run 15 seconds long, with about one-third running 30 seconds. Spot commercials air at intervals between two shows, while program commercials air within specific shows. Deals for placements are made by advertising agencies, which receive about a 15 percent commission based on the total contracted amount. Advertisers do not deal directly with broadcasters because agencies can better plan a company's publicity strategy and buy appropriate media, including TV time and print space. Thus broadcasters do not need large in-house staffs to deal with marketing activities (Shimizu 1993, 29).

Considering that the average household keeps its TV set on for more than eight hours a day, what kinds of images do these spot and program commercials project? Ramaprasad and Hasegawa (1990) analyzed 410 prime-time TV commercials that aired on four Japanese television stations in 1987. They found that Japanese commercials use the emotional appeal more than the informational appeal, often with very indirect product-selling approaches.

Sengupta (1994) studied 507 TV ads in 1992 and 1993 that portrayed 367 men and 480 women. Of these, 33.5 percent of men, but only 16.5 percent of women, were in working roles. The most prominent roles for working women were entertainment (35.4 percent), mid-level business (29.1 percent) and blue collar (15.2 percent). Men had the same top three categories but in a different order. Many more models did not work than worked. Furthermore, almost three-quarters of commercials (73.9 percent) showed single people, which reflects marketers' emphasis on young consumers.

Newspapers

Newspapers rank as Japan's second largest outlet for ads, taking up 21.7 percent of expenditures (see Table 8.3). When Japan's economy started to heat up in 1962, advertising income first exceeded sales revenue. Ads remained the backbone of newspaper revenue until the disastrous year of 1992, when the two sources evened out. Thereafter, ad revenues dropped against sales revenues, standing at 45.2 percent for ads vs. 54.8 percent for subscription/newsstand sales by 1994.

Table 8.4 shows the newspapers that carry more than 50,000 columns of ads per year. Not surprisingly, the national dailies carry the most ads, but those general-interest papers with the largest circulations (the *Yomiuri* and *Asahi*) did not rank as the top ad vehicles. Instead, the *Nihon Keizai*, the financial daily, with its more focused audience, was far and away the advertisers' favorite.

Advertising took 29.8 percent of total newspaper space in 1960, but since the mid-1960s, newspaper pages have maintained a space ratio of approximately 60 percent editorial copy to 40 percent advertising. The Japanese postal code stipulates an advertising space ratio of not more than 50 percent for special low postal rates.

Retail-sector advertising, such as for local grocery stores, generally takes the form of inserts delivered at home with the newspaper. These inserts provide a major portion of the independent newspaper dealers' incomes but no revenue at all for the newspaper companies. To recapture smaller local advertisers, newspapers are beginning to carry clip-out coupons.

Table 8.4. Leading newspapers, volume of advertising, 1990

Newspaper	Yearly total ads (columns)	Yearly total (pages)
National dailies		
Nihon Keizai (Tokyo)	127,343	15,054
(Osaka)	124,760	15,036
(Nagoya)	124,925	14,934
(Seibu)	124,898	14,922
(Hokkaido)	122,241	14,934
Asahi (Tokyo)	107,946	12,714
Evening edition	50,166	5,752
(Osaka)	91,230	11,266
(Chubu)	62,992	9,380
(Seibu)	65,645	9,418
(Hokkaido)	73,171	10,496
Yomiuri (Tokyo)	106,878	13,076
(Osaka)	91,479	11,452
(Hokkaido)	68,962	10,550
Evening edition	69,494	9,394
(Seibu)	78,395	11,266
Mainichi (Tokyo)	77,257	11,096
(Osaka)	74,373	10,540
(Chubu)	54,456	9,110
(Seibu)	59,224	8,958
(Hokkaido)	50,839	8,726
Sankei (Tokyo)	60,682	9,358
(Osaka)	64,425	9,364
Other		
Chūnichi Shimbun	89,418	12,072
Hokkaido Shimbun	80,456	11,186

Source: Dentsu (1991), *Japan 1992 Marketing and Advertising Yearbook.*
Note: "Leading" indicates more than 2,000 ad pages per year.

In a continuing ad campaign to play up the newspaper's strength as an advertising medium, the 1993 pitch drew upon the current soccer boom in Japan. Over a photo of Japan's National Soccer Team manager are the English words "Eye Contact." The copy reads: "The newspaper advertisement brings together the individual, the industry and society. Its goal is 'eye contact'" ("Soccer boom" 1993).

Until the economic bubble burst in the early 1990s, newspapers counted on large advertisements for mass-market goods and services rather than smaller advertisements aimed at specific audiences. As a result, "the bulk of the classified retail advertising has moved to specialty magazines, advertising inserts, and free community newspapers"

(Haruhara and Hayashi 1990, 32). Even the remaining classified bulwark, help-wanted ads, has been usurped by job magazines that carry such listings. In a slow and costly process, advertising agencies write most such ads, which newspapers set in type from handwritten copy. In order to fight back, newspapers are moving toward a remote-entry system whereby advertising agencies would input copy on computers linked online to newspapers. As in the United States, papers plan to introduce telemarketing and create new ad sources, including personals.

As newspapers fight for advertisers and readers, the Japan Newspaper Editors and Publishers Association (NSK) Code of Ethics and Advertising Publication Standards may be sorely tested. Adopted in 1976 and amended in 1991, the code challenges NSK members to carry only truthful, legal and dignified ads. The Publication Standards model for member newspapers prohibits, in a detailed 21-point list, any false, ambiguous, unscientific, obscene, unpatriotic or anonymous advertising.

Magazines

The ¥347.3 billion spent on magazine ads in 1994 represents only about a third of the amount that advertisers spent on newspapers. Still, it superseded radio expenditures (¥202.9 billion), which continued to fall as magazine revenues rose (see Table 8.3). Magazines make ideal vehicles for advertising because they can reach a specific, segmented market.

As Table 8.5 shows, in 1990 "good life" consumer magazines attracted the most advertising; the women's magazines *an·an* and *Hanako,* as well as the men's golfing magazines *Shūkan Par Golf* and *Shūkan Asahi Golf,* each carried more than 5,000 ad pages. But these four do not rank among Japan's highest-circulation publications. Indeed, the phenomenally popular *manga* comics, such as *Shōnen Jump* and *Big Comic Original* (see Chapter 6), carry relatively little advertising because their youthful readers do not have the disposable income of golf-playing executives or single women.

Magazine advertising can open a window onto contemporary Japan even for those who do not read or speak Japanese. For instance, the artificial manipulation of the human body does not seem as prevalent as in the West; a female model can have less-than-perfect teeth and even a flat chest. Also, one can't help but notice the many Caucasian models in both TV and print ads. Nakazawa (1993) studied 318 one- and two-page color ads in the February and March 1993 issues of nine magazines: three for both sexes (*Shūkan Asahi, Dime* and *AERA*), three for men (*Brutus, Popeye* and *Jiyujikan*) and three for women (*an·an, With* and *Fujin Gahō*). Of the

Table 8.5. Leading magazines, volume of advertising, 1990

Magazine	Yearly total ads (pages)	Yearly total (pages)
Weeklies		
Shūkan Asahi	3,147	9,796
Sunday Mainichi	2,296	10,532
Shūkan Yomiuri	2,976	9,878
Shūkan Shincho	2,923	8,060
Shūkan Gendai	3,145	11,642
Shūkan Bunshun	4,431	11,334
Shūkan Post	3,885	12,998
Shūkan Hōseki	2,970	12,126
Monthlies		
Bungei Shunju	2,782	7,546
Young men's		
Popeye	2,941	5,408
Hot-Dog Press	2,636	6,532
Dime	2,045	4,726
Women's, home		
Katei Gahō	2,482	5,876
Orange Page	2,534	4,472
Lettuce Club	2,391	4,664
Mrs.	2,034	5,240
Women's, general		
an•an	5,801	9,366
Shūkan Josei	3,699	11,444
Josei Jishin	4,765	13,868
Josei Seven	4,421	13,846
Bishō	2,191	6,016
non•no	2,801	7,042
Croissant	2,460	5,162
More	2,150	5,106
With	2,223	5,148
J.J.	2,001	4,272
Hanako	5,685	9,488
25 ans	3,186	6,580
Other		
Nikkei Pasokon	4,123	8,050
Pia	4,370	11,400
Shūkan TV Guide	2,968	13,200
The Television	2,243	9,210
Holiday Auto	2,987	6,880
Le Volant	2,882	5,096
Car Graphic	3,182	5,924
Shūkan Golf Digest	5,853	13,462
Shūkan Par Golf	6,207	13,668
Shūkan Asahi Golf	4,782	12,214
Diamond	2,025	7,598
Nikkei Business	3,438	7,100
President	2,107	5,240

Source: Dentsu (1991), *Japan 1992 Marketing and Advertising Yearbook.*

Note: "Leading" indicates more than 2,000 ad pages per year.

318 ads, 186 contained Caucasian models. Nakazawa (1993, 5) concluded that "Japanese base their standard of physical beauty on Western qualities."

What other images do magazine ads project? Cooper-Chen, Leung and Cho (1995) studied three magazines from 1990: *AERA* (weekly) in the general-interest category; *non•no* (published on the fifth and 20th of each month), which appeals to young working and college-age women; and *Nikkei Business* (biweekly) in the men's category. As in the real world, men and women occupy different roles in the ad world. Working men depicted in ads cluster in the high-level business and professional categories, but few women occupy the highest level (about 2 to 3 percent). For working women, the occupation "entertainer" ranks as the top female professional category. Advertisers perceive that Japanese like to see pretty female "talents" hawking products. But most ads do not depict professions; advertisers prefer to show people at play or without any context at all.

In both Japanese and U.S. magazines, similar products merit ad space—especially cosmetics. Cleaning products are noticeably absent on both sides of the Pacific. Busby and Leichty (1993) note the demise of products such as floor wax, detergents and disinfectants from their rank as the No. 1 U.S. products advertised in 1959. Likewise, in Japan such products are absent in both TV and magazine ads. Instead of products associated with drudgery, many ads show products associated with affluence, such as stereos, computers and CDs.

Print ads permit puns by grouping and accenting the *kana* symbols that represent syllable sounds. For example, an All Nippon Airways ad for Okinawa reads Ō Kī Nā Wā. The first two syllables mean "big," an image reinforced by a buxom model in the ad. The third syllable is an exclamation syllable. The fourth syllable means "wow!" So the pun version says, "How big! (and sexy) Wow!" (Tanaka 1994). Copywriters at agencies have abundant material to play with because of the complexities of the Japanese language.

Agencies

About half of all Japanese advertising spending emanates from the top 10 advertising agencies (see Table 8.6). Two among them, Dentsu and Hakuhodo, also rank among the top 10 ad networks in the world (see Table 8.7). Dentsu, the world's fourth (and formerly first) largest agency, had $9,818.9 million in annual billings in 1993. Both Dentsu and Hakuhodo "rely heavily (nearly 40 percent) on TV advertising for their chief source of power and profits" (Shimizu 1993, 28). One could write

Table 8.6. Japan's leading advertising agencies, 1994

Company	Gross income (thousands)	% Change from '93	Billings (thousands)
Dentsu Inc.	$1,479,566	17.4	$11,070,231
Hakuhodo Inc.	716,376	15.9	5,326,647
Tokyu Advertising	201,600	16.9	1,556,600
Asatsu Inc.	190,218	10.2	1,524,186
Daiko Advertising	182,561	11.5	1,443,665
McCann Erickson (Japan)	127,808	6.7	852,477
Yomiko Advertising	114,705	6.1	985,746
I&S Corp.	109,637	4.6	901,893
Dai-ichi Kikaku	105,626	5.4	868,124
Asahi Advertising	104,753	14.4	667,701
Man Nen Sha	94,799	8.1	610,500
Oricom Co.	80,170	9.0	566,173
Sogei	71,850	22.2	460,579
Nikkeisha Inc.	67,272	64.8	404,624
Kyodo Advertising	60,500	11.0	431,500
J. Walter Thompson Japan	56,141	24.7	374,314
Chuo Senko Advertising	54,600	11.0	390,300
Nihon Keizai Advertising	47,276	28.2	342,571
Leo Burnett Kyodo Co.	46,191	16.7	307,952
Dentsu, Young & Rubicam	43,430	7.3	330,612
Tokyo Agency International	40,290	8.5	315,688
Ad Dentsu Japan	31,502	9.7	236,659
Standard Advertising	24,754	8.4	156,319
Grey Daiko	16,539	12.4	110,315

Source: Agency report (1995).

Table 8.7. World's top 10 ad organizations, 1994

Name of group	Worldwide gross income (Unit: $ million)	% Change from '93
WPP Group	2,768.2	5.4
Interpublic Group of Cos.	2,211.0	4.0
Omnicom Group	2,052.6	7.5
Dentsu Inc.	1,641.7	17.0
Cordiant	1,431.5	6.8
Young & Rubicam	1,059.7	5.0
Euro RSCG	813.3	6.0
Grey Advertising	808.7	5.6
Hakuhodo Inc.	774.3	6.4
Leo Burnett Co.	677.5	8.8

Source: Agency report (1995).

an entire book on Dentsu, which outstrips in size the next five Japanese advertising agencies combined.

Dentsu

Dentsu, headquartered in the Tsukiji area of central Tokyo and operating out of 28 domestic offices, controls one of every four Japanese advertising dollars. It handles about half of all prime-time TV ads, more than one-fifth of the ads in the major newspapers and close to a third of those in the more important magazines. Activities of the company's 5,768 employees (as of January 1, 1991) go beyond advertising to include product research and development, corporate communication, media planning and development and consumer- and community-oriented activities. In public relations, Dentsu PR Center and Dentsu Burson-Marsteller dominate the field (see Chapter 9).

Dentsu also ranks as a major publisher, issuing the *Dentsu Advertising Yearbook, Japan Newspaper Yearbook, Advertising* (a monthly magazine) and *Dentsu-Ho* (a twice-weekly marketing/advertising trade newspaper with a circulation of 35,000), all in Japanese, and the *Japan Marketing and Advertising Yearbook* in English. In addition, the Dentsu Institute for Human Studies, a think-tank subsidiary, issues its own set of publications. *Kokuhō Hihyō* is an independent magazine that covers the Japanese advertising scene.

Dentsu's clout turns the usual client-agency relation on its head, such that advertisers and the mass media consider it "a privilege to be treated with consideration by Dentsu" and "follow its instructions rather than the other way round" (van Wolferen 1993, 232). The agency's resources enable it to regularly buy up magazine ad space, guaranteeing magazines a reliable income base; the practice frees the magazines from the weekly or monthly scramble for advertisers but gives Dentsu undue influence over content and the ad rates charged.

Dubbing Dentsu "the hidden media boss," van Wolferen (1993, 231) holds this unequivocal view: "Dentsu does more than any single corporation, anywhere in the world, to mould popular culture, both directly and through hordes of subcontractors . . . [and] is highly active politically." Its many subsidiaries and subcontracting firms include more than 100 film production companies and more than 400 subcontracting graphic arts studios. Furthermore, its *jinmyaku* [personal connections] cement its influence. According to van Wolferen (1993, 233), Dentsu hires family members of powerful TV, publishing, government and business executives to build a network of influence, a practice characterized as "taking hostages."

Dentsu's reach extends internationally through a network of overseas offices and subsidiaries in Bangkok, Sydney, Taipei, Hong Kong, Beijing, Shanghai, Moscow, Chicago, New York, Los Angeles, London, Stockholm, Paris, Brussels, Amsterdam, Dusseldorf, Madrid and Barcelona. In 1990, Dentsu acquired a 40 percent interest in Europe's Collet Dickenson Pearce International Group Ltd. (CDP Europe) to expand Dentsu's European network. CDP Europe, with annual billings of about $400 million, is headquartered in London and has offices in 10 cities, covering seven countries. In 1991, Dentsu and Young & Rubicam formed an equally owned partnership. Employing 1,700 people at 25 offices in 12 countries, the partnership had combined billings of some $900 million in 1990.

Dating back to 1901, Dentsu's roots in the Nippon Denpo news agency have fostered close ties with Japan's two modern-day news agencies, Kyodo Tsushin and Jiji Press (all three descended from the wartime Domei agency). Dating back to the 1950s, Dentsu has maintained a strong influence over commercial broadcasters ever since it helped to set up commercial TV stations. These links are reinforced by financial and personal cross-shareholding. According to van Wolferen (1993, 233), Dentsu "provides presidents and top-level executives for major newspapers, national and regional TV stations and other firms connected with the mass media, as well as its own subsidiaries."

As Japan's economy took off in the 1960s, so did Dentsu. On the basis of Dentsu's 1973 billings, *Advertising Age* in 1974 ranked Dentsu as the No. 1 agency in the world. In 1988 and 1989, it still stood as the world's largest. However, by 1990, mergers elsewhere and a recession in Japan reduced its rank. Because of the recession, "in an effort to make the most of their limited advertising budgets, companies have become increasingly selective in choosing an agency" (Doi 1992).

Effective April 1, 1992, Dentsu lost $76.5 million in Nissan Motor Co. billings to No. 2 Hakuhodo. The surprising move altered two long-standing practices: a single agency's handling of competing accounts (Dentsu traditionally worked with all seven Japanese automakers) and the long-term stability of accounts. According to an article in the financial daily *Nikkei*, Dentsu always assumed that "once clients were acquired, they would never be lost. Nissan's shift to Hakuhodo, therefore, was a big blow to the firm" (Doi 1992).

The publication of the *Nikkei* article in itself represented another change, with *Nikkei* taking off the kid gloves with which the media formerly handled all-powerful Dentsu. *Advertising Age*, which reprinted the *Nikkei* piece, called it "a sign of . . . Dentsu's lessening influence" (Doi 1992).

Other Ad Agencies

Even if Dentsu has recently lost a pound or two of influence, this 600-pound gorilla still affects all other agencies' operations. Some 3,000 smaller firms, which control the other 75 cents of Japan's ad dollar, get lower commissions than Dentsu. They have to differentiate themselves from Dentsu but not openly criticize the giant, as Dentsu probably still gets the majority of business from a client, which gives bits and pieces of the pie to smaller agencies.

If a client did make a switch, almost never did it "totally sever ties, a practice said to run counter to Japanese business philosophy" (Kilburn 1992, 1). Thus Nissan's move caused a major stir. Nissan, with a $255 million ad budget for Japan, had used four agencies before April 1, 1992: Dentsu, Nippo and Hakuhodo, each with 30 percent of Nissan's budget, and Standard, with 10 percent. After April 1, Nissan gained the efficiency of using three agencies rather than four.

Also characteristically, a large manufacturer develops a small agency that works almost exclusively for it. Nissan owns 40 percent of Nippo and contributes about 30 percent of its billings; it can count on Nippo's loyalty. Nissan seemed to dislike Dentsu's closeness to Toyota, which gives Dentsu $247 million of its $359 million ad budget. For similar reasons, BMW Japan had switched to Hakuhodo from Dentsu in April 1991, and VW Audi Nippon switched to Asatsu.

Hakuhodo's former partner, McCann Erickson Hakuhodo, does not handle competing clients (Toyota and Nissan, for example). The sole joint venture firm to break into Japan's top 10 (see Table 8.6), it does not, contrary to Dentsu's practice, act as a space broker (e.g., buying magazine pages and filling them with clients' ads). Instead, it develops a comprehensive marketing plan that differs for each client.

In 1960, McCann Erickson had U.S. clients such as Coca-Cola who wanted to establish themselves in Japan, but it lacked the credibility, connections and market knowledge needed to succeed in Japan. So it formed a joint venture with Japan's No. 2 agency, Hakuhodo, which understood the Japanese golfing and drinking protocols and had access to intermediaries who could introduce potential new business. The combination clicked. Billings grew from ¥500 million in 1961 to ¥60 billion in 1980 to ¥87 billion in 1990. In the early days, it often took five years to woo a client, but gradually the time shortened to a year or two.

Then, like most agencies, in 1993 it saw its first decline. The parent Hakuhodo firm, saddled by continuing expenses due to Japan's lifetime employment system, faced seriously dwindling revenues (it reportedly had a 67 percent drop in profits in 1992). In 1994 Hakuhodo sold its portion in the joint venture back to McCann Erickson. "In New York, with a

67% drop in profits, you would see people jumping out of windows," said Alex Young, director of the Osaka office, which opened in 1984 (Drew Freyman, personal communication, 1995). The Osaka office works closely with the Nestlé group and with Procter & Gamble, which relocated its headquarters to Kobe in 1988 (and suffered damage in the 1995 earthquake).

"Up to now, there has been no reason for change in the basic system of commerce, and therefore advertising," continued Young. "However, economic progress is now in doubt. People have begun to realize that the father figure has not been minding the store. Interdependence and information is breaking down Japan's ability to isolate its system of management from others."

Criticism of Advertising

Clients who switch agencies and the successes of Western joint ventures represent de facto internal criticisms of traditional advertising practice. Exposés and protests from the outside add other critical voices that sometimes lead to change.

Tobacco Advertising

In Japan, both smoking and cigarette advertising flourish. In fact, the Japanese have the world's biggest tobacco habit (Kitayama 1993). Cigarette sales taxes generate ¥15 billion a year (Gurdon 1994). Meanwhile, death rates from lung and larynx cancer and heart diseases are rising.

Japan's cigarette companies continue to actively advertise their products on television. Attractive television commercials featuring young people smoking account for more than ¥6 billion in advertising expenditures. As in the United States, anti-smoking groups accuse cigarette companies in Japan of targeting their advertising to minors and women. Minors younger than 20 are prohibited by law from smoking, but they can buy cigarettes freely from vending machines (Nagashima 1987).

A documentary on smoking, scheduled to air on 30 NTV affiliates on worldwide Kick the Habit Day, March 8, 1992, was titled "A 2.3-trillion-yen death wish: the tragedy of tobacco in Japan." After NTV's advertising sales department complained about the title, the production division softened it to "Why only Japan? Protesting laissez-faire attitudes towards cigarettes." Eventually, an executive director of NTV's news division canceled the program altogether, fearing that tobacco interests might pull their ads.

After NTV's union publication reported the saga, other media, including the Big Three newspapers and magazines, ran stories on the incident. NTV's affiliates, unions of other TV stations and anti-smoking groups protested the self-censorship, citing Article 3 of the Broadcasting Law, which guarantees freedom of program content. A media criticism journal called *Masu Komi Shimin* [Mass Comm Citizen] described the incident of advertiser pressure in detail (Suhara 1992). The program finally ran.

Alcohol Advertising

A respectably dressed office worker, still clutching his briefcase, lies sprawled unconscious across a subway bench. Nearby, two young men, their faces flushed from alcohol, prop each other up as they stumble toward the next sake bar. Usually prim Japanese "salarymen" staggering in a drunken haze are a familiar sight any night of the week in Tokyo (Jones 1993).

Alcohol is both a social lubricant and a safety valve in the pressure cooker of modern Japanese society, where strict self-control is the norm during the day. Traditionally, Japan has a tolerance for alcohol, recorded as far back as in the ancient Chinese chronicles. Today, Japan is the only industrialized country with rising rather than falling alcohol consumption. And with the rise in alcohol consumption comes a rise in alcohol abuse.

One official 1993 survey showed that 2.2 million adults were alcoholics, but volunteer groups estimated that as many as 10 million, or one in six, adults abuse alcohol. The national tax agency said that in 1991 Japanese gulped down a record 2.1 billion gallons of alcohol, or 23 gallons per adult (Jones 1993). Traditionally, only men drank alcohol, but as Japan has grown richer, the old taboo has faded, and now women and younger people drink more openly.

One in every 11 minutes of television advertising is devoted to promoting alcoholic drinks. A third of these commercials target women and younger people. Alcohol commercials feature film stars, singers and even Olympic medalists. In one popular television commercial, Scottish actor Sean Connery extols the delights of Japanese whiskey (Jones 1993). Stiffer regulations are being considered (see Chapter 10).

Citizens' Protests

Successful protests against specific ads have come from religious, consumer, minority and women's groups. In 1988, the Thai government complained about a cassette player ad featuring a Thai Buddhist statue. In the 1980s and 1990s, women's groups have protested ads that showed a naked, pregnant woman (for a campaign to launch a "comfortable" Toyota wide-body car); an actress sprawled on the ground with her hands tied behind her back (Onward clothing); cowboys on horseback menacingly circling a woman (whiskey); and a pair of female legs (Tokyo subways).

In 1993, Sanyo Electric Co. dropped an ad for a cordless phone that humorously showed a man with only his head sticking out of a big bag, calling for help by phone; a protest called the ad insensitive to the physically handicapped. Also in 1993, anti-nuclear groups protested an ad about plutonium policies that did not identify the government as the source and looked like an ordinary news article.

In the future, as Japanese consumers change from docile to demanding of better treatment in many facets of life, they will probably succeed in totally removing cigarette commercials from television. Other trends already occurring include both health issues and new technologies.

New Trends

Japan's first coupons appeared in newspapers in 1990, even though they have existed elsewhere for more than 100 years. The country's first "scratch-and-sniff" ad, which produced the aroma of fresh oranges, appeared in 1992 (for a Toshiba refrigerator); the *Yomiuri Shimbun* first had to gear up its printing technology to make the ad possible.

New media do not account for a financially large portion of advertising, but the growth rate of ads on CD-ROMs and through the Internet and other non-mainstream channels hit a phenomenal figure of 380 percent in 1992 (using 1985 as the base starting point). By comparison, magazines showed a growth rate of only 166 percent.

A CD-ROM prototype magazine developed by Dentsu may presage the future of advertising in Japan. *Ms,* which stands for *Multimedia Men's Magazine,* lets readers click onto various sections, such as Business, Love or Sports. In the Love section, "readers are asked to guess which one of several pretty women would change into a bikini on request. Choosing one of the women who does not doff her clothes launches a game to promote a range of Kao [personal care] products" (Kilburn 1994). In another approach already being tried, the print magazine *MacUser* comes with a disk that demonstrates Macintosh software products.

Since CD-ROMs serve well for long-term storage, they "may be more suitable for very long rather than short-term campaigns" (Kilburn 1994). Moreover, they are expensive and require highly skilled designers. But with Matsushita, Nintendo, Sony and Sega all pushing new CD-ROM game players, the user base will exist for this new medium.

In 1993, using traditional media, the national government began running AIDS prevention ads in young people's magazines, including *manga*. One in *Shōnen Jump* (for boys) and *Bessatsu Margaret* (for girls) shows a young man and two women with the headline, "Learning about AIDS is a compulsory subject for us." For TV spots, noted personalities deliver AIDS prevention messages. The ads represented part of an overall campaign in public awareness and persuasion. In Japan, as the next chapter will show, the field of public relations is closely related to advertising.

9
Postwar Public Relations

To Sumiko Suzuki and Taro Tanaka, the term "public relations" probably does not mean much, although the acronym "PR" has been adopted by the Japanese. Japan has only about 10 major public relations agencies. Even Japan's Ministry of International Trade and Industry deemed the situation critical, stating that 10 "is far too few for an economic superpower" (*Nikkei Weekly* 1994, 17).

Overview

One PR practitioner contends that "in Japan we are at the beginning of PR" (*Nikkei Weekly* 1993, 22). Another sees business and consequently business communications as now "undergoing revolutionary changes" (*Nikkei Weekly* 1993, 18). Still another foresees a dramatic shift from publicity to political counseling and research (A. Kuse, personal communication, June 18, 1993). The president of the Public Relations Society of Japan (PRSJ), Tsuneo Kuromizu, sees investor relations, risk management and environmental efforts as future counseling areas (*Nikkei Weekly,* 1991, 17).

For those who have access, Japan's *kisha* clubs (see Chapter 2) provide a ready-made publicity system. "We don't do news releases," explains Sakae Ohashi, president and founder of the Kyodo PR agency (personal communication, July 15, 1994). "We build opinion by approaching opinion leaders." All reporters covering, say, the electronics industry belong to the club attached to that industry's trade association. Through this "institutionalized symbiosis between journalists and the System's organization" (van Wolferen 1993, 124), practitioners from electronics manufacturers can convey messages about new products.

According to the *Nikkei Weekly* (1994, 17), "Japanese society as a whole, and thus corporations, do not have the same sort of PR needs as do

Western companies." Certain Western matters of concern never become issues in Japan. For example, good public relations in a firm requires public relations representation in the dominant coalition (White and Dozier 1992). In the Japanese lifetime employment system, whereby employees move in and out of public relations functions as they rise in a company, the representation happens naturally.

The overarching value of *wa* [harmony or concord] (see Chapter 1) affects public relations practice. Where the Westerner may see inefficiency, the Japanese sees avoidance of conflict: "In Japan patience is not so much a virtue as a way of life. . . . This is important in PR, where the question of when to make a press release can be more important than the content, and where the amount of time spent in preparing for a special event can appear out of all proportion to the significance of the event itself. Preparation is everything: surprises and sudden decisions are to be avoided, as they can run the risk of causing embarrassment or trouble" (Dentsu PR Center 1988, 13–14).

Harmony means that consumers do not engineer boycotts very often, that the media do not investigate business practices, that trust exists between employers and employees and that group welfare prevails over individual desires. However, the dark side of harmony means that executives prefer either cover-ups or doing nothing to going public with bad news. Furthermore, the trait of *ishin denshin* [taciturnity or nonverbal communication] is viewed positively, and non-talkativeness is a mark of maturity (Mizutani 1981; Tsujimura 1987). In tandem with the desire for consensus and *ittaikan* [feeling oneness], these aspects of Japan's "collectivism" (Lebra 1976) make for slow reactions to crisis situations, such as when Minolta faced Honeywell in court over patent infringement (see below).

In collectivistic cultures, "the boundary between an ingroup and an outgroup is very important" (Gudykunst and Nishida 1994, 22). In exchange for loyalty, the group looks after its members. Thus, in Japan, clients (members) remain loyal to the agency (group) unless monumental problems occur; on the agency side, not doing one's utmost for a client would be unthinkable.

This chapter explores these unique traits of public relations in Japan. These traits include the longevity of client-agency relations; mixing the roles of advertising and public relations, with an emphasis on public relations as publicity; compliant media that make publicity tasks somewhat easy; domination of both public relations and advertising by a few powerful agencies that handle competing clients; no system of professional accreditation; identity as a company employee rather than with public relations as a profession; little cross-firm sharing and networking by corporate public relations divisions; no strong, well-publicized ethical codes of conduct; a vertical career path within the company, with movement in and out of public relations; emphasis on where one studied rather than on what is crucial in entry-level hiring; almost no public relations majors or practicum courses at universities; little academic research on public relations, with surveys carried out by ad agencies; arrogant attitudes toward consumer protesters; and centralization in Tokyo, the site of the national media's head offices, corporate headquarters and major public relations agencies.

Public Relations up to the 1980s

Although public relations practice in Japan has developed a non-Western ethos, it started from Western sources. Allied Occupation forces created central and regional public relations offices to disseminate information, which established the link of public relations and publicity. By the time the Occupation ended in 1952 (see Table 9.1), Japanese government offices had set up similar *kōhō-bu* [public relations offices] to communicate with the public.

David Finn, co-founder of Ruder and Finn Inc. (Messerly 1966), commented on early "instinctual" corporate PR efforts: "You might say that public relations began here. . . . In one aspect, employee relations, America is just beginning to catch up to Japan. . . . Japanese newspapers and other companies have been sponsoring public service events . . . for years." By the 1960s, some large (e.g., the Mitsubishi group) and medium-sized firms had created public relations departments that focused mainly on publicity (*Nikkei Weekly* 1993). These corporate public relations managers established a voluntary association in 1964; in that same year, the Tokyo Olympics showcased Japan's postwar reconstruction. Another watershed international event for Japan, EXPO '70 in Osaka—the first world's fair in Asia—gave industries a chance to carry their message of pride and accomplishment to a global audience.

But in the 1970s, this flexing of industrial muscle also brought corruption, scandals, pollution and product deficiencies, prompting protests by normally docile citizens. Instead of just instinctual public relations efforts, corporations beefed up their public relations staffs and began to seek out help from agencies (Public Relations Society of Japan 1991).

As Table 9.1 shows, a burst of activity occurred in the 1980s. Japan's pioneer agency man, Sakae Ohashi, had gathered other firms together in 1975 to form an association. In 1980, Ohashi's group joined with the previously established corporate association to form the PRSJ.

In the 1980s, two trends marked the field: corporate identity and the

Table 9.1. Timeline for Japanese public relations

1945	August 14: Emperor broadcasts news of Japan's surrender (radio).
1946	Allied Occupation sets up offices to disseminate information.
1952	April 28: Peace Treaty takes effect; Occupation ends.
1955	Sakae Ohashi establishes first PR firm, named Kyodo in 1964.
1961	Dentsu PR Center established.
1964	Japan PR Association (JPRA) established in Tokyo. Mitsubishi Public Affairs Committee created to restore trust.
1973	Burson-Marsteller opens Tokyo office.
1975	Japan PR Industry Association (JPRIA) established.
1980	JPRA and JPRIA merge to form PR Society of Japan (PRSJ).
1982	First issue of *PRSJ Newsletter.*
1984	Osaka branch of PRSJ established (only group outside Tokyo).
1985	20 million visit Tsukuba EXPO's 29 corporate exhibits. Keizai Koho Center sponsors first Outstanding PR Awards.
1986	IPRA (International Public Relations Association) Board of Directors, from 16 countries, meets in Tokyo.
1988	Approved by Ministry of International Trade and Industry, PRSJ is incorporated; I. Tanaka, president of Dentsu PR Center, becomes president.
1990	First PR summit of municipal governments held at Kuse, Okayama; T. Kuromizu, president of Dentsu PR Center, named PRSJ president. Association for Corporate Support of the Arts established; First Mecenat Grand Prix for arts support awarded.
1991	Hakuhodo ad agency establishes Corporate Communication Unit. *Nikkei Weekly* publishes first annual PR supplement.
1992	Brazil Earth Summit increases corporate/municipal campaigns. PRSJ adopts an ethics charter. Dentsu ad agency establishes a Corporate Communication Unit.
1993	Japan Investor Relations Association established.
1994	Academics work to establish Japan Society for Public Relations.

growth of the borderless economy. The new (especially the young) Japanese consumer began to consider the company's level of corporate citizenship when buying products, in addition to the price and quality of a product. The borderless economy had both domestic and overseas public relations implications. To help foreign companies trying to break into the domestic Japanese market, about 15 foreign public relations firms set up branches or entered into joint ventures; they offered management services that foreign firms needed but domestic clients did not need. Furthermore, Japanese firms began adding non-Japanese or bilingual staff members.

Overseas, the many Japanese companies buying property or setting up production needed "to conduct ambitious PR activities to nurture feelings of friendship in local communities" (Public Relations Society of Japan 1991, 8). In the 1980s, corporate Japan faced "almost a classic marketing problem," said New York public relations expert John Scanlon. High-visibility acquisitions, such as Mitsubishi's investment in the Rockefeller Center and Sony's purchase of CBS Records and Columbia Pictures, had "touched off a deeper layer of American suspicion about Japan" (Scanlon cited in Conant 1990, 60).

In New York, the Nippon Club and the Japan Chamber of Commerce International (JCCI) have published an 85-page guide in both English and Japanese titled "'Joining In,' A Handbook for Better Corporate Citizenship in the United States." This publication includes a wide variety of information as well as a list of charities and non-profit organizations that Japanese corporations can contribute to, from the Red Cross and the Children's Defense Fund to the YMCA.

Yet, according to Conant (1990, 62), Japanese corporations find themselves in a public relations catch-22: "They have been advised to reach out and contribute to the community, but on more than one occasion their public relations ploys have been thrown back in their faces by critics. A paranoid culture sees the pariah everywhere: the underwriting of public television news programs was interpreted in an article in the *Columbia Journalism Review* as a way to subtly influence programming, grants to universities have been criticized in the *New Republic* as a devious way to turn American academia into a pro-Japan lobby."

The xenophobia seems to be easing in the 1990s (see Chapter 1), partly because Japan is beginning to open up its domestic markets to U.S. products and because its buying spree has stopped.

Public Relations in the 1990s

When the Occupation introduced public relations into Japan, the Japanese translated the term as *kōhō,* which literally means wide reporting or disseminating messages. The first character of the two-character word "advertising," which means "wide," was combined with the second character of "information," which means "report."

To this day, Japanese people confuse public relations with advertising because of the shared character of the two and also because of the nature of advertising itself. A successful ad campaign "frequently has a corporate image aspect, thus fulfilling what is often a basic PR function" (Dentsu PR Center 1988, 18); rather than pitching a particular product, soft-sell ads often aim to create a mood of reassurance about the corporation (see Chapter 8).

As for clients, they are willing to pay for advertising, but they think that public relations "should come free as an attached service," explains Yoshiaki Ishikura of the Nambokusha advertising and PR firm.

"Advertising is information. You can calculate the cost for reaching X number of readers. But you can't calculate the cost per person of PR" (personal communication, July 15, 1994).

According to PRSJ President Tsuneo Kuromizu, "We never charge on a time basis; clients don't understand this. We charge retainers plus actual expenses" (personal communication, July 15, 1994). He adds that "we need PR for PR. *Kōhō* has the meaning of propaganda; we need a new word." One answer to the dilemma involves doing away with Japanese words entirely and adopting the English term "corporate communications," or more simply, "CC."

The change, a major trend in the field, represents more than simply hanging out a new shingle. Corporations such as Zexel, Omron and TOTO have created new offices to handle all communications "that are directly related to managerial policies," including crisis management and training executives how to address the press (Dentsu 1993, 226). The two dominant Japanese ad agencies, Dentsu and Hakuhodo, have created CC bureaus by combining public relations and corporate identity divisions (see Table 9.1).

In addition to broadening the field beyond publicity, a second public relations trend of the 1990s relates to retrenchment. The 1993 handbook of the PRSJ listed 458 individual members in Tokyo and Osaka, but the 1994 figure dropped to about 430. The drop occurred because of the bursting of Japan's "economic bubble," which devastated the advertising field and wounded the public relations field. In fall 1992, one-third of companies had reduced their public relations budgets, with most of the rest staying at 1991 levels. The Dentsu PR Center took on a few new employees in 1995, its first new hires for about four years, according to Kuromizu.

Looking ahead, the class of 1997 should be the last to experience severe job competition. The number of 18-year-olds peaked in 1993, after which numbers will decline steadily. Resulting competition for students has fostered a boom in university identity (UI) communications—name changes, new logos, songs and high-profile forums (Rissho University, for example, invited Margaret Thatcher to its 120th anniversary in fall 1992).

A third trend involves crisis management. Missteps are changing the way many companies react to unexpected, negative events. In 1991, Normura Securities executives opted to sit out a scandal involving the brokerage house. In 1992, a U.S. district court ordered Minolta to pay Honeywell $96.35 million for patent infringement. Minolta reacted too slowly to gain any sympathy.

Politicians also "don't understand or care about PR," says PRSJ President Kuromizu. "They don't take the offensive and explain a crisis.

They just give up and resign" (personal communication, July 15, 1994). But if disaster strikes, one cannot just walk away. When a China Airlines airplane crashed at Nagoya in 1994, a Dentsu PR Center staff member saw it on TV and rushed to Nagoya. Dentsu "handled all the crisis communication with a team of 15 people," said Kuromizu. "For Virgin Atlantic Airlines [a Dentsu client], we have contingency plans already in place."

The media should get the whole story quickly and avoid endless follow-ups, believes Atsushi Kuse of Dentsu Burson-Marsteller (personal communication, June 18, 1993): "Consumers who bought a certain whiskey selling at duty free shops found foreign objects in the bottles. In three months we did a recall and relaunch. We offered a new product with a purity guarantee (80 percent chose this) or refund in cash. We [a crisis team of eight] also set up a consumer hotline."

Agencies

As of July 1993, PRSJ had 84 agency members, most of them one- or two-person operations. According to the Dentsu PR Center in 1988, Japan's top five agencies in terms of employees were Dentsu PR Center, International Public Relations, Kyodo PR, Ozma PR and PRAP Japan. Other large firms (with more than 50 employees) are Cosmo, Dentsu Burson-Marsteller, IR Japan and Omnicom PR Network. This small number of major agencies is subdivided into four types because of Japan's unusual mass communications history. In general, the Japanese firms excel at publicity, whereas Western firms emphasize non-publicity functions, according to Atsushi Kuse, vice president of Dentsu Burson-Marsteller (personal communication, June 18, 1993).

Agencies with Western Connections

If a foreign company wants to enter Japan, it may want to "start with PR: it's cheaper," notes PRSJ President Kuromizu (a full-page black-and-white ad in the national *Yomiuri Shimbun* costs about $450,000). In general, women professionals fare better at these Western-linked firms than at Japanese firms.

Joint ventures

Dentsu Burson-Marsteller Co., Ltd., of Tokyo, with about 50 employees, was formed in January 1989 when Burson-Marsteller (51 percent owner), which had operated in Tokyo for 15 years, joined with Dentsu (49 percent owner). The joint venture also has offices in New

York and Brussels. Its Tokyo staff of Americans and Japanese are almost all U.S.-trained.

Other firms in partnerships with large Western agencies include PRAP, associated with Ketchum, and International PR and Universal PR, both associated with the Shandwick group. Although the recession hurt some firms, PRAP did well in the early 1990s, says Executive Vice President Satoshi Sugita. With "international business our fastest growing segment," PRAP helped with the Toys "Я" Us store opening that featured George Bush and organized concerts for McDonald's (personal communication, July 11, 1994).

Branch offices

Firms with Tokyo offices are Edelman Public Relations Worldwide; Gavin Anderson & Co. (Japan) Inc.; Hill and Knowlton; Manning, Selvage and Lee; and the Rowland Co. The "bilingual and bicultural" Cosmo Public Relations Corp. of Tokyo, with 50 employees, has another office in New York. Clients include Hyatt Hotels, Hitachi and Sumitomo 3M.

Japanese Agencies

Ad agency–related

Dentsu PR Center, the largest public relations firm in Japan, is affiliated with Dentsu, one of the largest advertising and communications agencies in the world (see Chapter 8). Established in 1961, the center had total revenues of ¥11,000 million (more than $110 million) by 1993. With offices in Tokyo, Osaka, Nagoya and New York, it has 130 full-time domestic clients, including Canon, Fuji Film, Yamaha, Nippon Telegraph and Telephone (NTT) and Tokyo Electric. The firm's 20 foreign clients include Amway, Coca-Cola, IBM, Microsoft and Volvo. About one-third of its nearly 300 employees "maintain almost daily contact with the media people they know personally and professionally," according to an ad for the center. The president of Dentsu traditionally serves as president of PRSJ.

Dentsu's reach and clout (see Chapter 8), which may please its clients, worry some critics. Calling the Dentsu group "the hidden media boss," van Wolferen (1993, 234) states: "Dentsu is in a position to intimidate large firms, since it can make corporate scandals known and hush them up again. Moreover, companies hardly dare switch agencies because of rumours that Dentsu will report irregularities in their business to the authorities."

In addition to the independent public relations center, Dentsu itself has a public relations division, as does Hakuhodo, Japan's No. 2 ad agency. The divisions number 200 to 300 people. Similarly, smaller ad agencies have sections that do some public relations; for example, Nambokusha, 51 percent owned by Toyota, works specifically in the auto industry, with activities about 90 percent in advertising and 10 percent in public relations.

Independent

Newer and smaller firms can sometimes survive by carving out a special niche. IBI Inc., for example, established in 1972, specializes in investor relations and financial reports. Japan's first independent firm, Kyodo, can boast some clients (such as Kobe Steel) whose relationships with the agency date back 30 years. In addition to clients, the firm's president and founder, Sakae Ohashi, has long personal acquaintances with journalists. Presently employing 103 people, Kyodo has seen many former employees start their own companies. Clients include Japan Air Lines, Orient Watch, Chubu Electric Power and UNICEF Japan.

"Even corporations with large PR staffs need agencies," says Ohashi (personal communication, July 15, 1994). "They can't arrange the one-on-one media connections. We don't do corporate ID; we communicate it."

Corporations

Indeed, corporate public relations staffs are quite large. Shiseido, the largest cosmetics firm (and top magazine advertiser) in Japan, has 32 people in public relations. In addition, each of 105 domestic branch offices has a public relations program, and the firm has 25 people in its new Corporate Culture Division, started in 1990. The division evolved naturally from the firm's history of sponsoring events that linked Shiseido with France and art.

That same year saw the creation of a corporate arts association and awards program (see Table 9.1). By 1993, according to a survey, more than 50 corporations had created community or cultural affairs departments. Some such divisions, for example, that of the Mitsubishi group, have operated for 30 years but have recently changed direction. "For 16 years we brought one Asian journalist to Japan annually," said Shigetsugu Tateyama, secretariat director of the Mitsubishi Public Affairs Committee (personal communication, June 23, 1993). "Now we find grassroots programs to be more important. We want to target one or two Asian nations." Beginning in 1990, its Asian Children's Art Festival annually awards prizes and has traveled to Brunei, Hong Kong and Vietnam.

Although only a few corporations can afford community or culture divisions, corporate identity is "established as a business strategy, involving companies in nearly all sectors" (Dentsu 1993, 213). In 1990, *Weekly Diamond Magazine* even conducted a Corporate Image Survey; Honda Motor Co. won.

Some firms have used anniversaries, mergers or restructurings as occasions to change corporate symbols and promulgate new corporate doctrines. For instance, in commemoration of its 70th anniversary, Nikko Securities Co. established in 1991 the Nikko Shoken Dream Ladies, a women's soccer team—the first women's soccer team in a Japanese enterprise.

Most corporations seem satisfied that earlier investments in "CI" (corporate identity; the Japanese have adopted the English acronym) paid off in helping them weather the early 1990s recession (Dentsu 1993). In some cases, the chief executive himself established the firm's identity; for example, Sony's Akio Morita, Honda Motor Co.'s Nobuhiko Kawamoto and Shiseido Co.'s Yoshiharu Fukuhara "often appear in the mass media, acting as public relations officers for their firms" (Dentsu 1992, 264).

External communication has benefited from Japan's technological prowess. Tokyo Gas, Meidensha Electric and other firms send out video newsletters. Appropriately, Japan Data General sends its newsletter out by personal computer. Internal communication routinely uses satellites to convey the president's New Year's speech, changes in executives' postings and presentations at stockholders' meetings.

Companies are paying attention to the public in more traditional ways as well. The Japanese obsession with *manga* comics prompted Otsuka Pharmaceuticals to publish a *manga* about the human body, commissioning 10 famous cartoonists to draw educational strips.

The recession focused corporate attention on neglected public-private investors. As institutional investors pulled out of the market, firms turned to individuals to fill the gap. The Tokyo Stock Exchange has "established a system for officially honoring companies which have taken steps to increase the number of private stockholders" (Dentsu 1994, 219). In 1993, a new association, the Japan Investor Relations Association (see Table 9.1), aimed to "strengthen communications between enterprises and their shareholders" (Dentsu, 1993, 219).

Nomura Securities Co., the largest brokerage house in Japan, set up Nomura Investor Relations in 1991 after the firm was involved in a major scandal. Daiwa and Yamaichi securities firms likewise set up investor relations (IR) sections. The trading house C. Itoh established an IR team within its public relations department. The Sumitomo Corp. published a first-ever public relations booklet for individual shareholders. In the industrial field, Rohm, a semiconductor producer, was the first manufacturer to set up an IR office. Nippon Steel held a meeting attended by 400 institutional investors and securities analysts.

Municipalities

Politically, Japan is divided into 47 prefectures, within which even the smallest village units perform public relations functions. Large-scale nationwide health campaigns, such as AIDS prevention (see Chapter 8), are run by the national government rather than by non-profit groups like the Cancer Society.

Almost all municipalities conduct public relations efforts related to garbage (*gomi*), including attention to recycling. (In Japan, citizens must separate burnable and non-burnable items. Recycling is usually optional.) The Tokyo Metropolitan Government in 1989 created Gomira, an animated character symbolizing garbage, to help educate citizens about its garbage crisis.

Like corporations, municipalities employ CI (or MI–municipal identity) to promote themselves. In 1990, the PRSJ presented the top award in its pamphlet contest to Kuse Town, Okayama Prefecture, west of Kobe, at a seminar on the topic "PR: a must for local governments" (Dentsu 1992, 264).

Regional public relations efforts also exist. For example, the five cities and towns around the Koise River in Ibaraki Prefecture, northeast of Tokyo, held a campaign to purify Lake Kasumigaura, the second largest lake in Japan (Dentsu 1992). The recession has been a blessing in disguise for various rural districts. For example, Yamaguchi Prefecture created a "graduated from Tokyo" campaign to entice residents who had left home for urban universities to come back. The campaign was called in Japan "the U-turn phenomenon" (Dentsu 1993).

Aside from campaigns, what day-to-day activities engage a typical local public relations staff? The city of Ogaki near Nagoya has a staff of two who perform diverse functions (Michio Tsuchiya, personal communication, October 27, 1992). They pursue arrangements for Ogaki's five "friendly city" relationships, including a brochure printed in various languages and exchange programs; they produce a newsletter twice a month to be delivered to each house (other cities insert newsletters into newspapers); they publish the booklet *Ogaki City* (2,000 copies a year); they produce a 20-minute show for TV Gifu twice every month; they create both 10-minute radio announcements once a week and videotex messages for 1,000 NTT terminals; they update Ogaki Station's moving electrified sign announcing events and information; they supply information to the press (several items a day); they arrange a monthly mayoral press conference; and they give city building tours for schoolchildren.

Staff members are more likely to have backgrounds working for the municipality, often in varied jobs, than to have come from outside public relations positions. The exam taken by prospective employees asks, "What kind of job do you want?" One joins the city staff and may not get one's first choice. Every April, staffs rotate. The senior public relations staff members teach new people in an apprenticeship system.

Current Issues

As the year 2000 approaches, several interrelated factors are affecting segments of Japanese society, which in turn have implications for public relations. First, the "bubble" economy of the 1980s burst in the early 1990s, probably putting an end to the system of lifetime employment; consumer complacency; and quiet, obedient stockholders. Second, true multiparty politics began when, in the election on July 18, 1993, the Liberal Democratic Party (LDP) lost the majority it had held for 38 years (see Chapter 2); the public's disillusionment with political scandals and corruption has forced attention on ethics in all walks of life. Third, the falling birthrate and other indexes indicate female dissatisfaction with male-dominated Japanese society.

Statistics from PRSJ as of July 1993 in various employment categories showed a gender ratio markedly different from that of the United States: women are only 12 percent of corporate members; 19 percent of public relations firm members; 7 percent of ad firm members; 10 percent of production firm members; and 14 percent of 458 government association members. By contrast, U.S. public relations is rapidly becoming a feminized profession, with women constituting about 80 percent of college and university PR majors.

In their senior year, college students take various corporate entry tests. At large corporations, management will place some of the new hires in the public relations section but in later years may move them to entirely different sections. They will probably never be fired. The recession severely affected women's initial job offers, but even in good times, lifetime employment applied to them in only a limited way. "I never hire women graduates," said the president of one major agency. "They leave and get married" (personal communication, July 15, 1994). Indeed the common term for a public relations practitioner is the English phrase "PR man."

In 1990, a special section in the popular young women's magazine *Hanako* did much to publicize public relations as a career but little to emphasize its professional management function. Headlined "Fashionable Female PR Staff," the articles described "Fantastic Announcement Meetings, Exhibitions, and Press Conferences."

The ethics on both sides of the press–public relations relationship takes on special nuances in Japan, where people in business assume that a *honne* [true intention] lies behind the *tatemae* [surface expression]. One agency president called mass media ethics codes *tatemae* and journalists' actual behavior *honne*. "Japanese media violate their own ethics codes," he related (personal communication, July 15, 1994). "They ask PR people for tickets. When an agricultural association invites media people to tour the countryside, they routinely accept these free trips. Some 'black journalists' even write incriminating stories and then demand bribes not to release them. Others ask for interviews, write flattering stories and then take payment to run them." But such extreme behavior is not common.

"Most media people won't take money," says Toshiaki Ishikura of the Nambokusha agency (personal communication, July 15, 1994). "But golf, drinking or parties paid for by special interests are OK." According to Professor Takeshi Maezawa, who decries the custom, "In most newspapers, free tickets or invitations for trips, theaters or restaurants offered by news sources are not only acceptable but welcomed" (cited in Vanden Heuvel and Dennis 1993, 76).

Providing opportunities for journalists to write differs in degree from mass media's direct acceptance of public relations material. Prestige newspapers generally do not trust news releases, said an agency employee, but "you CAN be sure of placing material in small magazines. They willingly accept your news about new products. They like barter: a paid ad in exchange for running editorial copy. But such magazines have little credibility" (T. Ishikura, personal communication, July 15, 1994).

Conversely, what kind of pressure do ad or public relations people exert on mass media to change or soften content? Extremely intense and effective pressure can come indirectly from advertisers (see Chapter 8) or directly from ad/PR agencies. According to van Wolferen (1993, 234): "A Dentsu executive once boasted in a speech that the daily *Yomiuri* newspaper, after having invited consumer activist Ralph Nader to Japan, heeded a warning from Dentsu by breaking up a planned two-page special report and toning down the segment. Around the same time, the *Mainichi* newspaper, also under instructions from Dentsu, ran a 'moderate' story on the consumer movement."

However, according to an agency employee (personal communication, July 15, 1994): "The agency people may try to talk with the ad men at the newspaper, who then approach editors, but usually they won't change stories. They say the facts are the facts. The best we can expect is to take the product name out of the headline or omit the president's name."

Regarding political public relations in the now-defunct one-party system, a cozy relation existed between Dentsu and the LDP (van Wolferen

1993, 236–7): "The ninth bureau [of the LDP] absorbs over one-third of the PR budget of the prime minister's office and some 40% of that of the other ministries. Dentsu also has a near monopoly on disposal of the LDP's PR budget. . . . The role of the major 'advertising agencies' as servants of the system illustrates admirably the impossibility of drawing a line between the private and public sectors in Japan."

But precisely this kind of corruption and collusion set in motion changes that have probably altered "business as usual" in Japan as citizen complacency dissolves. In 1995, for example, a citizens' group protested that if tax monies were used to pay for receptions, any matters discussed should be public information. In the future, political communication, media strategy counseling and crisis public relations (contingency strategies and media plans) will see further development.

In another arena of citizen activism, environmental awareness is increasing. Beginning in about 1990, the public relations efforts of grassroots ecology groups affected the public relations activities of governments and corporations. One group of citizens, to publicize the dangers of tropical deforestation, even bought an ad in the *New York Times* directing readers to write to, among others, the president of Mitsubishi Corp. Eventually Mitsubishi Corp. set up a special environmental unit; Mitsubishi Motors published a *Green Book* in English, French and Spanish; and Mitsubishi Electric Corp. sponsored a "green" concert for John Lennon's 50th birthday at which Yoko Ono appeared (Dentsu 1992).

Aside from nature-friendly activities, environmentalism will put more emphasis on the overall quality of life: "The disadvantages to local residents of traffic jams, water pollution, and noise will undercut economic benefits by corporate operations. Increased tension between the two sides will make PR activities more important in community relations" (Dentsu 1992, 266).

As public relations gains identity as a field (and lifetime employment diminishes), more vertical job switching among employees doing similar jobs at varied firms will occur. Other changes will include a stronger role for professional organizations; industrywide publications of news and research beyond *Dentsu PR News* and PRSJ's newsletter; better recognition of quality efforts in the field through a prestigious, competitive awards process; more discussion of and attention to ethics; the movement of women into public relations top management positions; and a desire for businesses to communicate their cultural/social role. Also, as professionals seek continuing education and businesses seek trained entry-level hires, public relations education will be included in university curricula.

After their marriage on June 9, 1993, at the Tokyo Imperial Palace, Crown Prince Naruhito and Harvard graduate Masako Owada rode in an open car to their new residence, the Togu Karigosho Palace. While the wedding attracted massive media coverage, during the prince's search for a bride, a controversial media embargo prohibited reporting about possible candidates. (*Tokyo Shimbun* photo, used by permission.)

The massive earthquake in Kobe on January 17, 1995, which caused 18 pillars of the Hanshin Expressway to buckle, brought both praise and criticism for the way the news media covered the disaster. As a result, the media changed their contingency procedures for handling such cataclysms. (*Tokyo Shimbun* photo, used by permission.)

Two victims of sarin gas, which was placed in five cars of the Tokyo subway system during the morning rush hour of March 20, 1995, receive assistance. Shoko Asahara, leader of the Aum Shinrikyo cult, and others later went on trial for murder, while the mass media went "on trial" as well for their long-standing coziness with the cult. (*Tokyo Shimbun* photo, used by permission.)

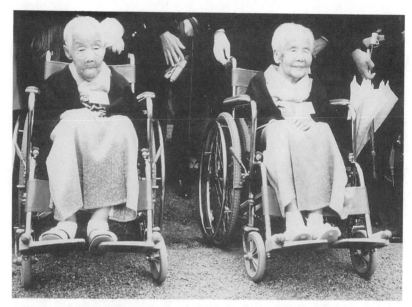

Twins Kin ("Gold") Narita (left) and Gin ("Silver") Kanie, who celebrated their 100th birthdays in 1992, became media stars first in their home Nagoya region and then nationally. (*Tokyo Shimbun* photo, used by permission.)

Yuko Ando, anchorwoman, Fuji TV network. (Photo courtesy of Fuji Television.)

Tetsuya Chikushi, anchorman, TBS-TV network. (Photo courtesy of Tokyo Broadcasting System Television.)

Yoshiko Sakurai, former anchorwoman, NTV-TV network. (Photo courtesy of Nihon Television.)

The *Asahi Shimbun,* Japan's "great daily," reads from top to bottom and right to left and has advertising along the bottom. This issue features a photo of U.S. President Bill Clinton meeting with Morihiro Hosokawa, Japan's first Socialist prime minister. (Photo by Anne Cooper-Chen.)

Weekly magazines often feature attractive young women on their covers. These pictured are the *Sunday Mainichi, Shūkan Post,* and *Shūkan Bunshū.* (Photo by Anne Cooper-Chen.)

Comic books, called *manga,* feature both modern themes such as "Last News," (left) and *samurai* "costume" dramas (right). (Photo by Anne Cooper-Chen.)

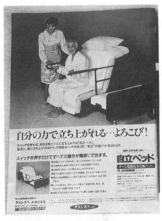

The Asian edition of *Time* magazine (right) for April 22, 1996, features some overlapping content but much exclusive material, such as the cover story on "Japan's New Anxiety." The U.S. edition's cover story for the same day on Jessica Dubroff (left) becomes an inside feature for the Asian edition titled "U.S.: Death of the Littlest Pilot." (Photo by Anne Cooper-Chen.)

Despite traditional reverence for the aged, in Japan magazine advertising rarely shows older women, except for specialized products like this. Television takes the largest share of Japan's advertising dollar. (Photo by Anne Cooper-Chen.)

Specialty magazines now popular in Japan include *Nikkei Business* (left), which opens and reads left to right, and the "guide/directory" publications of the Pia group, including *Kodomo Pia* for children and *Pia* for Tokyo residents; both *Pia* magazines read right to left. (Photo by Anne Cooper-Chen.)

The author (center) meets with Tsuneo Kuromizu, CEO of Dentsu PR Center and president of the Japan Society for Public Relations, and an assistant. Dentsu, formerly the largest agency in the world, dominates the advertising and PR fields in Japan. (Photo by Mizuo Kaneshige.)

Japan's rich media scene is evident at a newsstand in Tokyo. (Photo by Anne Cooper-Chen.)

Part 3
Cross-Media Issues

10
Law and Regulation

by Eddith A. Dashiell

Sumiko Suzuki, her husband and their two children have no family lawyer. Taro Tanaka does not have any college-bound friends who plan to go
to law school. In the non-litigious Japanese society, each lawyer serves
more than 8,500 people (1991), as opposed to the U.S. lawyer, who
serves only 365 people (1985). This lack of litigation and "low rights consciousness of the Japanese" (Youm 1990, 1110) extend to the mass media.

Overview

Residents of the United States and Japan belong to the 25 percent of the world's population whose mass media operate free of direct
government control and intervention (Merrill 1995, 70). Press freedom in
Japan, however, did not always have such constitutional protection.
Legal regulations tended to be greatly influenced by the more advanced
countries of the time. Before the Meiji Restoration (1868), Japanese laws
were under the heavy influence of China. Then came the period of
European influence (Nihon Keizai Shimbun 1984), with the 1889 Meiji
Constitution providing narrow protection of freedom of expression. Its
Article 29 stated, "Japanese subjects shall, within the limits of the law, en-
joy the liberty of speech, writing, publication, public meetings and associations" (Tanaka 1984, 19).

During World War II, the Japanese print and broadcast media served
as government propaganda organs and were subjected to legal restrictions and government pressures (Horibe 1985, 315). Following the end of
the war, the Occupation forces abolished the wartime restrictions on the
media and legally incorporated freedom of speech and expression in the
1946 Constitution (Foreign Press Center 1990, 18). Japan's present Con-

Eddith A. Dashiell is an associate professor at the E. W. Scripps School of Journalism.

stitution is a significant change from the Meiji Constitution in that it provides for the guarantee of a broad range of political rights and civil liberties. In contrast to the Meiji Constitution, which recognized free expression only "within the limits of the law," the 1946 Constitution guarantees unlimited press freedom.

Japan's Constitution expressly prohibits censorship of any kind. Paragraph 2 of Article 21 states that "no censorship shall be maintained, nor shall the secrecy of any means of communication be violated" (Horibe 1985, 318). Although the second half of the paragraph refers only to the means of communication, such as letters, telegrams and telephone messages, it can be interpreted as prohibiting all censorship of speech and publication. This broad protection stands in sharp contrast to the various types of prior restraint permitted during the era of the Meiji Constitution.

But even though overt censorship is banned under Article 21 of Japan's Constitution, self-censorship pervades the Japanese media (see Chapter 2). Non-governmental organizations have been established to check objectionable forms of expression, especially in the area of obscenity. The motion picture industry, for example, has its own regulatory organ called the Committee for the Maintenance of Ethics in Motion Pictures (commonly known as Eirin), and every motion picture is submitted for approval before it is shown at a theater (Tanaka 1984, 758).

Obscenity and Pornography

Japanese society is rather tolerant of erotica in print, pictures and other media. Pornography is everywhere in Japan—on trains, in department stores, on telephone poles and in newspapers and magazines. Television stations air sexually explicit scenes at any time of day; bookstores sell pornographic material alongside comic books and other magazines, on low shelves in full view of children. Pornography is even available from automatic vending machines on street corners. It is not unusual for someone riding the Tokyo subway to be sitting or standing beside a "salaryman" (Japan's typical office worker) calmly perusing one of the many sports newspapers that include X-rated photos, lewd drawings and stories of sexual fantasy (Stein 1993).

Pornography in Japan is so graphic that a growing number of overseas airlines are restricting the type of in-flight Japanese-language magazines they carry ("Nude photo" 1994). Japanese pornography, which depicts primarily nude women, is a booming business, estimated to generate as much as $10 billion a year.

The government, however, does restrict obscene materials according to Article 175 of the Criminal Code, and regulatory authority of obscenity is spread among many public and private agencies (Beer 1993, 233). While Japan's obscenity laws place no restraints on graphic scenes of sexual violence, including child rape and bestiality, the showing of pubic hair and genitalia has been strictly forbidden ("Pain mixed" 1993). Pubic hair and genitals are judged as obscene objects and are either cut out of Japanese films or obscured by fuzzy patches on the screen.

Pornography from Overseas

Although pornographic material obtained domestically is not subject to criminal punishment if it is for private use, importing pornographic material for any reason is banned under Article 21 of Japan's Customs Standards Laws. The Customs Bureau has censored imported "written material and pictures harmful to public order and public morals" (Beer 1993, 233). Neither Japanese nor foreigners are allowed to bring hard-core pornography into Japan. Those found in violation of this law could face a maximum of five years in prison or be fined a maximum of ¥50,000.

Imported pornographic magazines have been painstakingly scrutinized and the slightest hint of pubic hair scratched out by hand in each individual copy. The Japanese government has employed housewives and students to ink out any tufts of pubic hair in imported copies of *Playboy* and *Penthouse.* World-famous paintings have been impounded at Narita airport and sent back to their countries of origin because they offered up pubic hair to the gaze of the Japanese people, but Francisco Goya's renowned painting of a nude woman, "Naked Maja" (c. 1798), was allowed to go on display.

In 1992 customs officers at Narita airport held up imports of the American edition of Madonna's photographic collection *Sex,* letting it in only after censors had scratched out all the pubic hair from four photographs. Ironically, the photographs were not of Madonna but of men ("'Sex' doesn't" 1992). However, a Japanese version of Madonna's book went on sale with its photographs of male genitals almost untouched in defiance of Japan's obscenity laws ("Japan version" 1992).

By the time Madonna's book was released in Japan, the government had started to relax its interpretation of its obscenity laws, resulting in a partial lifting of the pubic hair ban. For example, the film censorship committee, Eirin, decided in 1992 to relax its practice of blurring out images of pubic hair and sex organs on screen. Eirin changed the wording of its censorship guidelines from strictly banning pubic hair and sex organs from films to banning them "in principle," leaving censors room for discretion. Questionable scenes would be judged individually within the context of the film. Foreign films would still be inspected by the customs office and be subject to customs obscenity standards ("Japan film" 1992).

Along with the reinterpretation of the obscenity laws was a sudden explosion of bare-it-all "hair nude" photos. The magazines, which are available at any rail station kiosk or newsstand, brazenly advertised their contents with banner "hair nude" headlines on the front cover to increase sales. Books featuring movie actresses posing in the nude–complete with pubic hair–began to line the shelves of bookshops.

How far the government will go in relaxing its interpretation of its pubic hair ban is still uncertain. For example, shortly after Japan appeared to be moving in a more open direction on obscenity, a Tokyo court in February 1995 fined a Japanese photographer and two others ¥500,000 for publishing more than 69,000 copies of a book of "hair nudes" that the court deemed to be "highly obscene" ("Japan metes" 1995).

The majority of academics hold the view that Japan's customs examination for pornographic material is censorship and therefore unconstitutional, but so far, the Japan Supreme Court has upheld the constitutionality of the customs laws. In September 1991, Ken Togo, a restaurant owner, was convicted and fined ¥84,000 for violating customs laws by trying to bring pornographic videos and magazines into Japan from San Francisco. Togo appealed his conviction to the Tokyo High Court, saying that controlling the importation of pornographic materials through customs inspections is a violation of the Constitution, which prohibits censorship. In July 1992, the Tokyo High Court acquitted Togo, ruling that the court cannot punish people for importing items deemed obscene if it was done for their personal viewing. In April 1995, however, the Supreme Court rejected the Tokyo High Court's obscenity decision, ruling that customs officials have a constitutional right to control the importation of obscene material even if the material is for private use ("Supreme Court" 1995).

Manga and Domestic Pornography

Japan has been criticized for the prevalence of pornography compared with other countries. Many Japanese adults protest their country's attitude toward pornography, which portrays women almost exclusively and reflects demeaning attitudes toward women (see Chapter 12).

In early 1991, Isako Nakao, a mother of three, was "tricked" by a cute cover and innocent-sounding title into buying a *manga* comic for her son. In a clean, attractive "big-eyed" animation style, it contained work by an artist using the pseudonym U-Jin who presented stories of high school students having sex in every conceivable manner. The contents of the strip, *Angel*, enraged Nakao, who formed the first of many mothers' groups aimed at fighting to control sexually explicit comics and curb their sale to young people.

Their efforts eventually led to "voluntary" labeling of adult comics by the publishers, including Shogakukan, whose biweekly magazine *Young Sunday* was publishing *Angel*. Many distributors will not carry a comic with the *seinen* [adults only] label because it can mean a 50 percent drop in sales. Although the battle put some smaller publishers out of business, they were glad that the national government did not get involved.

Many of the mothers' groups want government-imposed restrictive standards and explicit warning labels, such as *yugai tosho* [harmful book]. For the time being, the groups publish their own lists of "forbidden comics" (one recent list contained 83 percent of all comics released that month), which they send to comic stores and distributors.

"It's hard to defend comics like Angel," lamented one editor, "but many well-written comics with erotic themes have suffered as well" (Smith 1993, 1). An industry group of comic book publishers, the Conference on Publishing Ethics (CPE), established in 1963, favors voluntary restrictions such as an "adult comic" label. Hideo Shimizu (1991, 5), CPE president and a professor emeritus at Aoyama Gakuin University, emphasizes a "juvenile's right to read and to express their own views" as taking precedence over parental censorship.

Regulation of Broadcasting

Along with newspapers and magazines, broadcasting is one of the major mass media in Japan that also shares the print media's constitutional guarantee of freedom of speech and expression. This guarantee, however, is qualified, for Japanese broadcasting is regulated in much the same way as broadcasting is regulated in the United States.

Like the United States, Japan has some broadcasting regulations designed to prevent monopoly of the airwaves and to encourage broadcasters to operate their radio and television stations in the public interest. In the United States, the 1934 Communications Act is the basis for U.S. broadcast regulation. In Japan, the legal framework for broadcasting is found in the Broadcast Law (dealing with policies) and the Radio Law (dealing with technical matters), both promulgated in 1950. Article 3 of the Broadcast Law clearly guarantees freedom of broadcasting by providing that "broadcast programs shall never be interfered with or regulated by any person, except in the case where he does so under the power provided by law."

Ministry of Posts and Telecommunications

When the Occupation forces in Japan restructured the Japanese broadcast system after World War II, they dismantled the existing monopoly system and replaced it with a competitive one, based on the American model, that an independent government agency would oversee (Weinberg 1991, 661). For a brief time, that government agency was the Radio Wave Management Commission, patterned after the U.S. Federal Communications Commission.

In 1952, the Japanese government decided to delegate the authority of broadcast regulation to the Ministry of Posts and Telecommunications (MPT). The MPT is responsible for publishing ordinances, notifications and general guidelines such as basic standards for the establishment of a broadcast station and the broadcast frequency allocation plan (Foreign Press Center 1990, 55–56).

Even though Japanese broadcast regulations were drafted according to an American model, the MPT has constructed a system of broadcast regulations sharply different from and more restrictive than the U.S. system. For example, the MPT interpreted Article 59 of the Radio Law as prohibiting cable operators from providing overseas programming unless "the companies delivering this programming are either entirely or primarily Japanese owned" ("Star becomes" 1996). Thus the Japanese, unlike most other Asians, could not watch BBC-Asia, the varied offerings of STAR-TV from Hong Kong, MTV or CNN-I. However, a monumental change occurred in April 1996 when the MPT gave permission to STAR-TV, Ted Turner's TNT and the Cartoon Network to begin satellite broadcasts—"the first wave of what could become a flood of foreign programming" ("Star becomes" 1996). At last, Japanese television will face true competition.

The U.S. FCC awards broadcast licenses after holding formal hearings that include competitive applicants. The MPT has substituted the American approach of formal, competitive hearings for its own approach: *ipponka chōsei*, commonly translated as "coordination." When there are a number of applicants for a single license, the MPT facilitates the creation of a joint venture representing all influential applicants rather than engaging in a competitive selection process (Weinberg 1991, 662, 664–65).

Japan's system of bargain-oriented license allocation has been criticized for centralizing media power, promoting blandness in broadcast content and encouraging an active political role in the licensing process. While the U.S. approach has succeeded to only a small degree in diversifying media control, the Japanese approach rejects the basic philosophy of diversity and is "designed to keep control of broadcast licenses within the circle of the socially and politically influential" (Weinberg 1991, 729).

Japan Broadcasting Corp. (NHK)

Japan's first radio broadcast was made by the Tokyo Broadcasting Station on March 22, 1925. This soon became Nippon Hoso Kyokai (the Japan Broadcasting Corp.), or NHK, modeled after and still resembling the BBC (see Chapter 7). After the Broadcast Law was enacted in 1950, NHK was restructured to become Japan's public broadcaster. Article 44 of the Broadcast Law outlines the requirements that NHK must meet, including political impartiality, through offering different viewpoints on controversial issues, and nurturing new culture while preserving the culture of Japan's past.

Like cable subscribers in the United States, those who receive NHK programming in Japan must pay a receiving fee. Article 32 of the Broadcast Law requires everyone with a radio or television equipped to receive NHK's broadcasts to pay this fee. These receiving fees are paid on an equal basis by all owners of television sets. The monthly fee is approved by the Diet each fiscal year and can be paid by automatic account transfer or to door-to-door collectors (few Japanese have checking accounts).

NHK, however, does waive the receiving fees for various social welfare facilities, educational institutions and the needy. People suffering from impaired hearing or vision and those with severe physical disabilities receive a 50 percent discount on their receiving fees. There is also a two-month exemption for victims of natural disasters ("Receiving fee" 1992).

NHK covers almost all of its operating expenses, including those for radio broadcasting, with revenues from these receiving fees and accepts no financial assistance from the government and commercial or other organizations. In theory, this receiving fee system guarantees NHK's financial independence, insulating it from influence by the current government, special interests and ratings.

However, the Japanese government has from time to time tried to influence how NHK covers news. For example, the government had threatened to ban live broadcasts of banquets at the prime minister's official residence after NHK aired an unauthorized videotape of U.S. President George Bush becoming ill during his visit to Japan in 1992. NHK technicians were preparing for the live broadcast of the banquet when they noticed that President Bush had collapsed under the table; they started taping the scene with a crewless camera. NHK waited 45 minutes before airing the video because it wished to honor a promise to make all footage available simultaneously to other television companies that were unable to be present because of space restrictions ("NHK barred" 1992).

Government officials said NHK had violated a verbal agreement to broadcast only the speeches by President Bush and Prime Minister Kiichi Miyazawa as well as a toast. NHK officials said they decided to use the footage despite the violation of the agreement with the press section because not using the tape would be equivalent to abandoning NHK's responsibility as a broadcasting organization. The prime minister's office then banned NHK from airing any more live broadcasts of the prime minister's banquets because the airing of unauthorized broadcasts could violate privacy. Chief Cabinet Secretary Koichi Kato, however, overrode the ban, and NHK's live broadcasts of the prime minister's banquets have continued ("Gov't won't" 1992).

Regulation of Advertising

Japan has two types of advertising regulations—one legal and the other voluntary. The government plays a dominant role in advertising regulations in Japan. Like the United States, Japan has a national governmental agency that oversees the regulation of advertising. In the United States, it is the Federal Trade Commission; in Japan, it is the Fair Trade Commission (FTC).

The two major laws in Japan covering advertising are the Anti-Monopoly Law and the Premium and Representation Control Law, which the FTC enforces. The Anti-Monopoly Law provides the general framework for controlling advertising by prohibiting actions detrimental to competition against the public interest. The Premium and Representation Control Law is designed to protect consumers' interests by preventing exorbitant giveaways and unfair labeling of products and by promoting fair competition (Nihon Keizai Shimbun 1984).

In addition to the national laws regulating advertising, many other laws, ministry ordinances, resolutions, notifications and edicts provide grounds for regulatory actions by central and local governments. As many as 300 such regulations are in force, some of them extremely complex and even contradictory. Interpretation of the regulations can differ quite a bit depending on which regulatory agency applies them.

Broadcast regulation in Japan allows a maximum of six commercial minutes per 60-minute TV program. However, by airing many short programs, networks can boost TV commercial time (see Chapter 8). Japan's FTC has said that comparative advertising is acceptable provided the message can be verified and isn't libelous or slanderous. But for cultural reasons, advertising presents only subtle comparisons, implying, for example, that "another car" has less interior room. The Pepsi commercial featuring M.C. Hammer discussed in Chapter 8 was the first in Japan that overtly compared competing products.

Alcohol Advertising

The legal drinking age in Japan is 20, but liquor stores have few qualms about selling to underage customers and rarely require identification. A survey published in November 1993 found that one in six high school students in Osaka had a serious drinking problem. Critics blame heavy television advertising and the availability of liquor as the main reasons for the high alcohol consumption (Jones 1993).

Alcohol is relatively cheap in Japan and easily available thanks to automatic vending machines. Some 200,000 vending machines throughout Japan–even on mountaintops–dispense canned and bottled beer along with soft drinks. Some also offer kegs of beer and bottles of sake (rice wine) and whiskey (Jones 1993).

In response to the growing number of alcohol-related problems among young people, a subcommittee of the Public Health Council in 1993 proposed the elimination of vending machines that sell alcoholic beverages and a rethinking of alcohol advertising. The committee proposed a limit on the time of day television commercials for alcoholic beverages could be aired and a limit on the use of popular personalities in the commercials and ads ("Council proposes" 1993).

Regarding warning labels, in 1992 a citizens' group asked for government regulations requiring alcohol containers to carry warnings about specific health risks. Since 1989, Japanese alcohol products exported to the United States have had to carry warning labels to comply with U.S. regulations. However, Suntory omits the warnings that already appear on, for example, Budweiser beer when it repackages the product into cans with Japanese-language labels. One consumer advocate said that the "different warning between Japan and other countries means discrimination against domestic consumers" ("Japanese companies lax" 1993).

Cigarette Advertising

Today's U.S. college students have never experienced a time of socially acceptable smoking, smoke-filled restaurants and airports and TV and radio commercials for cigarettes or other tobacco products (Congress banned such advertisements in 1971). Japan is the only industrialized country that has almost no restrictions on cigarette advertising or sales. In fact, the government used to own Japan Tobacco Inc., the nation's only manufacturer of cigarettes. The government also depends on tobacco as a major source of tax revenues. Critics contend that the Japanese government, which engages profitably in manufacturing and selling cigarettes, has no incentive to restrict smoking and cigarette advertising (Nagashima 1987).

While the government does not legally restrict cigarette advertising, the Tobacco Institute of Japan (domestic and foreign cigarette makers such as Phillip Morris, R.J. Reynolds, and Brown and Williamson) has placed voluntary restrictions on advertising and sales promotions that target adolescents and encourage females to smoke. Under the regulations, television stations can air cigarette commercials only late at night (between 10:54 p.m. and 5 a.m.) to limit adolescents' exposure to the ads.

Cigarette manufacturers print medical warnings on cigarette packaging, including the amount of tar and nicotine (National Trade Data Bank 1995). The wording of the warning, mandated by federal law in the United States, in Japan remains voluntary—and softer. A spokesman for Japan Tobacco said, "Warnings for exports are straightforward, but we don't think we should go that far in Japan" ("Japanese companies lax" 1993).

An anti-smoking push has begun in Japan that could have an effect on cigarette advertising. In March 1995, a government panel submitted a proposal to Japan's Health and Welfare Ministry for the tightening of controls on television cigarette advertising. The proposal was in response to a request by the World Health Organization for each country to draw up an anti-smoking action program to be realized by the year 2000. While noting the ultimate need to totally ban television commercials for cigarettes, the panel asked in the interim for a reduction of the number of cigarette commercials and to review the time slots for when cigarette ads are allowed ("Health ministry panel" 1995).

The panel also proposed controlling operating times of cigarette vending machines; raising cigarette prices; separating smoking and non-smoking areas on public transportation, other public areas and offices; and requesting medical institutions, schools and juvenile welfare organizations to ban smoking altogether. The panel, however, stressed that decisions about controls on cigarette advertising and sales should be left to the industries themselves, not to the government.

Advertising Self-Regulation

As with the cigarette industry, other corporations and industries also have their own voluntary private regulatory organs. The Japan Advertising Review Organization, founded in 1974, operates under criteria that direct advertising and labeling to follow these guidelines:

- be of a fair and truthful nature
- not be harmful to the audience
- fully consider effects on children and youth

- be decent and fully consider the nation's mores and customs
- fully conform to the related laws and regulations and strongly uphold the social order

The Japan Advertising Review Organization conducts reviews at the request of consumers and passes judgments on advertisements such as "lacking in explanation," "extravagant," "false," "libelous," "heinous effects on youth" and "lacking in social and moral responsibility" (Nihon Keizai Shimbun 1984).

Within broadcasting, corporations are required to conform to the broadcasting criteria formulated by the National Association of Commercial Broadcasters (Nihon Keizai Shimbun 1984). For newspapers, each has its own advertising regulations. In 1976 (amended in 1991), the Japan Newspaper Editors and Publishers Association (NSK) adopted a list of 21 publication standards, which it advises members to use as a reference. Its three-point ethics code simply directs newspaper advertising to tell the truth, not damage the "dignity of newspaper pages" and not violate any laws (Nihon Shimbun Kyokai 1995, 58).

Of all the industries that have self-regulations regarding advertising, those of the pharmaceutical and banking industries rank as exceptionally stringent. Japan's Federation of Pharmaceutical Manufacturers Associations' voluntary regulations of advertisements for over-the-counter drugs are among the strictest rules on advertising. The Federation of Bankers Associations of Japan introduced regulations in 1954 designed to prevent excessive competition among banks when they offered almost the same services under tight government regulations on financial institutions. By 1993, however, the federation began lifting its self-restriction on commercial bank advertisements in an effort to promote banking industry competition. The federation began to ease regulations on the volume of advertisements in newspapers and magazines and on television, allowing each bank to advertise its original financial products freely ("Bankers' group" 1992).

Defamation

News sparks people's interest, and much of the news covered by the media includes scandals and rumors. Problems arise, however, when the news harms reputations. Defamation or libel has been defined by the U.S. courts as the unprivileged publication of a false and defamatory statement about an individual that harms that individual.

Like U.S. libel law, Japanese libel law attempts to balance the freedom to criticize a person's reputation in the media with the value of protecting that person's good name. The media have a constitutional right to freedom of expression, but Japan's libel law gives individuals the opportunity to sue the media if they feel their reputation has been falsely damaged by the media.

The Japanese interpret the concept of reputation differently from Americans. While Americans define reputation in terms of their rights as individuals, the Japanese mostly view reputation within the context of their membership in a family or group. Drawing from the Confucian tradition, the Japanese perceive a defamatory accusation as a "loss of face" to their group rather than a harm to their individual rights (Youm 1990, 1103). Japanese law defines defamation as "reducing the respect of another in the community or lowering him in the estimation of his fellows" (Horibe 1985, 327).

In U.S. libel law, the Supreme Court of the United States has ruled that individuals deemed to be public officials or public figures should have a higher burden of proof before they can win a libel suit. This "actual malice" test requires that public figures prove that the media published or aired the defamatory article with knowledge that the story was false or with reckless disregard for whether the story was true or false. In Japan, there is no such actual malice test.

Compared with the United States, few libel lawsuits are filed in Japan. The Japanese dislike the confrontation, publicity, expense and trouble of suing, even for a justifiable reason (Youm 1990, 1110). But the lack of special laws regulating the media and the small number of libel suits filed do not mean that the Japanese media can safely play fast and loose with defamation law.

Sometimes irresponsible publications pay a high price for injuring the reputation of an individual (Youm 1990, 1111). For example, Kazuyoshi Miura, a murder suspect who had been the target of frenzied media coverage, filed a series of libel lawsuits. After a five-year trial, Miura was convicted of hiring a gunman to shoot his wife in the head and himself in the leg at a parking lot in Los Angeles in 1981 ("Miura wins" 1994). From his jail cell while appealing his life sentence, Miura filed more than 230 libel suits against various media organizations, including the Kyodo wire service, over their often sensational coverage of the murder case.

Miura has won many of the suits. In October 1992, the Tokyo District Court ordered the *Sankei Shimbun* newspaper to pay ¥1 million in damages to Miura, ruling that the headline "Miura, a devil incarnate, to be sentenced to death" damaged his reputation (Maezawa 1992). Ironically, one publication lost a libel suit filed by Miura after it described his behavior as "Excessive Action–18 Suits" (Maezawa 1992).

Miura has not been the only one to sue the Japanese media and win.

The Tokyo District Court in January 1994 ordered six press organizations to pay a total of ¥4.5 million in compensation for libeling a woman by alleging she murdered her husband, the head of a prominent Japanese company. From March until August of 1988 the magazines reported the case under sensational headlines, one of which read: "Madness! Princess of old noble family murders husband" ("Six media" 1994).

Japan strives both constitutionally and statutorily to strike a balance between protecting the media's freedom of expression and protecting an individual's right to a good name. Although the frequency of libel action is still negligible in Japan compared with the frequency in the United States and other countries, the Japanese media is increasingly feeling the effect of libel law. Therefore, defamation in Japan should soon become a more important issue for the media (Youm 1990, 1111).

Privacy

The Japanese language has no equivalent for the word "privacy." Japanese speakers usually use the Japlish word *puraibashii* in *katakana* (the Japanese alphabet used for foreign words) for "privacy" (Horibe 1985, 331). The right to privacy (*puraibashii no kenri*) was first recognized by the Japanese courts in a 1964 Tokyo District Court decision involving Yukio Mishima's *After the Banquet* (*Utage no ato*), a novel mixing fact and fiction in its depiction of the marital affairs of Hachiro Arita, a noted Tokyo politician. Mishima had received Mrs. Arita's consent, but not Mr. Arita's, before serializing the story in a major magazine. The Aritas, outraged over the novel, successfully sued Mishima for what became the largest damage award at the time—¥800,000, approximately $2,200 (Beer 1993, 235).

With this district court decision, respecting and protecting an individual's right to privacy was no longer merely a matter of ethics. Rather, the court elevated individual privacy to a legal right, to be protected against unlawful infringement. The court defined the right of privacy as "the legal right and assurance that one's private life will not be unreasonably opened to the public" (Horibe 1985, 331).

Beginning in 1989, for private individuals, the Japanese media established a policy of trying to respect the right of privacy as a matter of public morality, while at the same time emphasizing the importance of press freedom. In many cases, Japanese media will refrain from releasing names and addresses, even when there are no explicit agreements, such as with rape or kidnapping cases, to protect the victims' right to privacy. The Japanese media also do not publish the names of AIDS patients or the names of children born from in vitro fertilization, nor do they give the names of mentally disturbed people in trouble with the police (Foreign Press Center 1990, 25).

Newspapers usually adhere to the 1989 policy, but magazines often do not. Thus newspapers are not usually sued for invasions of privacy, but several cases involving magazines or movies based on the lives of living people have raised privacy and freedom of expression issues.

The Media and the Courts

Except in certain circumstances, the Japanese Constitution mandates public trials, and no Japanese law prohibits the media from reporting pretrial, trial or post-trial proceedings, including testimony presented regarding and the circumstances surrounding the case. In the absence of a jury system in Japan, the media cover trials rather freely based on the belief that professional judges are not apt to be influenced by news reports (Horibe 1985, 324).

Actual press reporting of trials has provoked much hostile criticism from attorneys, focusing particularly on reports concerning criminal suspects. Critics claim that the press treats suspects as if they had already been found guilty, thereby violating the presumption of innocence. Despite this harsh criticism, the media continue to report freely on trials.

Court Note-Taking

Traditionally, only members of the Japanese court press club were permitted to take notes during official court proceedings. Although other democracies such as the United States have long taken for granted the freedom to take notes in court, Japan and South Korea virtually banned note-taking in court. The note-taking ban meant that courtroom guards would regularly scan the crowds for authors, novelists, law students and foreign correspondents scribbling notes, often taking their pens and sometimes removing the offenders themselves. Judges could grant special permission for note-taking, but as a rule they routinely denied such requests, saying note-taking in court was disruptive (Sanger 1989).

Seattle, Wash., attorney and writer Lawrence Repeta challenged the courts' note-taking ban after his application requesting permission to take notes in court was denied seven times. With the help of the Japan Civil Liberties Union, Repeta sued the government, an action unusual enough by itself in Japan. Repeta's court battle was a long one, and he lost each time until his case reached the Supreme Court. In March 1989, the Supreme Court ruled in his favor, saying that "the freedom to take notes should be respected" and ordinary note-taking could not be construed as obstructing "the fair and smooth conduct of a trial." Employees at the

Tokyo District Court quickly taped over signs warning spectators to keep their pens in their pockets. Repeta's victory at the Japan Supreme Court was a "rare rebuke to the country's often hidebound legal system, and a rarer embrace of a foreigner's challenge to the status quo" (Sanger 1989).

Juveniles and the Courts

Japan's Juvenile Act is a good example of a legal restraint on the media. Under the act, the media cannot report the names of juvenile suspects, and the law forbids the publication of articles and photographs that would identify a minor who is before a family court or who is being prosecuted for a crime (including an adult on trial for a crime committed as a minor). This ban prohibits any mention of the individual's name, age, occupation, address or physical features as well as other information that might reveal the juvenile's identity.

The purpose of this law is to keep preadult mistakes from forever scarring that person's life and blocking avenues of rehabilitation. For years, the media observed this ban faithfully, making exceptions only in those rare instances in which the public safety imperative took precedence and they were asked to cooperate with the police in the search for a dangerous juvenile. In recent years, however, that trend has begun to change, with the Japanese media starting to publish the names of minors charged or convicted of violent crimes (Horibe 1985, 323–24).

Reporters' Privilege and Access

In the United States, journalists are in a constant battle with the courts over whether they have a constitutional or statutory right to keep their sources, notes, tapes or films confidential. States have passed shield laws designed to protect reporters' rights to keep their sources confidential. In Japan, in the absence of such a statute, it has been up to the Japanese courts to decide the constitutionality of such a privilege.

A reporter's privilege (*shōgen kyozetsuken*–literally, the right to refuse to testify) was first recognized in a 1979 civil case by the Sapporo District Court, but the issue has been debated for decades (Beer 1993, 239). Historically, the Japanese courts have ruled that a reporter's communications with a confidential source are not privileged if that information could obstruct criminal justice and lead to improper favoritism in the treatment of reporters and other writers. On the other hand, the courts have protected the journalist's privilege when the reporter's refusal to divulge information on a source does not impede a defendant's right to a fair trial (Beer 1993, 239).

The Freedom of Information Act in the United States declares all federal government documents (with nine exceptions ranging from national security to individual privacy) open for public inspection. Japan has no national law requiring the government to give such access to Japanese citizens or the media. In the 1980s, however, a national movement for greater openness in the bureaucratized government resulted in local governments passing their own laws giving the public access to official documents, and a growing number of reporters are taking advantage of these freedom of information ordinances (Beer 1993, 237).

In Japan, most reporting is directed by official pronouncements and *kisha* club briefings, with reporters doing little actual digging for information (see Chapter 2). Reporters' use of and access to public documents is limited to a few local jurisdictions that have freedom of information laws. As reporters in these localities started accessing public documents, they noticed discrepancies between the information contained in the documents and the information given by officials ("Reporters use" 1993, 5). However, in the absence of national freedom of information laws, most Japanese reporters have no way to reconfirm what they write.

Cameras in the Courtroom

U.S. courts have been struggling with the issue of allowing cameras in the courtroom for decades, and Japanese courts also struggle with the issue. In Japan, taking photographs in a courtroom requires approval by the presiding judge, but in almost all but some exceptional cases of civil lawsuits, taking photographs has been banned because of the court's consideration to defendants' human rights and the possible adverse effect on judges and people connected with the trial ("Court complains" 1983). The Japanese media, however, have been requesting the court to ease the control on taking pictures in courtrooms, asserting the public's right to know ("Court complains" 1983). In 1988, a Japanese court ruled for the first time that cameras could be used in the courtrooms ("Privacy of AIDS" 1988).

Copyright Law

Japan has a strong interest in U.S. musical "oldies" of the 1950s and 1960s. Music software companies sell at low prices compact discs and tapes of Elvis Presley and other famous musicians, often played in Japanese discos. Japan's love for music coupled with the advanced technology of high-speed music copying has caused some copyright problems for the U.S. music industry. In September 1995, the United States informally asked Japan to reinforce copyright protection of music, saying the present Japanese legal framework for copyrighting music is too lax and prone to abuse when it comes to "neighboring rights." Neighboring rights empower manufacturers of music recordings to prohibit copying and broadcasting by third parties (Bureau of National Affairs 1995).

Today's Japanese copyright laws reflect the rapid advances in copying and communications technology and a series of revisions made in international copyright conventions. Most of the focus of Japan's copyright laws centers on Japan's relationship with the United States in terms of trade and new technology.

Japan's copyright law was amended in 1991 to prohibit unauthorized duplication and distribution of foreign music or video recordings produced after 1968. The amendment also grants rights to foreign performers and producers of sound recordings. The new law also extends from 30 to 50 years the duration of rights of performers, producers of sound recordings and broadcasting organizations. Owners of foreign-made recordings have the right to prohibit sound-recording rentals for the first year of sale and the right to be paid compensation for use of their copyrighted work for 49 years.

In Japan, the limited taping of a copyrighted work without the permission of its author or creator is permitted under Article 30 of Japan's copyright law. However, the law has been amended so that all authors can be compensated for the use of their work that has been copied for private purposes with digital equipment or other recording devices as specified in government ordinances (Fuzhen 1993, 19). In the United States, recording for home use or for educational purposes is considered "fair use" and is not an infringement of U.S. copyright law (Economist Intelligence Unit 1994).

Copyrights in Japan are either transferable or non-transferable, and protection usually runs for 50 years after the death of the creator. No formalities are required to enjoy protection under the laws, but the works must be original. Types of property eligible for protection include literature, music, drama, art, architecture, maps, movies, pictures and computer programs, as well as secondary works such as translations and edited works such as newspapers and databases. Works should be registered when transferred (Economist Intelligence Unit 1994).

Disputes between the United States and Japan over the use of advanced multimedia technologies have escalated in recent years. Japanese companies have been charged with and sometimes sued for copyright violation, false advertising and trademark counterfeiting (Economist Intelligence Unit 1994). In fact in May 1995, the United States placed Japan and seven other countries on its "priority watch list" because of Japan's failure to adequately protect American copyrights, patents and trademarks ("Clinton warns" 1995).

Japanese manufacturers, including the media, have become more active in protecting their intellectual property rights, and their current, defensive stance in this area is likely to grow more aggressive.

Government Influence and Voluntary Restraint

While freedom of expression is a constitutional guarantee and Japan's mass media are allowed to operate free of direct government control, there is evidence of indirect control on the part of the government in how it influences Japanese media coverage. Historically, the Japanese media have always had close connections with the political regime, and this close relationship under the *kisha* club system has played a major role in how the Japanese media operate (see Chapter 2).

The Japanese media's use of self-regulation in the coverage of private, sensitive or potentially embarrassing information about government officials and the royal family is fairly common. For example, the media refused to specify the nature of Emperor Hirohito's illness during the last few months before his death in 1989, although they gave daily reports on his vital signs. An extreme form of self-censorship occurred in 1992 when the palace pressured the media to agree to a news blackout while it embarked on a search for a bride for Crown Prince Naruhito (see Chapter 3).

When Emperor Akihito's younger son, Prince Akishino-no-miya, and Princess Kiko were married in 1990, Kyodo wire service photographer Toshiaki Nakayama took a photograph of the bride gently brushing the prince's hair out of his eyes. Many considered the photograph endearing, but the ultraconservative Imperial Household Agency, which administers the lives of Japan's royal family, felt it violated protocol. The agency condemned the photograph as disrespectful and forced Nakayama eventually to leave the court's *kisha* club. Disgusted by the media's silence over the incident, Nakayama resigned from the Kyodo wire service (Jones 1993).

Nakayama's resignation was perhaps influenced by the fact that Japan's journalists do not develop an overarching sense of loyalty to the profession, partly because of the system of training for journalism careers. The next chapter will explore that system and its implications.

11
Journalism Education, Training and Research

Taro Tanaka wants to study journalism with an eye toward a career as a newspaper sports reporter. He has his choice of only 21 universities that house departments of journalism or mass communication (compared with more than 400 in the United States). Among those universities, not even one boasts a daily student newspaper where he can test the waters of his chosen profession. Then when he graduates, Taro will find that his studies in journalism give him no advantage over other applicants for jobs on newspapers–a symptom of the lack of cooperation between J-schools and the profession. That uneasy-to-nonexistent relation derives from the long history of mass media companies, with their system of in-house training for lifetime jobs, and the relatively brief history of journalism education in Japan.

History of Journalism Education
Before World War II

The first book on journalism in Japan was *Shimbungaku* [Journalism Study], published by Kimihira Matsumoto in 1899. In the preface, he wrote: "No one doubts the necessity of a lawyer being trained in law, an economist in economics, and a doctor in medicine. Similarly, no one should doubt the necessity of a journalist being trained in journalism" (Haruhara 1994, 18).

Then in 1922 a newspaper reporter at the Tokyo *Nichi Nichi Shimbun* (the present-day *Mainichi Shimbun*), Hideo Ono, published a book called *The Development of Japanese Newspapers*. The next year Ono, the founding father of Japanese journalism education, traveled to Europe and the

This chapter draws heavily on a paper (1995) by Hideo Takeichi, professor of journalism at Sophia University, Tokyo.

United States to survey the state of journalism research and training overseas. He had important meetings in Germany with Professor Karl d'Esterat of Munich University and in the United States with the dean of the School of Journalism at the University of Missouri, Walter Williams, who became a close friend.

In Japan, journalism education began in 1929 when Ono set up the Newspaper Studies Room at Tokyo University's College of Liberal Arts. This study room—part extracurricular club activity, part academic research society—was open to all students interested in journalism. In 1932, Ono established the department of journalism at Sophia University. Sophia's journalism department offered solely night classes from 1932 to 1939, during which period the number of students doubled. In 1939, the night classes were switched to regular daytime classes.

Otherwise, little of note occurred in pre–World War II journalism education and research, mainly because Japan did not have a fully developed democratic society to serve as a context for a vibrant, independent press. Indeed, content research shows that Japanese newspapers in the early 1930s "invented chauvinistic and sentimental stories" *before* the military took over the government (Ito and Tanaka 1992, 17). Tight controls took hold only after 1937 (Ikei 1981).

After World War II

In 1946, under the guidance of the Allied Powers' General Headquarters (GHQ), the Japan Newspaper Editors and Publishers Association (NSK) promulgated the Canons of Journalism, which opens with these words: "To rebuild a democratic and peaceful Japan, the mission assigned newspapers is of great importance."

Recognizing the importance of journalism education, GHQ also helped to establish journalism programs at Keio University, Waseda University (within the faculty of politics and economics), Nihon University (within the faculty of law) and Doshisha University (within the faculty of humanities). In addition, the faculties of sociology at Hosei, Kansei Gakuin, Kansai and Toyo universities offered majors in mass communication. Research institutes were created at Keio University and Tokyo University.

In the 1970s, graduate school programs in journalism also appeared. Sophia University established Japan's first master's program in journalism in 1971 and first doctoral program in 1974. Today, universities with their own graduate programs include Tokyo University, Waseda University, Seijo University, Tokai University and Doshisha University.

Curriculum

The journalism curricula at Japanese universities changed significantly between 1932 and the 1960s. In the prewar period, news reporting and journalism theory classes focused on newspapers almost exclusively. Besides classes in the journalism major, the school also required students to take supplementary general education classes.

In the mid-1960s, when television became a mass medium, a few schools introduced broadcast classes. Discussions about the postindustrial *johoka shakai* [information society] prompted schools to offer new classes on the information age and new media. According to Ito and Tanaka (1992, 34), "More practical and training-oriented courses are offered in newer, smaller and less prestigious universities and colleges." However, no one passes up a chance to attend one of the top universities in Japan, such as the four profiled below, no matter what one's career goals.

Journalism at Four Universities

Compared with the United States, where 60 percent of 20- to 24-year-olds were enrolled in universities and other post-secondary schools in 1991, Japan had fewer (30 percent) of its young people in higher education (Topolnicki 1991, 90). Of Japan's 515 four-year universities and colleges and 595 two-year junior colleges (1991), only one has a free-standing school (called in Japan "faculty") of journalism, newly created at Tokyo Economics University in 1995 (see Table 11.1).

Sophia University

After the end of the war, in 1948 the journalism department at Sophia University formally joined Sophia's College of Liberal Arts. Professor Ono received a boost to his teaching staff when a previously part-time professor, Kenzo Kasuya, became the second full-time professor in the department. In 1959, one of the founders of the Japan Broadcasting Corp. (NHK) Broadcasting Studies Institute, Taizo Inoue, a part-time lecturer, assumed a full-time professorship. The number of broadcast classes increased so dramatically that the department could offer a broadcasting as well as a newspaper specialization.

Of the 76 credits needed for graduation, 74 were for required courses. In the late 1960s, a period of campus unrest swept universities throughout Japan. In 1967, Ono's successor as chairman of the journalism department, Yasuhiro Kawanake (M.A., Marquette University; research work, University of Illinois), initiated a broad overhaul of the curriculum.

Table 11.1. Academic programs and mass communication courses

•Freestanding Faculty of Journalism : 1
  (Tokyo Economics University, created April 1995)

•Graduate programs: 11

•Courses (no separate program)
  Four-year national public universities: 15 schools
  Prefectural and municipal public universities: 6 schools
  Private universities: 126 schools
  Public and private junior colleges: 65 schools

•Junior colleges with independent journalism department: 3
  (Information Communication Department at Shohbi Gakuen Junior College, the
  Communication Department at Ohita Prefectural Arts and Culture Junior College, and
  the Public Information and Mass Communication Department at Naniwa Junior
  College)

•Number of journalism classes
  Undergraduate, four-year public and private universities: 1,400
  Graduate schools: 120

Source: Summer issue of the quarterly journal *Comprehensive Journalism Study* (edited by
the Comprehensive Journalism Research Institute).

The new curriculum included mass communication theory, comparative
international journalism, ethics and law. It reduced the number of required credits to only 32 and permitted electives outside the journalism
department. The minimum 136 credits needed for graduation are distributed as follows: 36 credits in general education, 16 in foreign language (eight in English and eight in a second language), four in health
and physical education and 80 in the journalism major in five areas.

Recent additions include classes dealing with new media and a special
topics class that varies each semester (for instance, "Science Reporting,"
"Photojournalism," "Women and the Media," "Local Newspapers" and
"Speech Communication"). Sophia has a staff of eight full-time professors
and 10 part-time lecturers, including both undergraduate and graduate
teachers.

Keio University

The information on Keio University and on Waseda and Tokyo
universities below comes mainly from Ito and Tanaka (1992, 29–34).

The forerunner of Keio University, a private school, was founded in
1858 by Yukichi Fukuzawa (1835–1901), a reformer, educator and journalist whose picture graces the ¥10,000 note. In the late 1800s, he was

editor of one of Japan's most prestigious newspapers, the *Jiji Shimpo*. In 1920, Keio became a full- fledged university. Keio's Program for Journalism Studies, started in 1946, became the Institute for Communications Research in 1961.

In addition to regular research activities, the institute, headed by Masami Sekine, offers courses to any student enrolled at Keio. Every year the institute accepts about 60 students (20 sophomores and 40 juniors) in a special certificate program of skills and theory courses. In 1990, the institute, located at the Mita campus in Tokyo, had four professors, one associate professor, 20 adjunct professors, nine part-time researchers and three overseas visiting fellows. Although the institute does not offer graduate courses, graduate students can join the institute's research project teams. The Graduate School of Sociology and Graduate School of Political Science, also located at Mita, offer courses in communication studies.

As Table 11.2 shows, the Institute for Communications Research publishes two academic journals on communications, one in Japanese and one in English. The *Keio Communication Review* (*KCR*), established in 1980, is the only journal in English that presents academic research on all mass media in Japan. (NHK's *Studies of Broadcasting* has a more limited focus.) Both Japanese and non-Japanese researchers contribute articles to this unique publication, which comes out once a year in March.

Although *KCR* is produced at Keio's Mita campus, its founding editor, Youichi Ito, teaches communication courses in the Faculty of Policy Management at the Shonan Fujisawa campus. (In 1996, *KCR*'s 19th year of publication, Professor Minoru Sugaya assumed the editorship.) In 1990, the policy management school moved to the newest of Keio's five campuses, about an hour from central Tokyo. Students at the new campus can study TV production, animation and multimedia systems in state-of-the-art facilities.

Waseda University

Waseda University, also a private institution, dates back to 1882. It boasts nine undergraduate schools, eight graduate schools, 10 institutes and laboratories, four centers and various other affiliated bodies. Its Institute of Social Sciences, founded in September 1940, and Institute for Research in Contemporary Political and Economic Affairs, founded in 1978, pursue communication research projects and sometimes sponsor open lectures for students on these subjects.

Although students cannot major in journalism per se, Waseda has a reputation as a feeder school for Japan's national mass media. In 1990,

Table 11.2. Major research institutes

	Year of establishment	Bulletins/journals		
		Title	Language	Frequency
University				
Institute for Communications Research, Keio University	1961	*Keio Gijuku Daigaku Shimbun Kenkyujo Nempo*	Japanese	Semiannual
		Keio Communication Review	English	Yearly
Institute of Journalism and Communication Studies, University of Tokyo	1949	*Tokyo Daigaku Shimbun Kenkyujo Kiyo*	Japanese	Semiannual
Industry				
NHK Broadcasting Culture Research Institute	1946	*Hohso Kenkyu to Chosa*	Japanese	Monthly
		NHK Hohso Bunka Chosa Kenkyu Nempo	Japanese	Yearly
NAB (National Association of Commercial Broadcasters in Japan) Institute	1962	*Occasional Research Report*	Japanese	Irregular
Research Institute of Japan Newspaper Publishers and Editors Association	1976	*Nihon Shimbun Kyokai Kenkyujo Nempo*	Japanese	Yearly
Nikkei Advertising Research Institute	1967	*Nikkei Kohkoku Kenkyujoho*	Japanese	Bimonthly
Dentsu Institute for Human Studies	1987	*Human Studies*	Japanese	Semiannual
Research Institute of Telecom-policies and Economics	1967	*Kaigai Denki Tsushin*	Japanese	Monthly

Source: Ito and Tanaka (1992, 27).

172 Waseda graduates were hired by the five national daily newspapers and two major news agencies, compared with only 61 from Keio and 28 from Tokyo University.

Tokyo University

Unlike Keio and Waseda, Tokyo University, or "Todai," Japan's most prestigious university, is federally supported. Todai's history dates back to 1877. Its Shimbun Kenkyu Shitsu (Program for Journalism Studies), started in 1929, was reorganized as the Institute of Journalism and Communication Studies in 1949. It publishes a twice-yearly journal (see Table 11.2).

The institute's staff of eight professors, five associate professors and four senior instructors often carries out research with members of other organizations. Each year the institute admits via a competitive exam some 30 students, who have completed the second year or its equivalent in any university. In 1990, the institute had 98 students enrolled in its two-year program.

Keio and Todai have the only university-affiliated research institutes. Table 11.2 also lists industry-sponsored institutes, such as those of Dentsu, NHK and the newspaper associations that have been referred to in other chapters.

Research and Professional Organizations

Sophia's Professor Ono added another "first" to his résumé with his election as inaugural chairman of the Japan Society for Studies in Journalism and Mass Communication (JSSJMC), established in 1951. By June 1995, the society had about 1,100 members, including university journalism educators and media practitioners. The newer Japan Society of Information and Communication Research has many members from industry. The Communication Association of Japan is like the Speech Communication Association of the United States (see Table 11.3).

The JSSJMC resembles the older (established in 1912) 3,000-member, U.S.-based Association for Education in Journalism and Mass Communication (AEJMC). Both issue publications. JSSJMC produces a biannual academic publication, *The Journal of Mass Communication Studies,*

Table 11.3. Membership of major academic associations

	Year of establishment	Membership
Japan Society for Studies in Journalism and Mass Communication (JSSJMC)	1951	1,100
Communication Association of Japan (CAJ)	1970	172
Japan Society of Information and Communication Research (JSICR)	1983	1,083
Japan Society of Advertising (JSA)	1969	431
Japan Society of Publishing Studies (JSPS)	1969	321
Japan Society of Image Arts and Sciences (JASIAS)	1974	500

Source: Ito and Tanaka (1992, 24).

Note: The data for JSA and JASIAS are as of 1987; for JSSJMC, as of 1995; and for JSPS, CAJ and JSICR, as of 1991.

which reached its 46th issue in 1995, and AEJMC's *Journalism Quarterly* reached volume 72 (288 issues) in 1995. Five or six times a year, both societies also publish newsletters for members. The JSSJMC holds two large weekend academic congresses each spring and fall. In addition, 10 other smaller study meetings and lectures occur throughout the year. Similarly, AEJMC holds one annual four-day summer conference, with numerous regional meetings organized by its 10 divisions.

But when it comes to research presentations at these meetings, the similarity ends. The number of research presentations at JSSJMC's biannual congresses has increased from 10 in the early 1950s to about 20 by the 1980s. At first, presentations were all based on individual research, but soon collaborative research presentations, workshops and symposia were added. On the basis of their relative sizes, one might expect the AEJMC conference to offer about 60 research presentations; instead, at the 1995 convention, the program included more than 500 presentations. The nearly 2,000 attendees also had their choice of going to 126 panels and workshops, 79 business meetings, 46 exhibitions, a keynote speaker or a plenary session.

Research productivity in Japan does not match membership size; indeed, "planning committees of academic associations often find it difficult to secure enough presenters at annual conventions" (Ito and Tanaka 1992, 23). AEJMC paper presentations, by contrast, represent only about 40 percent of submissions, since judges select the best papers through a blind reviewing system.

Ito and Tanaka (1992, 26) attribute Japan's low research presentation rates to (1) the production of less original research because of the time and energy spent in translating books and articles from overseas; (2) a culture that discourages forwardness and talkativeness, as in oral presentations; (3) a culture that discourages conflict with researchers from other institutions, as in refereed competitions; (4) the lifetime employment system, which carries no "publish-or-perish" incentive; and (5) the sense of loyalty to one's employer, prompting professors to publish work in *kiyō* [in-house journals].

Although standards at in-house journals are lax, the institutions behind them have great strength. According to Ito and Tanaka (1992, 29), in Japan "'vertical' organizations such as independent universities and research institutes are powerful, while 'horizontal' organizations such as academic associations are weak. . . . Thus, journals published by 'horizontal' organizations like academic associations continue to be weak, with only a small pool of articles from which to choose."

The main horizontal publication, JSSJMC's *The Journal of Mass Communication Studies,* published at Tokyo University, includes about 15 articles per issue. Originally, it came out only once a year, but a publication subsidy from the Ministry of Education has permitted two issues a year since 1993 (see Table 11.4).

Topics of oral presentations and articles in the journal focused on newspapers in the 1950s. Starting in the 1960s, the number of theoretical and TV studies increased. From the late 1960s to the 1970s, research widened to encompass mass communication and society, including environmental reporting. Much research in the 1980s dealt with regional communication, such as rural mass media, and new media. From the 1980s into the 1990s, the focus broadened to embrace global issues. Other topics of the 1990s include the information industry and mass communication policies.

Especially after the start of Japanese satellite broadcasting, communication problems between Japan and its neighbors arose, reviving memories of military incursions. For example, Korean scholars called direct broadcast satellite spillover a Japanese "cultural invasion." However, in the early 1990s JSSJMC and the Korean Society for Journalism and Mass

Table 11.4. Journals published by major academic associations

	Journals		
	Title	Language	Frequency
Japan Society for Studies in Journalism and Mass Communication (JSSJMC)	*Shimbungaku Hyōron*	Japanese	Semiannual
Communication Association of Japan (CAJ)	*Human Communication Studies*	Japanese and English	Yearly
	Speech Communication Education	Japanese and English	Yearly
Japan Society of Information and Communication Research (JSICR)	*Jōhō Tsūshin Gakkaishi*	Japanese	Quarterly
	Jōhō Tsūshin Gakkai Nempō	Japanese	Yearly
Japan Society of Advertising (JSA)	*Kohkoku Kagaku*	Japanese	Semiannual
Japan Society of Publishing Studies (JSPS)	*Shuppan Kenkyū*	Japanese	Yearly
Japan Society of Image Arts and Sciences (JASIAS)	*Eizohgaku*	Japanese	Quarterly

Source: Ito and Tanaka (1992, 25).

Communication Studies began to take turns in sponsoring an annual joint meeting.

In 1988, as another outreach effort, on the 75th anniversary of Sophia University's establishment, the journalism department sponsored an international symposium. Titled "Journalism Education in Asia," it included invited foreign researchers from Thailand, the Philippines, Korea and Mainland China.

Many scholars see a need for interaction between Japan's isolated academy and overseas mass communication researchers. Scholars and journalists from Japan could help study multinational problems such as satellite broadcasting or binational problems such as reporting Japanese-American trade friction.

Unfortunately, few sources exist to fund international conferences or support international exchanges in research. The Scientific Studies Fund of the Ministry of Education, the International Exchange Fund and the Japan Society for the Promotion of Science provide funds for research in various fields. The only endowment currently available for journalism is the Japanese Broadcasting Fund. The only university research entity providing funding for journalism and mass communication research is the Social Information Research Institute at Tokyo University. Cooperation from the media industry is minimal in research funding and other areas as well.

Hiring Procedures and Career Paths

For some years following the end of World War II, journalism educators at universities and mass media industries maintained a friendly relationship. For example, an annual fall meeting sponsored by NSK brought together about 10 representatives from each group. Regretfully, in the mid-1980s, those annual meetings were discontinued because of a deadlock over newspapers' hiring practices. Year after year, universities asked newspapers to change their employee selection process to give some special consideration to the skills, ethical sense and commitment shown by students who had studied journalism at a university. However, the press persists in its reliance on spring entrance exams, refusing to recognize this education as a plus when screening for new employees.

Graduates in any major—even medicine or agriculture—can take the exam. More than 3,000 people apply for the 70 to 80 entry positions offered each year at national newspapers. To be employed by a newspaper, an applicant need only score high on the written exam (in writing, foreign language and general knowledge) and make a good impression on the evaluation committee in a 10-minute interview.

Although on the surface this system appears fair, it screens out most women because of preset quotas weighted in favor of men. For example, the *Yomiuri Shimbun*'s planned hiring for April 1995 includes 85 men and 10 women; the *Asahi*'s, 98 men and 13 women; and the *Mainichi*'s, 32 men and eight women ("News companies" 1994). (After university graduations in February, almost all companies take on new hires in April.)

Furthermore, the reliance on test scores overlooks an applicant's aptitude for and commitment to journalism. Even smaller newspapers have such an overwhelming number of applicants for each opening that they have no compelling reason to give preferential treatment to graduates with a degree in journalism. As newspapers expect most of their reporters to work for them until retirement, they actually prefer "white handkerchiefs"—non-journalism majors whom they can mold into "their kind" of reporters. Through in-house training, newspapers also hope to instill a sense of loyalty to the company. Consequently, newspaper companies may feel threatened by recruits who have already studied about media's role in society and the future of journalism and have a loyalty to the profession beyond that to a specific company.

The mass media simply expect a university to give students a general educational background and a modicum of writing skills. The practical training comes in a recruit's first few years on the job. He (rarely she) begins supervised work in various bureaus, moving every few years. At some point the young reporter works in the central headquarters.

Increasingly in the last decade, newly hired recruits at first-rate newspapers, news agencies and TV networks have quit within one or two years. Clearly, these people scored well on the entrance exam but did not have an affinity for day-to-day work as journalists.

Universities for their part could do more to bridge the chasm that separates industry from the academy. They could make their graduate courses a viable option for midcareer editors and reporters who seek further education. They could strive to improve the quality of journalism teaching. They could set up a system that funds study and training for midcareer editors and reporters, such as the Niemann Fellowships at Harvard University.

There have been a surprising number of disturbing incidents in recent years that illustrate a lack of professionalism, even at senior levels. The next chapter will explore the implications for society and the media of the present system that trains company loyalists instead of journalists.

12
Current Issues,
Future Prospects

Sumiko Suzuki, like many other Japanese, has lost the trust she once had in the mass media. In a poll in 1993, 30-somethings rated newspaper credibility much lower than people older than 40 (Iwasaki 1994, 37). Journalists, too, may have lost faith in themselves. According to van Wolferen (1993, 129): "An uncomfortable sense of not living up to the professed standards of journalism . . . is fairly common. The problem is complicated by the press's self-imposed but socially accepted (and expected) function in preserving the social order and guarding public morality."

A Crisis in Ethics?

The structure of mass media as many-headed businesses, as well as a de-emphasis on journalism education (see Chapter 11), contributes to a lack of professional ethics. Certainly journalists anywhere, such as those involved in faking a fire for a 1992 "Dateline NBC" story on GM pickup trucks, can fall prey to ethical lapses. But the serious consequences of some media practices have recently made the entire profession suspect.

Commercial Television

Critics in Japan decry the tabloid TV "wide shows," something like the U.S. show "Hard Copy," that appear on all commercial TV networks for their sensationalism and *yarase* [setting up or faking scenes]. Intense competition drives networks to dangerous extremes for feature story material (Hadfield 1996).

The most serious ethical lapse in Japanese TV history contributed to the murder of three people. In 1989, TBS interviewed Tsutsumi Sakamoto, the lawyer for plaintiffs bringing charges against the Aum

Shinrikyo cult (see Chapter 3). Subsequently, TBS agreed to show raw footage of the videotaped interview to three senior Aum staff members. Kiyohide Hayakawa, Aum's No. 2 man, got TBS to agree not to air portions of the tape that showed Aum in a negative light.

A week later, in November 1989, members of Aum broke into the Sakamotos' apartment and killed the lawyer, his wife and their 1-year-old son. (In 1996 Aum members confessed to the murders and went on trial.) Police put up posters and asked for any information about the Sakamotos, but TBS said nothing. If it had, police might have brought the Aum murderers to trial sooner and even prevented the deaths of people from Aum's sarin gas attacks years later.

In exchange for quashing critical portions of the Sakamoto interview, TBS got exclusive stories on Aum's activities in Germany and underwater training at its headquarters near Mt. Fuji. In March 1996, TBS denied the tit-for-tat deal under questioning in the Diet. However, a few days later TBS admitted showing Hayakawa the unedited tape. Investigators had found details about seeing the tape and the deal with TBS in Hayakawa's personal notes.

On May 1, 1996, TBS broadcast a four-hour program without commercials describing its internal investigation. The TBS president, after admitting that TBS had made a deal with Aum, took responsibility and resigned. But critics demanded much harsher punishment for possible complicity in murder (Hadfield 1996).

Other notorious cases of ethical lapses have also had serious ramifications. In June 1993, when the Liberal Democratic Party (LDP) was fighting to stay in power, TV Asahi's news director, Sadayoshi Tsubaki, suggested that his staff should slant their programs in favor of the newly emerging political parties and push for the end of LDP rule–a possible violation of the broadcasting law's third article, which provides for political neutrality in broadcasting (see Chapter 3). Tsubaki, who had a degree in education, had never studied journalism. When he joined TV Asahi, then an education channel, he "did not know what journalism was. This episode effectively exposed his weaknesses" (Takeichi 1995, 19). In 1994 the Ministry of Posts and Telecommunications (MPT) warned but did not punish TV Asahi.

NHK

One might attribute shady practices to the need of commercial mass media to deliver audiences to advertisers, but some of the worst recent incidents have involved the publicly funded Japan Broadcasting Corp. (NHK). Because citizens pay subscribers' fees for supposedly high-quality programming, NHK's lapses seem more shocking.

In February 1993, an *Asahi Shimbun* story described how an NHK-TV documentary that aired in fall 1992 included staged and fictitious scenes. The NHK special, "Unknown Kingdom in the Himalayas," included 60 misrepresented scenes, according to a member of the four-man documentary team. For example, a healthy staff member pretended to be suffering from altitude sickness; the crew artificially triggered a rock slide; and a local boy was paid for incanting a "prayer for rain." Viewers knew nothing of the crew's interventions in these events.

The NHK program depicted life in the tiny self-governing state of Mustang on Nepal's Tibetan border high in the Himalayas. The NHK crew, the first foreign camera team allowed to film in Mustang, shot the questionable scenes under instructions from an NHK senior director. Other misrepresentations included scenes of the crew arriving by foot (they arrived by helicopter) and crossing a river on foot through the water (there was actually a bridge).

NHK admitted the truth of the allegations and set up a special inquiry committee headed by its vice chairman. The executive producer apologized for "factual mistakes, errors and overeagerness that caused misunderstanding," adding that the morals of all broadcast journalists were being questioned because of this "distortion of facts" ("NHK documentary" 1993).

Another NHK special in May 1990, which featured a young Thai girl, was also found to include misrepresented scenes. Commenting on the NHK and other cases, Masahiro Kinoshita, head of the Broadcast Bureau of MPT, called for "self-cleansing efforts" by TV journalists ("NHK documentary" 1993).

Watchdogs and Critics

Print journalists also do not stand blameless. Magazines often walk a thin line between investigation and sensationalism (see Chapter 6). In 1989 the same *Asahi Shimbun* that broke the NHK story published a photograph of graffiti carved onto live coral off Okinawa Island. It was later discovered that an *Asahi* photographer had defaced the coral himself to get a "good picture" to illustrate a story on how scuba divers were destroying coral reefs. As a result of the coral incident, *Asahi* established an Advisory Press Council of outside experts to review the contents of the paper (Tamura 1993, 33).

Also outside the industry, a number of magazines, such as *Hōsō* [Broadcasting] *Report*, a 72-page bimonthly, carry exposés on topics such as the mass media's fawning coverage of celebrity weddings TV programs that never aired because of informal censorship. Other periodicals of media criticism include *Jyanarizumu Sōgō* [Journalism Study], *Hōsō*

Hihyō [Broadcast Criticism], *Masu Komi Shimin* [Mass Comm Citizen] and *Tsukuru* [Creation].

Three media critics participated in a roundtable discussion that was featured in *Hōsō Report* (Aoki, Hara and Honda 1992): Katsuichi Honda, author and free-lance journalist (a former reporter for *Asahi Shimbun*); Toshio Hara, author (a former president of the Kyodo News Agency); and Sadanobu Aoki, editor, *Hōsō Hihyō*, a former reporter for the *Sankei Shimbun*, who moderated the discussion. The following excerpts were translated by Michiyo Tanaka.

> **Honda:** Japanese journalism is not diversified; its problem is standardization.
>
> **Hara:** Japanese media have had a tendency not to cover grassroots movements. When Emperor Hirohito died, Japanese media expected foreign media to analyze his war responsibility, but they did not.
>
> **Honda:** I say, "Journalism is dead."
>
> **Hara:** During the Gulf War, Japan just relayed pieces of American stories to the Japanese audience. But U.S. journalists admitted the shortcomings of their coverage such as transmitting censored videotapes. Afterwards, they jointly protested to the Department of Defense. The Japanese news media don't cooperate with each other in that sense.
>
> **Honda:** With the collapse of the Soviet Union, intellectuals lost confidence.
>
> **Hara:** So-called "progressive" journalists, such as those at the *Asahi Shimbun*, had a fantasy image of socialism. The anti-communist and status-quo journalists, such as those at the *Yomiuri* and *Sankei*, gained confidence.
>
> **Aoki:** Nowadays major media's executives act like members of government policy advisory groups; such coziness would never occur in the United States.
>
> **Hara:** You wonder whether they represent the news media or the government.
>
> **Aoki:** The close relationship between national newspapers and TV networks means that the government, which controls broadcast licenses, can easily put pressure on newspapers, too.
>
> **Hara:** As many as 30 to 40 private broadcast companies make political contributions—acting like business enterprises, not journalistic institutions.
>
> **Aoki:** We need an independent administrative commission like the Federal Communications Commission in the United States.
>
> **Honda:** Newspaper companies function like banks. *Asahi* runs a mail-order business and a fitness club. How can we call that journalism? Former newspaper executives move over as directors of those non-journalistic subsidiary companies.

Hara: We should use a byline system like Western countries, which enhances individual professionalism. Team-work reporting simply enhances company loyalty. But it is not necessarily true that Western journalism is better than that in Japan.

Hara: Japan's first place in newspaper readership derives from its door-to-door delivery system. Many who have tried to issue new newspapers have failed because of this delivery system. All in all, people simply don't expect much from papers.

Nor do other critics expect much of television. A recent non-fiction book (Watanabe 1995) discusses the use of television by power elites and methods of news manipulation. Taking a fictional approach, Konaka (1972) used his personal experiences as an employee of NHK for six years to write a novel about power, conflict, betrayal and conformity from the point of view of Kodera, who changes from a company man to a union organizer.

Accountability

Some viewers expect and are demanding more. TV consumers' groups such as Forum for Citizens' TV (FCT), led by Midori Suzuki, hold seminars and conduct week-long monitoring studies of TV programs and commercials on all network stations. On the basis of data from these studies, the group, started in 1977 in Tokyo, announced in December 1992 a seven-point "Charter of TV Viewers' Rights" (Suzuki 1993).

1. *Right to a free flow of information.* With satellite broadcasting, producers should be mindful that their programs reach not only Japanese but also people outside Japan.

2. *Right of free speech and universal media access.* Unfortunately, at present the voices of ethnic and cultural minorities, women (except for young, pretty females), the handicapped and the aged are not being heard.

3. *Right to know.* Rather than just reporting stories of celebrities and routine events, TV should communicate political, economic and social truths.

4. *Right to hear opposition points of view,* especially on environmental and consumer issues. The people need to have an independent ombudsman so that irresponsible remarks do not go unchallenged.

5. *Right to quality programming,* free from the tyranny of ratings, especially in the case of children's programs.

6. *Right to criticize.* Viewers should be taught to watch programs criti-

cally and not merely succumb to Japan's pervasive TV culture. Among media-rich countries, only Japan has no "TV literacy" movement because of the mind-set that what's good for industry supersedes what's good for the public.

7. *Right of participation.* The public should have a voice in electing NHK's chairperson and managing directors. The airwaves might then truly belong to the public.

Women and Mass Media

As addressed in the FCT charter, the visibility of women as TV anchors masks overt (not even covert) discrimination in the most highly masculine society in the developed world (Hofstede 1984). Beginning in the mid-1980s, women ascended to several TV anchor slots (see Chapter 7). However, Japan's two most popular news programs, TV Asahi's "News Station" (with Hiroshi Kume) and TBS's "News 23" (with Tetsuya Chikushi), still have male anchors.

Employment of Women

Japan has an Equal Employment Opportunity Law, but it carries no stiff penalties, so media and other companies routinely flout it. For example, for 1995 hiring, newspapers and companies set and made public the following limits on the percentage of women they would hire ("News companies" 1994): *Asahi Shimbun,* 12.9 percent; *Mainichi Shimbun,* 20.0 percent; *Yomiuri Shimbun,* 10.5 percent; *Nihon Keizai Shimbun,* 6.3 percent; *Sankei Shimbun,* 11.7 percent; Kyodo News Service, 28.1 percent; Jiji Press, 13.0 percent; and NHK, 21.4 percent.

In other words, even at the most generous institution, the Kyodo News Service, men will constitute nearly 72 percent of new hires, qualifications notwithstanding. In the worst case, each man has more than nine times the chance that each woman has of getting a job. The glass ceiling that confronts U.S. women would be a welcome improvement in Japan.

In the combined newspaper industries, according to research by CGN-Japan (a group of female media scholars), the total percentage of women employees is 8.0 percent; however, the number employed by the Big Five national papers remains lower, at 6.8 percent. In general, the higher the circulation of the paper, the fewer women are employed.

This section is based on a 1995 paper by Miiko Kodama, professor of journalism at Musashi University, Tokyo.

Women work most often in the general affairs and accounting sections and least in the printing and shipping sections. No woman at the Big Five serves as an executive, and only four of 496 (0.8 percent) occupy such positions in the smaller prefectural papers. As for managerial positions, 0.7 percent is the average held by women, with 0.5 percent at nationwide papers and 0.7 percent at prefectural papers.

Of the 34,289 people working in the broadcasting industry, women account for 13.4 percent on average, with only 7.1 percent at NHK and 13.4 percent in key commercial stations. The proportion of women at commercial radio stations remains at 20.2 percent; at AM and shortwave radio stations, 24.6 percent; and at FM stations, 26.0 percent. Here, too, the larger the station, the lower the percentage of women.

At major TV stations such as NHK and key commercial stations, women occupy only 8.7 percent of the total work force, clustering more in the fields of general affairs, accounting and business and less in technological fields. "Announcer" covers jobs such as anchor, reporter, master of ceremonies and commentator. NHK has a low rate of female announcers because NHK does not send women to the local branches. As for managerial positions, 2.2 percent on average are held by women, with commercial stations having more female managers than NHK.

Media Images of Women

Many protests have attacked images of women in advertising. *Manga* comics routinely portray women in sadistic and sexually explicit ways; men's magazines and sports dailies offer up megadoses of pornography (see Chapters 6 and 10). Quantitative studies related to portrayals of women are cited throughout this book. Qualitative conclusions based on continuing content analyses of Japanese media include five principles.

1. Women and men are evaluated differently. Considering the language, the use of the noun form alone suggests the standard, meaning male, while the added adjective "female" or "woman" suggests something special. For example, Margaret Thatcher was not a prime minister but a "woman prime minister."

2. Women are objects. The camera's perspective is usually male. One story on new corporate hires showed the legs of new female employees and then panned up to their faces. Glamorous women are often depicted, while handsome men seldom are. Women are evaluated from a man's point of view in the media.

3. Women are subordinate. Standard news story style uses a man's full name ("Mr. Suzuki said") but only a woman's first name ("Sumiko said").

This shows the remnants of paternalism. In Japanese, a husband can still be called *shujin* (literally, master), and a wife, *kanai* (literally, "back in the house").

4. A woman's ability is low. Media sometimes use expressions such as "even a woman can do it" (it's so easy) and "even a man cannot do it" (it's so hard).

5. A woman's place is in the home. In commercial films, a woman's role is often in the house, where she is shown washing dishes, taking care of children and helping with the man's work. The media may comment that "marriage brings a woman happiness" but will never consider what marriage brings a man.

Gender Issues in Journalism Education

No research has been conducted relating to gender, media and Japanese university education except for a brief survey by Miiko Kodama (1995). Of 120 people who received questionnaires distributed at the Annual Conference of the Japan Society for Studies in Journalism and Mass Communication (JSSJMC) (July 2–3, 1995), 100 replied.

Reflecting attitudes of Japanese society generally, Japanese media professors' consciousness toward women's issues is extremely low. Two decades ago, female faculty members were seldom found in Japanese universities at all, except in home economics and language departments. Today in JSSJMC, about 10 percent of members are women.

Only about 5 percent of those surveyed had taught a gender/women's issues and media class. All women who replied to the questionnaire had done something concerning gender/women issues; by contrast, only about 30 percent of men had.

Toward the Future

Although Japanese women in the media are still disadvantaged, one can find some positive signs. First of all, the ratio of women in the media has been increasing in the last 15 years, especially since 1985 when the Equal Employment Opportunity Law was instituted. Female reporters increased from 1.12 percent (1985) to 8.48 percent (1994) at newspapers, from 5.8 percent (1986) to 15.2 percent (1994) at commercial stations, and from 0 percent (1982) to 7.5 percent (1995) at NHK. A great increase in the percentage of women probably also occurred in production companies, although statistics are not available. (Production companies provide about 70 percent of television programs through their contracts with stations.)

The increase in women at academic institutes should have an influence on the media in the future. For the last several years, the CGN-Japan group has held monthly meetings to discuss the issue of women and the media. At the 1995 World Conference on Women in Beijing, CGN-Japan held a workshop on women and media in Japan. CGN also passes on its research data and proposals to media organizations, women in the media, readers, viewers and citizen watchdog groups, such as FCT, which also addresses discrimination against minorities in its charter.

Minority and Ethnic Concerns

Some protest campaigns have targeted specific ads, such as those that demean the handicapped. Citizens may unconsciously tolerate or encourage unfair media treatment of anybody different because of Japan's cultural homogeneity (see Chapter 2), whereby "the nail that sticks out must be hammered down."

Coverage of Minorities

Where U.S. and African blacks found a *manga* series on Little Black Sambo offensive, many Japanese found the caricature *kawaii* [cute] (see Chapter 2). The series in the weekly *Shūkan Josei* was pulled after a rash of protests and an apology from the publisher (*"Jungle taitei"* 1992).

Another form of anti-black discrimination was evident in the coverage of the so-called "yellow cab" phenomenon. Prompted by a 1991 book by Shoko Ieda, in 1993 TBS aired a 90-minute documentary about Japanese ("yellow") women living in and around New York City who were often "taken for a ride" by black men and sometimes infected with AIDS. (An earlier 1992 Asahi TV broadcast on the subject included staged scenes.) It was a very popular media issue; "the media showed more enthusiasm for investigating this issue than they have ever had for any of the country's countless political scandals" (Ma 1996, 65).

Subsequently, Japanese women in the New York area held meetings to protest coverage of the phenomenon and the "eagerness with which that kind of story is received in Japan" (Tanaka 1993, 88). Michiyo Tanaka (1993, 89), one of the protesters, states: "In a nearly homogeneous society like Japan people are more chauvinistic and less sensitive to discrimination and racism. It is therefore easy for them to believe that evil comes from a foreign country. . . . It is not healthy that the Japanese media repeat stories about yellow cabs without questioning their credibility."

In a random telephone survey of 200 people, the protest group did not find even one New Yorker who had heard of the term to refer to anything other than a taxi. The finding contradicts Ieda's statement in her book that Americans commonly call Japanese women "yellow cabs." Nonetheless, Ieda's *Yellow Cab II* was published in 1995.

Discussion of any kind in the mass media of one Japanese minority—the *burakumin* (Japan's "untouchables")—remains almost taboo. People of *burakumin* heritage had ancestors who engaged in butchering and leather working. Unless they can keep their heritage secret, they have to marry only other *burakumin* and face housing and job discrimination.

On July 28, 1989, a watershed TV Asahi program about discrimination against the group aired on the early morning show "Towards Morning: Live TV" (*"Hōsō kai"* 1992). After the show aired, more than 1,300 calls flooded the station; many Japanese did not even know such a group existed. A follow-up show on November 11 had to give background on the group, whose story does not appear in school textbooks or in any other mass medium.

Another show on May 29, 1992, featured the results of a poll of 300 mass media professionals in Tokyo and Osaka. Of the 189 who replied, 46 percent said discrimination against the *burakumin* is gradually decreasing, while another 46 percent said it was about the same (the rest gave unclear answers or thought it was getting worse). In reply to the question, "Do you think mass media are helpful in decreasing discrimination in general?" 43.9 percent answered "no," and only 36 percent said "yes" (the rest gave mixed or unclear replies). Perhaps because of similar sentiments—that mass media aim for the homogeneous middle—minorities in Japan (as in many countries) have established their own communication systems.

Minority/Immigrant Media

The present total of registered and unregistered foreigners in Japan is estimated at 1.6 million, buoyed by large increases in immigration during the go-go 1980s. The number of registered Chinese in Japan increased from about 75,000 in 1985 to more than 214,000 in 1994; Brazilians of Japanese heritage, from about 2,000 to more than 150,000; and Filipinos, from about 12,000 to almost 78,000. By contrast, the number of U.S. citizens living in Japan increased only slightly, from about 30,000 to 43,000 (the numbers include both students and those on work visas).

No non-Japanese group, however, comes close to equaling the nearly 1 million Koreans already in Japan (about 1 percent of the population). Koreans, even those born in Japan, fall under the category "registered foreigner." No ethnic Koreans may run for any public office. All legal immigrants (even a Fulbright senior research scholar studying on a cultural visa, such as this book's author) must visit the local government office to be fingerprinted.

Aside from English-language publications (see Appendix 2), which serve "a large, unspecified group of foreigners" (Shiramizu 1995, 6), about 60 periodicals in languages other than Japanese serve the immigrant population. They range from large, ad-supported weeklies—with circulations of more than 50,000—in Chinese, Portuguese and Korean, to small, less frequently published community newsletters. While up to 20 publications exist in the Big Three languages (Korean, Portuguese and Chinese), those in other languages are fewer: Spanish, 4; Tagalog, 4; Malay, 1; Thai, 1; Bengali, 1; and French, 1.

With fewer immigrants arriving in the mid-1990s, the ethnic press has shifted from serving the needs of newcomers (housing, medical and legal matters) to providing news of sports, entertainment (in Japan and the home country) and cultural activities, including places to travel in Japan. Except for "media which receive subsidies from their home government, virtually none of the independent media lean editorially to any particular political party"; for example, the Chinese media "give equal balance to both Beijing and Taipei viewpoints" (Shiramizu 1995, 7).

In exposing specific problems that immigrants face, the ethnic media sometimes play the role of ombudsman. To that end, some publications carry summaries of stories in Japanese. Once when a Japanese official slapped a Chinese woman, the ethnic media covered the story with banner headlines; eventually, "reporters for the major Japanese newspapers learned about the story and treated it as a lead story" (Shiramizu 1995, 7).

Ethnic media may explore practices that mainstream Japanese media regard as simply business-as-usual. The article on *chikan* [commuter train groping] in the Chinese weekly *Zhong Wei Dao Bao* (circulation 32,000) "reflected the bewilderment Chinese people feel about this," said the weekly's editor. "The failure of either the victim or witnesses to react are surprising to foreigners" ("Ethnic press" 1994).

To help these publications and act as a liaison to Japanese society at large, the first ethnic press symposium was held in Tokyo in 1994. The Ethnic Media Press Center was created in 1995.

The print media, being more numerous, play a greater role in solidarity than non-Japanese radio programs (Shiramizu 1995, 6–7); however, some ethnic radio exists in mini-FM form (see Chapter 7). Radio Sarang, which began in 1992, broadcasting from a church basement in Osaka, stands out as the prime example of ethnic broadcasting. Sarang, which means "love" in Korean, broadcasts in an area where 40,000 Koreans live. It mixes talk and music in various languages, about 20 percent being in Korean. Eventually it hopes to elevate its status from mini-FM to legal community radio, "even though they know that a Korean will never be licensed by the MPT. They therefore plan to let one of their Japanese members apply for a license" (Sonnenberg 1994, 20).

Direct Broadcast Satellite (DBS) Spillover: Cultural Imperialism?

Another source of Korea-Japan friction involves the flood of Japanese mass media that flows into neighboring Korea, including magazines, books, *manga* and videos. Korean law forbids the showing of Japanese TV programs on Korean networks (Vanden Heuvel and Dennis 1993, 18), but it cannot block the footprint of NHK's DBS programs, which cost nothing if one buys a small receiving dish.

"Korea has yet to purge itself of what is pejoratively called 'Japanese culture' forced upon [Korea] during the colonial rule," assert Kim and Kim (1993, 70). Older Koreans especially–who remember Japan's 36-year occupation–fear a new wave of domination.

Outside any apartment building in Seoul, one can see the parabolic DBS antennas dotting many balconies. A 1990 survey (Kim and Kim 1993) showed that audiences watched NHK only 10 percent of the time that they watched Korean programs–for an average Korean, about 18 minutes of NHK in three hours of viewing a day. The top reason for viewing NHK was "to be able to watch while the Korean channels are off the air" (the government believes that Koreans should work during the day and sleep at night, so weekday TV broadcasting occurs only in the morning and evening). The second reason was "to get informed about the world," and the third reason was "to learn Japanese" (Kim and Kim 1993, 72–73).

The Japanese for their part say the Koreans "should improve their own program qualities to keep the Korean audience away from Japan's DBS" (Kim and Kim 1993, 71). Change seems inevitable. Korea now has 27 cable channels, although Seoul had only 370,000 subscribers as of 1995. NHK, unencrypted, offers fee-free service for those who have a dish.

Taiwan, another former Japanese colony in which anyone born before about 1935 can speak Japanese, does not feel as threatened. Some 30,000 to 40,000 Taiwanese households receive NHK satellite offerings. As a counterweight to NHK, Taiwan has 24-hour TV alternatives available, many cable channels and a high cable penetration. The effect of distance and the smaller number of Taiwanese who live in Japan make Taiwan's relation with Japan less painful.

Broadcast Technology and Policy

Japan achieved postwar prominence in consumer electronics, outperforming and virtually bringing to an end the U.S. TV manufacturing industry. Now it hopes that its newest innovation, 3-D television, will entice consumers as successfully as did the Walkman. But while Japan's electronics companies "are doing well, their workers are not" (Desmond 1996, 17). Japan imports 2.5 times as many TV sets as it exports–sets that are manufactured at overseas Japanese-owned factories by Thais, Malays and other non-Japanese workers.

The world's first two-channel DBS service and the development of high-definition TV (HDTV) stand out as other innovations in which Japan can take pride. Similarly, the early success with these technologies has brought some problems.

Broadcast Satellites

NHK and WOWOW

The DBS service established by NHK in 1989 has met with some success. Of the nearly 40 million TV households in Japan, 7.2 million (18 percent) officially subscribe to NHK's two channels; Tokyo households increased their ownership from 14.2 percent in 1991 to 24.7 percent in 1993 (Ishii 1996). Priced at ¥930 (less than $10) per month, they offer world news, sports, music entertainment and movies. Unofficially, "as the channel is not encrypted, others naughtily watch without paying" ("Slow march" 1995, 49).

Fewer households subscribe to the encrypted commercial WOWOW channel, which began operation in April 1991; it enrolled its 2-millionth subscriber in January 1996. Families can use their NHK dish to receive it, but the pricier WOWOW offers only one channel and requires purchase of an ¥18,000 ($180) decoder. The consortium of 261 shareholders that manages WOWOW, Japan Satellite Broadcasting (JSB), currently faces a deficit of hundreds of millions of dollars.

The MPT has not yet achieved the proper balance between government-supported DBS and privatized, free-market DBS (Gershon and Kanayama 1994). Approximately 96 percent of NHK's DBS revenues come from viewer subscription fees, with the remaining 4 percent coming from other commercial activities and government subsidies.

NHK radically changed its public service stance when it started to sell DBS subscriptions, acting exactly like a commercial venture. In essence, it has the enviable role of an unregulated monopoly: insulated from marketplace realities and receiving government subsidies, but still able to charge usage fees.

In 1994, after another revision of the Broadcast Law, NHK started still more commercial ventures. It sells to 18 Asian countries a variety of programs, including "Today's Japan" and "Asia Now," in Japanese (nine hours, 30 minutes) as well as English and Cantonese (two hours, 30 minutes). Rather than coming to consumers directly, the programs go by satellite to national TV systems, such as Vietnam TV and New Zealand TV, or cable operators, such as Kiwi Cable and Hong Kong's Wharf Cable (Kanayama 1995).

By contrast, both political and market forces influence (and may drive out) WOWOW, which shows mainly movies. For about the same $20 a month that WOWOW charges, consumers can rent (at about $3 each) a couple of videos a week of movies they choose themselves.

The MPT controls WOWOW by placing retirees, who offer "administrative guidance," in lucrative *amakudari* [descent from heaven] (see Chapter 2) post-retirement jobs. Not only must WOWOW pay the retirees' generous salaries out of its profits but also those of other executives (likewise former MPT officials) at related foundations and companies, such as firms dealing with decoder devices. The "questionable relationships are so complicated it would take ... a super decoder to unravel" (Morikawa 1993b).

Communication Satellites

The decision to move ahead with DBS came at a time when Japan's economy was booming; the 1988 gross domestic product growth rate topped 6 percent. By 1992, when communication satellite (CS) services hit the marketplace, the growth rate fell to about 1 percent; by 1993, it was negative. At this writing in 1996, the economy has edged up slightly, but consumers are guarding their resources carefully. For the fifth straight year, as of December 31, 1995, Japan had the world's best balance sheet ("Japan remains" 1996).

The Japan Communications Satellite Co. (JCSAT) leases out 60 percent of its space to customers; one prep school, for example, broadcasts college entrance exam lessons to sites outside its Tokyo home base. Japan Satellite Systems (JSAT) carries the five commercial channels.

To get the six communication and three broadcast satellite services, consumers must buy three different types of parabolic antenna as well as decoder boxes. Then each month the average subscriber pays $87.50 to receive all nine DBS services (Gershon and Kanayama 1994). No wonder the latecoming CS had only 1 million subscriptions via cable and 130,000 in direct reception by 1996.

HDTV

In contrast to the relative success of DBS dishes, so far only 55,000 HDTV sets, costing about $5,000, have been sold. The images, which are twice as sharp as those we now watch, mean that even on gargantuan sets, picture quality does not suffer. The sound equals that of compact disks, avoiding the hisses and pops of analog systems such as records and tapes.

HDTV development, which began in the early 1970s, has so far cost Japanese government and industry more than $1 billion. In 1984, NHK announced the development of the Multiple Sub-Nyquist Sampling Encoding (MUSE) system, capable of transmitting HDTV programs with only one satellite channel. Experimental broadcasts began in 1989. So far, Japan remains the only nation where people can actually watch HDTV regularly.

In 1993, the U.S. FCC dropped NHK's analog system from contention as a candidate for adoption as the U.S. standard format. In 1996, the MPT released a report predicting that "ground-wave, satellite and CATV broadcasting will be virtually digitalized by the year 2010" ("Digitalization" 1996). Europe has already decided to switch from an analog to digital standard.

Broadcasting and electrical industry officials favor the existing analog system. The MPT feels Japan will suffer if it persists in a mode that is different from that of the rest of the world, but it will also suffer from abandoning a system into which it has invested monumental time and money, with its audience of 10 million.

Consumers would benefit from one world standard because of higher volume and lower production costs per TV set. MUSE transmits images using analog waves, whereas a digital system transmits sound and images in a code using ones and zeros. Thus TV images and computers could blend more easily to provide multimedia services.

The MUSE system already processes the image in the studio and in the home set digitally. Meanwhile, manufacturers have begun to move ahead to the HDTV age. Hitachi America is developing a decoder that can receive HDTV transmissions at reduced resolution on a traditional TV set (McConnell 1995). Sony has developed a projection system that uses Texas Instruments' digital Micromirror display technology (Lachrenbruch 1995).

In 1996, as expected, the U.S. FCC did adopt the digital system designed by a seven-company group called the Grand Alliance. Thus HDTV sets will probably become available in the United States in 1998. Japan, for its part, will have to predict future HDTV commercial usage in order to decide how many channels to allocate to HDTV when it launches its newest satellites in 1997 and 1999.

In 1996, the MPT gave permission for 34 companies to participate in PerfecTV to conduct digitalized multichannel broadcasting on consignment using communications satellites. The service was scheduled to start in October 1996.

Policy and Philosophy

The HDTV setback "showed the drawbacks in this country's system of Government-backed cooperative industrial development. The system allows for great staying power and steady progress down a particular path, but does not adjust well when the technological road turns" (Pollack 1994, C5). Even with a clearly wrongheaded policy, the MPT had too much at stake to suddenly kill it, but eventually, in March 1997, the MPT indicated it would abandon analog and go digital. In general, "the Japanese are better off when change is slow" (Simons 1996, 19).

After the technical experts agree on an innovation, it advances to the appropriate government ministry through "liaison committees maintained jointly by the companies involved to provide monitoring and lobbying efforts for those industries with the ministry" (Self 1991, 4). As we saw in Chapter 2, reporters from mass media, who work in the *kisha* clubs attached to the ministries and industries, sometimes act as go-betweens in negotiations like these.

Step 3 of consensus creation involves input from a "public cluster" (Self 1991, 4) of university professors and other leaders. Step 4 involves other ministries. Finally, in step 5, the general public can put in their two cents worth, but only after the *nemawashii* [rooting] process has resulted in an announced policy; at this late stage, "the policy is not likely to die or be significantly changed in all these public hearings. By this time, it has achieved a robust consensus" (Self 1991, 4). In almost a mirror image of the "people last" approach, "U.S. telecommunication policy-making style is rapid and risky and above all public" (Self 1991, 3).

Nowadays the layers of decision makers face forces they cannot control as easily as they can stave off imports of rice: signals from some 20 satellites whose footprints cover Japan. In an ironic echo of Korea's protests to Japan, Japan complained about unwanted signals, notably from STAR-TV. In 1992, the MPT "sent a mission to the company and the Hong Kong government. Ministry officials had to come back with the official explanation that the images received in Japan are merely a 'spillover'" ("Satellite TV" 1993).

Home-grown commercial TV networks liked the MPT's "closed-door, single-nation broadcasting policy" and fear that "foreign programs may undermine the broadcasting industry by stealing some of its advertisers" ("Satellite TV" 1993). But critics of business as usual, such as the LDP maverick Ichiro Ozawa, believe that protectionism and regulation do not bring security. Ozawa (1994, 47) wrote in his book *Blueprint for a New Japan*, "Freedom from regulation entails abolishing anachronistic and meaningless rules."

Finally, in April 1995, the MPT gave permission to Rupert Murdoch's STAR-TV and Turner Entertainment Networks Asia to sell their programming via cable. Although the Japanese may well "prefer domestically made programs to imported ones" ("Slow march" 1995, 50), at least viewers will get a chance to see and make their own judgments about what other Asians have been watching for years.

New Media

While most of the rest of the developed world—especially the United States—was plugging into the Internet, the MPT was thinking about it. In 1993, "the ministry eventually came around to the idea that such things were inevitable" ("Japan's Internet" 1995) and that Japan lagged behind. It awarded the first two Internet licenses to foreign companies.

The two largest on-line services in Japan, PC-Van and Nifty-Serve (modeled on CompuServe and America Online), claim to have about 1 million subscribers each. A growing number of connection services also exist. Although Japan started late, Internet use grew by 86 percent in 1994 (impressive, but less than overall Net growth). Clearly, Internet diffusion remains in its early stages.

One study concluded that of all the world's computers linked to the Net, the United States had 70 percent of them ("Third World" 1996). By January 1996, the United States had 5.5 million (58 percent) of the world's 9.5 million hosts (each university system, for example, counts as one host), while Japan had just 3 percent. With half the U.S. population, Japan "should" have 29 percent of the world's hosts. Apart from slow MPT response time, four factors have slowed the adoption of this innovation ("Japan's Internet" 1995):

- low home PC ownership—about one in 10 households (vs. one in three U.S. households)
- the problems of Nippon Telephone and Telegraph (NTT): tremendous

expense of phone lines, insufficient growth capacity, overload of existing capacity and slow response (eight months to get a leased line instead of a few days)
• the dominance of English on the Internet
• expense of the connection services and usage charges

Ishii (1996, 22) also points to "psychological barriers against communication by computer. . . . Japanese people prefer word processors to personal computers because of a lack of computer skills" and unfamiliarity
with a computer keyboard. A larger proportion of offices than homes
have PCs, but only employees at very large companies will come in contact with them in their work (84.5 percent of firms with more than 300
employees have PCs, but only 20.6 percent of firms with fewer than 10
employees).

In a two-wave survey of Tokyo residents in 1991 and 1992, Ishii (1996)
found that home ownership of word processors went up from 37.6 to 43.3
percent of households, but PC penetration remained low (17.3 to 17.6 percent). He also found that people who adopt new PCs earlier are wealthier, better educated and likely to have used them at work as well as spend
less time watching TV.

Now that many newspapers provide information on-line ("33 news
firms" 1996), a picture of the typical user has emerged: a young man. In
a 1996 survey, 95 percent of users were men, and 80 percent were 20 to
34 years old.

Ikeda (1994a) studied four forums on Nifty-Serve, each with more
than 10 subgroups on which users could remain anonymous: FI,
International Exchange; FJ, Amateur Journalism; FA, Animation; and
FC, PC Use. Unique, distinguishing characteristics included for FI, 46
percent had greetings (informal messages); FA, 22 percent used icons and
20 percent used mimetic words; FC, 31 percent gave names; FA, 40 percent had emotional expressions; FJ, 77 percent had opinion-expressive
contents, FI and FC, name card exchanges; FA, interpersonal basis; and
FJ, opinions. Unique Japanese icons include (^_ ^), a smile with an Asian
look and (__), a deep bow.

Nifty-Serve can give its customers up-to-the-minute, portable news if
they spend $640 more for a Zaurus handheld terminal with a liquid crys-
tal display (starting March 1, 1996). At home, linked to one's own phone;
away from home, linked to a public phone line; or on the go, linked to a
cellular phone, the user can gain access to 300 articles (edited down to
150 Chinese characters) and opinion pieces (in their entirety) from the
Mainichi Shimbun, updated twice daily. The information, arranged in 17
categories (such as breaking stories, politics, economics, international af-

fairs, horoscope, weather and sports), will take two to three minutes per category to download.

On a CBS News "48 Hours" program (*New York Daily News*, 1995), an executive of the *New York Daily News* expressed certainty about the future of print newspapers "until they invent a screen you can carry into the john." The Zaurus, although meant more for subways than bathrooms, weighs only 250 grams (7 ounces) and measures 16-by-9.5 centimeters. The additional Nifty-Serve fee for the *Mainichi,* $5 per month, does not include any extra telephone charges.

Both the *Sankei Shimbun* and *Nihon Keizai Shimbun* also have developed experimental electronic newspapers. The *Sankei* teamed up with Fuji Television, Mitsubishi and Mitsubishi Electric to create in December 1995 a company called Denshi Shimbun KK. In a delivery system different from *Mainichi*'s, which uses part of the TV spectrum, it will send articles to portable terminals. Rather than abstracts, the system will carry 90 percent of the articles in the final morning edition (but no ads, photos or graphics). Users must have a "station" connected to their TV set, to which they connect a tiny viewer. After downloading data, they can put the viewer in a pocket and read the articles later. The receiver and terminal cost $400, in addition to $12 a month for the e-news subscription.

Nihon Keizai Shimbun, cooperating with NTT, started in March 1996 a multimedia news service that includes moving pictures and sound–and advertising. At experimental terminals, the Nikkei Hyper Press provides information from six menus, based on key words that a user punches in. Stock prices and foreign exchange rates are updated every few minutes.

Unfortunately, laments Tsuyoshi Yamamoto of the *Sankei Shimbun,* the papers are "not able to fully convey the news value" of disparate articles ("Three electronic" 1996). In pulling down separate articles, one does not get the editor's judgment, as reflected in page placement and headline size. But the papers go beyond electronic databases because they are meant to go with the user, not force the user to sit at a terminal with a modem. As we saw in Chapter 4, 12 newspapers provide Internet services, as do many U.S. papers. Indeed, four Japanese newspapers offer English-language services via Nexis/Lexis (see Appendix 2).

"It is often said that Japan is behind the United States by 10, maybe even 20, years in the multimedia area, due most probably to the consciousness peculiar to the Japanese," believes Takamitsu Sawa (1994), a professor at Kyoto University. He thinks the United States has truly entered the information age, while Japan remains in the last stages of industrialization. "Will Japan be able to remain an 'economic power' in the new age of highly information-oriented societies?" asks Sawa (1994). No, he answers, because Japan's interlinked educational, political, social and corporate systems, which produced excellent results in the industrial 1980s, "will not be suitable in an advanced information society. And the corporate seniority system will obstruct the employment of highly able but young people at high wages." These antiquated systems would need a 180-degree turnaround, overhauled to stress individualism and to cope with quick change.

"The Japanese prefer uniformity . . . 'media' means the mass media to many Japanese," believes Sawa (1994). "There is no large potential demand for multimedia [new media] in this country." Japanese prefer to receive mass media that everyone else is watching/reading/hearing rather than to make choices. It gives them a sense of security and control. On the other hand, the change from feudalism to modern nationhood in the 1800s resulted from a similar self-assessment that Japan, lagging behind, had to catch up.

The high-tech parabolic dish outside Sumiko Suzuki's apartment may soon bring more programming variety into her life. It shares balcony space with the decidedly low-tech clothesline that she likes to use, consulting the T-shirt symbols on the previous night's weather forecast. Meanwhile, Taro Tanaka dreams of covering the 1998 Winter Olympics in Nagano during his senior year. When journalists descend on Japan from all over the world, seeds of new mass media ideas may be planted. As the 1964 Tokyo Olympics created change in Japan, so too could 1998 be the beginning of some needed reforms and continuation of what Japan does well.

Appendix 1: Timeline

Japanese Media Milestones to the End of World War II

Asia

 China: paper, 49 B.C.; ink, 1300 B.C.; writing, 5000 B.C.

 Printing: China, wood-block printing, 900s A.D.; Korea, metal movable type, early 1400s

 Classical written Chinese: elites in Japan, Korea, Vietnam; low literacy in China: 1 to 2 percent around 100 B.C.; 5 percent in 1800

 Ming Dynasty (1368–1644), block-printed court news sheets; Ch'ing Dynasty, 1700s, a few popular illustrated newspapers

Asia/Japan Contact

 c. 400, Korean scribes employed at Japanese court

 552, Buddhism reaches Japan

 610, import via Korea of Chinese paper-making techniques (adaptation results in Japanese rice paper)

 701, first legal code, modeled on Chinese law, includes provision on shop signs (first advertising regulation)

 600s to 800s, Chinese writing adapted to spoken Japanese

 late 600s, cartoon caricatures by Buddhist monks

Nara Period (710–84)

 712, compilation of *Kojiki* (historical record)

 713, compilation of *Fudoki* (local gazetteers)

 720, compilation of *Nihon shoki* (historical record)

 760, compilation of *Manyoshu* (poetry collection)

Heian Period (794–1185)

 c. 800s, Kugutsu wandering "minstrels" perform, spread news

 905, compilation of *Kokinshu* (poetry collection)

 c. 1002, writing of *Makura no Sōshi* [Pillow Book] by Lady Sei Shonagon

 c. 1008–20, writing of *Genji Monogatari* [Tale of Genji] by Lady Murasaki

 Bishop Toba (1053–1140) creates Animal Scrolls (cartoons)

Kamakura Period (1185–1333)

 1205, compilation of the *Shinkokinshu* (poetry collection)

 Buddhist artists create Hungry Ghost Scrolls (cartoons)

1241, store front advertises Toraya bean paste buns

1274, first mass ads (*hikifuda*) distributed by department store

Yoshino Period (1336–92)

Muromachi Period (1392–1573)

1400s, *Noh* plays by Zeami gain popularity, convey information

1541, Francis Xavier arrives in Japan to spread Christianity

1543, Portuguese import firearms, begin trade in south Japan

Period of National Reunification (1568–1600)

Edo Period (1600–1867)

c. 1615, tile engraved *kawaraban* (pre-newspapers)

mid-1600s, mass-produced *otsu-e* wood-block pictures

1720, relaxation of ban on Western books

Hiraga Gennai (1728–79), first writer of ads for payment

Hokusai (1760–1849), wood-block artist; coined term *manga* [comics]

Utagawa (1797–1861), wood-block artist

1811, establishment of the Translation Bureau for Dutch Books

1800s, through private schools, male literacy at 50 percent (*hankoh:* schools for samurai; *terakoya*: temple schools for children; *juku*: schools where scholars taught Western learning)

1851, Shozo Motoki creates first book printed in Japan, a Dutch-Japanese dictionary

1862, delegates from Japan learn much at London Exposition; Yukichi Fukuzawa publishes *Seiyō Jijō* [Conditions of the West]; Ohchi Fukuchi later starts a daily newspaper

1863, government publishes first monthly newspaper *Kanpan Batavia Shimbun*, excerpted from the Java *Courant*

Meiji Period (1868–1912)

1870, Yokohama *Mainichi Shimbun* established

1872, Tokyo *Nichinichi Shimbun* established

1872, Code of Education aims at universal literacy

1873, first modern advertising (and trading) firm appears

1900, 80 percent of children in primary schools (temples, etc.)

1870, first daily newspaper (government mouthpiece)

1874, *Yomiuri* established in easy-to-read language

1870s, papers "misbehave"; government cracks down

1879, *Asahi Shimbun* founded in Osaka

Taisho Period (1912–26)

1923, Kanto earthquake; Tokyo papers suffer, while Osaka papers prosper (Big Three dominance begins)

1924, Takayanagi establishes TV laboratory

1925, radio begins

1925, Yagi develops antenna to receive VHF/UHF signals

1926, Japan Broadcasting Corp. (Nippon Hoso Kyokai, NHK) radio established

1926, Takayanagi sends letter "I" via prototype TV

Showa Period (1926–89)

  1928, live broadcast of enthronement of Emperor Hirohito

  1930, Emperor visits Takayanagi's TV laboratory

  1930, first shortwave relay broadcast from London

  1930s, anti-foreign propaganda; Info Committee in cabinet

  1936, live broadcast of 11th Olympic Games from Berlin

  1936, news agencies merged to form government organ

  1937, military censors news

  1937, NHK experimental TV station sends transmission

  1940, NHK broadcasts first TV drama

  1940s, United States and United Kingdom use Yagi antennas to detect Japan's
  ships

  1945, Emperor Hirohito broadcasts surrender over radio

  1945, Allied General Headquarters institutes Press Code and Radio Code
  placing restrictions on media but releasing it from control by military

  1946, promulgation of new constitution with guarantees of free speech and
  free press

Appendix 2: Information Sources in English

English-Language Daily Newspapers

Asahi Evening News
5-3-2, Tsukiji, Chuo-ku, Tokyo 104-11
Jointly edited by *Asahi Shimbun* and Asahi Daily News Co.
Est. 1954.
Evening circulation: 38,800 (estimated)

Japan Times
4-5-4, Shibaura, Minato-ku, Tokyo 108
Independent
Est. 1897
Morning circulation: 65,596

Mainichi Daily News
1-1-1, Hitotsubashi, Chiyoda-ku, Tokyo 100-51
Published by Mainichi Newspapers
Est. 1922
Morning circulation: 46,000 (estimated)

The Daily Yomiuri
1-7-1, Ohtemachi, Chiyoda-ku, Tokyo 100
Published by the *Yomiuri Shimbun*
Est. 1955
Morning circulation: 51,498

FAX publications: *Asahi Shimbun Japan Access* and *Yomiuri Report from Japan*

Weekly and Biweekly Publications

Tokyo Weekender (biweekly)
2nd floor, Tuttle Building
2-6, Suido 1 chome
Bunkyo-ku, Tokyo 112
Newsprint tabloid; free in Tokyo and Yokohama or by subscription. Distributed in Tokyo's 23 wards with the *Daily Yomiuri.*

The Japan Times Weekly (every Saturday)
The Japan Times, Ltd.
Head office: 54, Shibaura 4 chome, Minato-ku
Central P.O. Box 144, 352, Tokyo 100-91

The Nikkei Weekly
1325 Avenue of the Americas, Suite 2500
New York, NY 10019
1-800-322-1657
Business news broadsheet; 70 percent written for the *Nikkei.*

Monthly Magazines Published in Japan (general interest; local publications also exist)

Tokyo Business Today
1-2-1, Nihonbashi Hongoku-cho
Chuo-ku, Tokyo 103

PHP
PHP Institute Inc.
3-10, Sanban-cho, Chiyoda-ku, Tokyo 102
Publishes: international edition, Asia-Pacific edition

Tokyo Journal
Cross Cultural Communications, Inc.
Cross Cultural Communications Building
12-2, Minami Motomachi, Shinjuku-ku, Tokyo 160
International edition: *Japan Journal*

Eye-Ai Magazine
Sennari Building, 5th Floor
5-6-20 Minami-Aoyarna
Minato-ku, Tokyo 107
Covers culture, entertainment, popular music, arts

Hiragana Times (monthly)
Subscriptions: YAC Planning Inc.
Kowa Building, 4F
2-3-12 Shinjuku
Shinjuku-ku, Tokyo 160

Editorial offices: 902 Towa Shinjuku Corp.
24-3 Shinjuku,
Shinjuku-ku, Tokyo 160
For students in their 20s, all nationalities; also publishes *Housing in Tokyo*

JIJ–Japan International Journal (monthly)
Business World Corp.
2-8-6 Shiroganedai
Minato-ku, Tokyo 108
Est. 1990 for single, employed young people

Winds (monthly)
In-flight magazine of Japan Air Lines
No address available

Other Publications

The Japan Quarterly (quarterly)
Asahi Shimbun Publishing Co.
Editorial office: *Asahi Shimbun*
5-3-2 Tsukiji
Chuo-ku, Tokyo 104-11

Japan Views
Asia Foundation Translation Series
465 California St.
San Francisco, CA 94104

Nexis/Lexis Sources

Asahi News Service: NEWS; ASAHI
Daily Yomiuri: WORLD; DAYOMI
Mainichi Daily News: WORLD; MAINWS
Nikkei Weekly: NEWS; NWEEK

Internet Addresses

Kyodo News: http://www.kyodo.co.jp/
Japan Times: http://www.japantimes.co.jp/

*Verified circulation

References

A Day in the Life of Japan. 1985. NY: William Collins.

Ad expenses mark first fall since 1965. 1993. *Asahi Evening News* (February 16): 6.

Adams, Kenneth, and Lester Hill, Jr. 1991. Protest and rebellion: fantasy themes in Japanese comics. *Journal of Popular Culture* 25 (1): 99-187.

Advertising spending down in 1993. *NSK News Bulletin* 17, 1 (March): 4.

Advertising spending increases 5% in 1995. 1996. *NSK News Bulletin* 19, 1 (March): 5.

Agency report. 1995. *Advertising Age* (April 10): S-29.

Akao, Mitsushi. 1995. Three quarters of reporters felt satisfaction in their jobs—from NSK's 1993 Survey of Reporters. In *The Japanese Press '95,* 41-44. Tokyo: Nihon Shimbun Kyokai.

Akhavan-Majid, Roya. 1990. The press as an elite power group in Japan. *Journalism Quarterly* 67 (4): 1006-14.

Amano, Yukichi. 1994. In linguistic lockup. *Japan Views* (January): 15-16 (reprinted from the *Tokyo Shimbun,* November 16, 1993).

Ambrose, Stephen. 1988. *Rise to Globalism: American Foreign Policy since 1938,* 5th ed. New York: Viking Penguin.

Aoki, Sadanobu, Toshio Hara, and Katsuichi Honda. 1992. *Tei dan: jidai to jya-narizumu he no toitake* [Three way discussion: roundtable on contemporary journalism]. *Hōsō Report* 118: 2-14.

Bankers' group to scrap regulations on banks' ads. 1992. Kyodo News Service (January 14).

Barr, Cameron. 1995. Japan media berated for cozy ties with police in probe of gas attack. *Christian Science Monitor* (May 16): 6.

Beer, Lawrence. 1993. Freedom of expression: The continuing revolution. In *Japanese Constitutional Law,* edited by Percy R. Luney, Jr., and Kazuyuki Takahashi. Japan: University of Tokyo Press.

Bell, Daniel. 1973. *The Coming of Post-Industrial Society.* New York: Basic Books.

Benedict, Ruth. 1946. *The Chrysanthemum and the Sword.* New York: Houghton Mifflin.

Blustein, Paul. 1991. Japan's cola wars test: Can Hammer rap Coke? Pepsi tests taboo against comparative ads. *The Washington Post* (May 9): B9.

Brislin, Tom. 1995. Weep into silence/cries of rage: bitter divisions in Hawaii's Japanese press. *Journalism and Mass Communication Monographs* 154.

Bureau of National Affairs. 1995. Intellectual property: U.S. asking Japan for better protection of music copyrights. *Daily Report for Executives* (September 20): A182.

Busby, Linda, and Greg Leichty. 1993. Feminism and advertising: traditional and nontraditional women's magazines, 1950s-1980s. *Journalism Quarterly* 70 (2): 247-64.

Chamoto, Toshimasa. 1993. *Mizu kava hihan o fūjitei kiku tabu no boketsu o horu sanbi no koshitsu hōdō* [The chrysanthemum taboo and suicidal self-censorship: fawning reporting that glorifies the imperial household]. *Hōsō Report* 121: 28-32.

Chiasson, Lloyd. 1991. The Japanese-American encampment: an editorial analysis of 27 West Coast newspapers. *Newspaper Research Journal* 12 (2): 92-107.

Christopher, Robert. 1983. *The Japanese Mind*. New York: Fawcett Columbine.

Clinton warns trading partners. 1995. *The Legal Intelligencer* (May 2): 7.

Conant, Jennet. 1990. Secrets of the Nippon Club. *Manhattan, Inc.* 7 (4): 57-63.

Cooking up a new kind of magazine. 1993. *Asahi Evening News* (February 18): 5.

Cooper-Chen, Anne. 1997. Japan's Great Daily: editorials in the *Asahi Shimbun* during a year of political change. *Keio Communication Review* 19: 67-84.

_____. 1995. Japan's clouded window: news on NHK and TBS television, 1993. Paper presented to the Association for Education in Journalism and Mass Communication convention, Washington, D.C.

_____. 1994. *Games in the Global Village: A 50-nation Study of Entertainment Television*. Bowling Green, Ohio: Popular Press.

_____. 1992. A week of world news: TV gatekeeping in Japan, the United States, Jamaica, Sri Lanka and Columbia. *Keio Communication Review* 14: 69-84.

Cooper-Chen, Anne, Eva Leung, and Sung-ho Cho. 1995. Sex roles in East Asian magazine advertising. *Gazette* 55 (3): 207-23.

Cooper-Chen, Anne, and Lara Sims. 1996. Two pacific powers view the world: news on CBS and TBS television, 1993. Paper presented to the Association for Education in Journalism and Mass Communication convention, Anaheim, Calif.

Council proposes withdrawal of beer vending machines. 1993. Kyodo News Service, *Japan Economic Newswire* (October 1).

Court complains about publication of Tanaka's photo. 1983. Kyodo News Service, *Japan Economic Newswire* (October 14).

Cult's broad reach. 1995. *Newsweek* (May 8): 54.

Dai ka sairyu kara ichinen–hisaichi Shimabara kara no shogen [One year after the big fire–testimony from the Shimabara disaster site]. 1992. *Hōsō Report* 117 (July/August): 2-6.

Demand for faxed facts flourishing. 1992. *Asahi Evening News* (November 11): 5.

Dentsu. 1993. *Marketing and Advertising Yearbook, Japan 1994*. Tokyo: author.

_____. 1992. *Japan 1993 Marketing and Advertising Yearbook*. Tokyo: author.

_____. 1991. *Japan 1992 Marketing and Advertising Yearbook.* Tokyo: author.

Dentsu PR Center. 1988. *Communicating: A Guide to PR in Japan.* Tokyo: author.

Desmond, Edward. 1996. The failed miracle. *Time* (April 22): 16-20.

DeVos, George, and Audie Bock. 1974. *Themes in Japanese Society as Seen through the Japanese Film.* Berkeley: Regents of the University of California.

Digitalization of broadcasting. 1996. *NSK News Bulletin* 19 (2): 5.

Doi, Teruyuki. 1992. Rare event in Japan: Dentsu gets bad press. *Advertising Age* 63 (24): 22.

Dulles, F. R. 1965. *Yankees and Samurai.* New York: Harper & Row.

Economist Intelligence Unit. 1994. 4.02 protection of intellectual property (August 1).

Edelhart, Mike. 1983. "Dallas" bombs in Tokyo. *Psychology Today* 17 (4): 22-23.

Edelstein, Alex, Youichi Ito, and Hans Kepplinger. 1989. *Communication and Culture: A Comparative Approach.* White Plains, N.Y.: Longman.

Ethnic press in Japan. 1994. *Mainichi Daily News.* (November 16): 14.

Fallows, James. 1989. *More Like Us.* New York: Houghton-Mifflin.

Feldman, Ofer. 1995. Political reality and editorial cartoons in Japan. *Journalism Quarterly* 72 (3): 571-80.

_____. 1993. *Politics and the News Media in Japan.* Ann Arbor: University of Michigan Press.

Flournoy, Don, Debra Mason, Robert Nanney, and Guido Stempel. 1992. Media images of Canada. *Ohio Journalism Monographs Series* 3.

Foreign Press Center. 1990. *Japan's Mass Media* (No. 7, About Japan Series). Tokyo: author.

Fujitake, Akira, and Tsutomu Yamamoto. 1994. *Zusetsu Nippon no komyunkeshyon* [Mass Communication in Japan]. Tokyo: Nihon Hoso Shuppan Kyukai.

Fukunaga, Hiroshi. 1993. Editorial: Ducks, sumo and Japanese journalism. *Tokyo Business Today* (April): 5.

Fuzhen, Wang. 1993. Japanese copyright: history and contemporary challenges. *The Japan Foundation Newsletter* 20: 14-19.

Gershon, Richard, and Tsutomu Kanayama. 1994. Direct broadcast satellites in Japan. Unpublished paper, Western Michigan University.

Gonzenbach, William, David Arant, and Robert Stevenson. 1992. The world of U.S. network television news: eighteen years of foreign news coverage. *Gazette* 50: 53-72.

Gov't won't ban live broadcasts of banquets, Kato says. 1992. Kyodo News Service, *Japan Economic Newswire* (January 13).

Gudykunst, William, and Tsukasa Nishida. 1994. *Bridging Japanese-North American Differences.* Thousand Oaks, Calif.: Sage.

Gurdon, Hugo. 1994. Kamikaze smokers ignore health risks. *Sunday Telegraph* (June 5): 19.

Hadfield, Peter. 1996. TBS president resigns. Segment on "Monitor Radio" (May 1).

_____. 1991. Japan: keeping in with the club. *Index on Censorship* 7: 15-17.

Hagiwara, Shigeru. 1995. Rise and fall of foreign programs in Japanese television. *Keio Communication Review* 17: 3-26.

Hall, Edward. 1976. *Beyond Culture*. New York: Doubleday.

Haruhara, Akihiko. 1994. The current state of journalist training in Japan's universities. *Shimbun Kenkyu* (May): 18-24.

Haruhara, Akihiko, and Toshitaka Hayashi. 1990. Newspapers. In *Japan's Mass Media* (No. 7, About Japan Series): 9-37. Tokyo: Foreign Press Center.

Hasegawa, Kazumi. 1995. Does the U.S. comparative advertising TV practice work abroad? The case of Japan and the United States. Paper presented to the International Communication Association, Albuquerque.

Head, Sydney. 1985. *World Broadcasting Systems*. Belmont, Calif.: Wadsworth.

Health ministry panel drafts anti-smoking action program. 1995. Kyodo News Service, *Japan Economic Newswire* (March 29).

Henningham, John P. 1979. Kyodo gate-keepers: a study of Japanese news flow. *Gazette* 25 (1): 23-30.

Hillenbrand, B. 1992. America in the mind of Japan. *Time* (February 10): 20-23.

Hirose, Hidehiko. 1994. The press club system in Japan: its past, present and future. *Keio Communication Review* 16: 63-75.

Hiroto, Kosuge. 1993. Only on Monday. *Japan Views* (November): 5. From *Mainichi Shimbun* (September 14).

Hofstede, Geert. 1984. *Culture's Consequences: International Differences in Work-Related Values*. Abridged edition. Beverly Hills: Sage.

Horibe, Masao. 1985. Press law in Japan. In *Press Law in Modern Democracies: A Comparative Study*, edited by Prina Lahav, 315-38. New York: Longman.

Hoshiyama, Yukimitsu. 1994. Kisha clubs open doors to foreign press. In *The Japanese Press '94*, 29-31. Tokyo: Nihon Shimbun Kyokai.

Hōsō kai no taboo ni chosen shita "Asa made: nama terebi" no san nen ["Til dawn: live TV": three years of challenging a broadcast taboo]. 1992. *Hōsō Report* 118: 46-49.

Ikeda, Kenichi. 1994a. A social psychological approach to "networked" reality. *IEICE Transactions* E77D (12): 1390-96.

_____. 1994b. Mass media's construction of reality and voting behavior in the 1993 general election in Japan. Paper presented to the International Association for Mass Communication Research, Seoul.

Ikei, Masaharu. 1981. *1930–nendai no masumidia: manshujihen eno taio o chusin to shite* [Mass media in the 1930s: focus on coping with the situation of the Manchurian incident]. In *Saiko: Taiheiyo Senso Zenya*, edited by K. Miwa. Tokyo: Souseiki.

Images of Japan. 1996. "ABC News Nightline," No. 3886 (April 10).

In pursuit of sarin and the truth. 1995. *NSK News Bulletin* 18, 2 (June): 1-2.

Inoue, Teruko. 1989. *Josei zasshi o kaidoku-suru* [Analyses of women's magazines]. Tokyo: Kakiuchi Shuppan.

Ishii, Kenichi. 1996a. Factors influencing the adoption of new information media in Japanese families. *Media Asia* 23 (1): 22-28.

_____. 1996b. Is the US overreported in Japan's mass media? *Gazette* 57: 135-44.

Ishikawa, Sakae, and Naoyuki Kambara. 1993. Diversity in Japanese television: a preliminary analysis of seven VHF channels. *Keio Communication Review* 15: 17-27.

Ito, Kinko. 1994. Images of women in weekly male comic magazines in Japan. *Journal of Popular Culture* 27 (4): 81-95.

Ito, Takeshi. 1993. Headlines from the magazines. *Mainichi Shimbun* (May 30): B9.

Ito, Youichi. 1994. An application of the tri-polar kuuki model to the withdrawal of the United Nations peace cooperation bill in Japan. Paper presented to the International Association for Mass Communication Research, Seoul.

———. 1993a. Mass communication theories in Japan and the United States. Chap. 8 in *Communication in Japan and the United States,* edited by William Gudykunst. Albany, N.Y.: State University of New York Press.

———. 1993b. The future of communication research: a Japanese perspective. *Journal of Communication* 43 (4): 69-79.

———. 1993c. Communication and cultural change: a Japanese perspective on globalization. Chap. 12 in *Organizational Communication and Management: A Global Perspective,* edited by Andrezj Kozminski and Donald Cushman. Albany, N.Y.: State University of New York Press.

———. 1991a. Birth of *jōhō shakai* and *jōhōka* concepts in Japan and their diffusion outside Japan. *Keio Communication Review* 13: 3-12.

———. 1991b. *Jōhōka* as a driving force of social change. *Keio Communication Review* 12: 33-58.

———. 1990a. "The trade winds change": Japan's shift from information importer to an information exporter, 1965-1985. In *Communication Yearbook 13,* edited by J.A. Anderson, 430-65. Newbury Park, Calif.: Sage.

———. 1990b. Communication and cultural change: a Japanese perspective on globalization. Chap. 12 in *Organizational Communication and Management,* edited by Andrezj Kozminski and Donald Cushman. Albany, N.Y.: State University of New York Press.

Ito, Youichi, and Norichika Tanaka. 1992. Education, research institutes and academic associations in journalism and mass communications in Japan. *Keio Communication Review* 14: 15-35.

Itoh, Teiji, and Gregory Clark. 1983. *The Dawns of Tradition.* Tokyo: Nissan Motor Co.

Iwasaki, Chieko. 1994. Newspaper credibility mildly recovers, newspaper's function to watch politics–from NSK's 1993 nationwide newspaper survey. In *The Japanese Press '94,* 37-42. Tokyo: Nihon Shimbun Kyokai.

Jameson, Sam. 1992. Violence chilling freedom of speech in Japan. *Yomiuri Shimbun* (October 17): 8A.

Japan film censors to relax obscenity standards. 1992. *The Reuter Library Report* (October 28).

Japan metes out fine to pornographers. 1995. United Press International (February 24).

Japan remains richest country in terms of assets. 1996. *Athens (Ohio) Messenger* (May 26): A9.

Japan version of Madonna book slips past censors. 1992. Reuters (December 1).

Japanese air force. 1969. *Time* (May 2): 82.

Japanese companies lax on warning labels. 1993. *Asahi Evening News* (February 14): 4.

Japanese readers take to electronic books. 1996. *Asian Mass Communication Bulletin* 26 (2): 21.

Japan External Trade Organization-JETRO. 1991. *U.S. and Japan in Figures.* Tokyo: author.

Japan's Internet tangle. 1995. *The Economist* (July 15): 50.

Jones, Gareth. 1993. Japan media, muzzled by palace, slammed as servile. *The Reuter Library Report.* (March 12).

JR rejects weekly's sale at station stores. 1994. *NSK News Bulletin* 17(3): 8.

Jungle taitei zeppan yohkyu kara "Shūkan Josei" shazai jiken made [From the demand to cease publication of Jungle Emperor to the apology by *Shūkan Josei*]. 1992. *Hōsō Report* 118: 12-15.

Kambara, Keiko. 1990. The Japanese have a word for it. *Christian Science Monitor* (January 25): 12.

Kanai, Yoshiko. 1996. *Hanako* and the consumer society. *Japanese Book News* 13 (Spring): 1-3.

Kanayama, Tsutomu. 1995. Program distribution to Asia-Pacific region. Unpublished paper, Ohio University.

Kato, Hidetoshi. 1993. Television in Japan. Unpublished paper, National Institute of Multimedia Education, Chiba, Japan.

_____. 1988. *Essays in Comparative Popular Culture.* Papers of the East-West Center Communication Institute, 13.

Katsumata, Yoshikazu. 1996. Credibility of newspapers gradually rises. In *The Japanese Press '96,* 41-45. Tokyo: Nihon Hoso Kyokai.

Katz, Elihu, Tamar Liebes, and Sumiko Iwao. 1991. Neither here nor there: why "Dallas" failed in Japan. *Communication* 12: 99-110.

Kawakami, K., and Ofer Feldman. 1988. Media use, political attitudes and participation among Japanese university students. Paper presented to the 14th World Congress of the International Political Science Association, Washington, D.C.

Kilburn, David. 1994. Dentsu takes a CD-ROM spin. *Advertising Age* 65 (14): 18.

_____. 1992. Nissan axes Dentsu as Hakuhodo gains. *Advertising Age* 63(7): 19-20.

Kim, Chie-woon, and Won-Yong Kim. 1993. An assessment of the influence of DBS "spillover" as a factor of conflict between Korea and Japan. *Keio Communication Review* 15: 69-80.

Kin and Gin still media medalists. 1992. *Asahi Evening News* (October 10): 5.

Kinoshita, June. 1991. Allure in Tokyo. *Allure* (July): 88-95.

Kitamura, Hideo. 1987. Television is a fiction and viewers are observers. *Studies of Broadcasting* 23: 141-53.

Kitayama, Seiichi. 1993. Japan aiming to relinquish smoking title. *The Nikkei Weekly* (September 27): 6.

Kliesch, Ralph. 1991. The U.S. press corps abroad rebounds: a 7th world survey of foreign correspondents. *Newspaper Research Journal* 12 (1): 24-33.

Kodama, Miiko. 1995. Japanese women in the media. Paper presented to the Association for Education in Journalism and Mass Communication, Washington, D.C.

Komatsubara, Hisao. 1971. Japan. Chap. 6 of *The Asian Newspapers' Reluctant Revolution,* edited by John Lent. Ames, Iowa: Iowa State University Press.

Konaka, Yotaro. 1988. *Nyusu Kyastahs Senso* [TV News Wars: The Anchors]. Tokyo: Tokyo Shimbun.

_____. 1972. *Ohkoku no geijin-tachi* [Artists of the Kingdom]. Tokyo: Kodansha.

Kristof, Nicholas. 1995. In Japan, brutal comics for women. *New York Times* (November 5): B1, 6.

Lachrenbruch, David. 1995. Sony's "micromirror" projector. *Electronics Now* 66 (9): 6.

Ladd, Everett. 1995. Time to recognize US-Japan success story. *Christian Science Monitor* (June 21): 19.

Larson, James. 1984. *Television's Window on the World*. Norwood, NJ: Ablex.

Lebra, Takie. 1976. *Japanese Patterns of Behavior*. Honolulu: University of Hawaii Press.

Lewenstein, Marian. 1987. Global readership. *Presstime* (September): 10-12.

Luther, Catherine, and Douglas Boyd. 1995. Under the veneer of democracy: American occupation control over broadcasting in Japan, 1945-1952. Paper presented to the Association for Education in Journalism and Mass Communication, Washington, D.C.

Ma, Karen. 1996. *The Modern Madame Butterfly*. Rutland, Vt.: Tuttle.

Machlup, Fritz. 1962. *The Production and Distribution of Knowledge in the United States*. Princeton, N.J.: Princeton University Press.

Maezawa, Takeshi. 1992. Mediawatch. *The Daily Yomiuri* (December 22): 8.

Magazines teach dads how to play with kids. 1993. *Asahi Evening News* (January 8): 5.

Maloney, Kate. 1991a. Japan blends 20th century with tradition. *Chautauquan Daily* (July 9): 6.

_____. 1991b. Japanese diplomat looks beyond trade issues. *Chautauquan Daily* (July 13): 4.

May, William. 1988. Seishin: the Japanese spirit and Japanese sports newspapers. Paper presented at the International Association for Mass Communication Research, Barcelona.

McConnell, Chris. 1995. Hitachi unveils SDTV decoder. *Broadcasting & Cable 1995* 125 (37): 51.

Media disagree over merit of news blackout. 1993. *Asahi Evening News* (June 4): 3.

Merrill, John, ed. 1995. *Global Journalism*. White Plains, N.Y.: Longman.

_____. 1990. Global elite: a newspaper community of reason. *Gannett Center Journal* 4 (4): 93-101.

Merrill, John, and Harold Fisher. 1980. *The World's Great Dailies*. New York: Hastings House.

Messerly, Anne. 1966. Japanese praised by David Finn of U.S. *Asahi Evening News* (November 14): 3.

Meyer, Thomas. 1989. That's incredible. *American Way* (Summer): 24, 26, 29.

Miller, Jay K. 1994. Broadcast news in Japan: NHK and NTV. *Keio Communication Review* 16: 77-103.

Miura wins libel suits against Kyodo, 3 newspapers. 1994. Kyodo News Service, *Japan Economic Newswire* (August 23).

Mizutani, O. 1981. *Japanese: The Spoken Language in Japanese Life*. Tokyo: Japan Times.

Monthly folds after denying Holocaust. 1995. *NSK News Bulletin* 18 (1): 4.

Morikawa, Kathleen. 1993a. Sensational magazines need sensitivity lessons. *Asahi Evening News* (February 27): 5.

_____. 1993b. Unscrambling WOWOW's mysterious debt. *Asahi Evening News* (March 27): 9.

Mowlana, Hamid, and Mehdi Rad. 1992. International flow of Japanese television programs: the "Oshin" phenomena. *Keio Communication Review* 14: 51-68.

Mulcahy, Richard. 1994. Change in the media discourse of Japan's international role: an analysis of the role conceptions in the *Asahi Shimbun* in 1982 and 1992. Paper presented to the International Association for Mass Communication Research, Seoul.

Murrow, L. 1992. Japan in the mind of America. *Time* (February 10): 16-20.

Nagashima, Hidesuke. 1987. Smoking remains national habit in Japan. Kyodo News Service, *Japan Economic Newswire* (April 30).

Nakane, Chie. 1988. Japan in the context of Asia. *Japan Foundation Newsletter* 15 (4): 2-6.

_____. 1970. *Japanese Society*. Berkeley: U of California Press.

Nakasa, Hideo. 1987. Scandal vs. social responsibility: the growing criticism of journalism in Japan. *Studies of Broadcasting* 23: 27-49.

Nakazawa, Noriko. 1993. Effectiveness of Western models in Japanese advertising. Paper presented to the Association for Education Journalism and Mass Communication, Kansas City, Mo.

National Trade Data Bank. 1995. Japan: Tobacco market overview. *Market Reports* (March 21).

New twist in game mag war. 1992. *Asahi Evening News* (December 25): 5.

New York Daily News segment. "48 Hours" (CBS-TV) April 13, 1994.

News companies to continue holding down employment. 1994. *NSK News Bulletin* 17 (4): 8.

Newspaper closures increasing. 1992. *NSK News Bulletin* 15 (3): 1-2.

Newspaper price hikes and personnel cuts. 1994. *NSK News Bulletin* 17 (1): 6.

Newspapers confident against wave of future media. 1995. *NSK News Bulletin* 18 (2): 6.

NHK barred from banquet broadcast after Bush video. 1992. Kyodo News Service, *Japan Economic Newswire* (January 10).

NHK documentary on Himalayan region includes staged scenes. 1993. *Asahi Evening News* (February 3): 1.

Nihon Keizai Shimbun. 1984. Historical review of advertising regulations in Japan. *Japan Economic Journal* (October 2): 41.

Nihon Shimbun Kyokai (NSK). 1995. *The Japanese Press '95*. Tokyo: author.

Nikkei Weekly. 1994. Special supplement on public relations (March 7): 17-24.

_____. 1993. Special supplement on public relations (March 1): 18-22.

_____. 1991. Special supplement on public relations (June 29): 17-18.

Nishihara, Shigeki. 1987. *Yoron chōsa ni yoru dōjidaishi* [Chronology by Public Opinion Polls]. Tokyo: Brehn Shuppan.

Nishino, Yasushi. 1994. Diversity in television programming in Japan. *Studies of Broadcasting* 30: 115-30.

Nude photo magazine fad bothers non-Japanese airlines. 1994. Kyodo News Service, *Japan Economic Newswire* (October 29).

Okabe, Roichi. 1991. A quantitative and qualitative analysis of CBS's depictions of Japan from rhetorical perspectives. Paper presented at the Conference on Communication in Japan and the United States, California State University, Fullerton.

Overview of publishing industry. 1994. *Japanese Book News* 7 (Summer): 21.

Ozawa, Ichiro. 1994. Book excerpt: "Toward a Bolder Japan." *Time* (June 13): 38, 47.

Pain mixed with pleasure for Japan's "sex" printer. 1993. *The Reuter Library Report* (February 26).

Politician-owned cable TV networks arouse suspicion. 1993. *Asahi Evening News* (June 16): 4.

Pollack, Andrew. 1994. Japan may abandon its system for HDTV. *New York Times* (February 23): C1, C5.

Privacy of AIDS patients a major problem, editors say. 1988. Kyodo News Service, *Japan Economic Newswire* (May 27).

Public Relations Society of Japan. 1991. *Japan PR Directory.* Tokyo: author.

Publishing in 1994. 1995. *Japanese Book News* 10: 21.

Purdy, Roger. 1987. The ears and voice of a nation: the Domei news agency and Japan's news network, 1936-1945. Unpublished dissertation, U of Calif., Santa Barbara.

Ramaprasad, Jyotika, and Kasumi Hasegawa. 1990. An analysis of Japanese television commercials. *Journalism Quarterly* 67 (4): 1025-33.

Ranard, Andrew. 1990. O-batalian vs. Oyagi-gal in the great manga war. *International Herald Tribune* (July 14-15): 16.

Receiving fee system. 1992. *NHK Factsheet.* Tokyo: Nippon Hoso Kyokai.

Reid, T. R. 1995a. Japlish. Segment on National Public Radio's "Morning Edition" (June 2).

———. 1995b. Japan, land of the rising daughter. *Washington Post* (May 31): B1, B10.

Reischauer, Edwin O. 1981. *Japan: The Story of a Nation.* 3rd ed. Tokyo: Tuttle.

Reporters use access to information laws to gather news. 1993. *Asahi Evening News* (May 29): 5.

Saito, Shinichi. 1995. Does television cultivate the image of America in Japan? Paper presented to the Association for Education in Journalism and Mass Communication, Washington, D.C.

———. 1994. Television and perceptions of American society in Japan. Paper presented to the Association for Education in Journalism and Mass Communication, Atlanta.

Sakaiya, Taichi. 1985. *Chika Kakumei* [The Chika Revolution]. Tokyo: PHP Kenyu-sho.

Sakata, Hyde. 1995. General trends of the Japanese press. In *The Japanese Press '95,* 13-20. Tokyo: Nihon Shimbun Kyokai.

Sales/distribution agent workers up again. 1995. *NSK News Bulletin* 18 (1): 9.

Sanger, David. 1993. Japan's old guard flails at the talking heads. *New York Times* (November 7): D16.

_____. 1989. U.S. lawyer makes Japan sit up and take notice. *New York Times* (March 16): 4.

Sasaki, Noriko. 1995. International news coverage of Japanese newspapers. Unpublished paper, Ohio University.

Sata, Masunori. 1991. Conclusion. Chap. 7 of *A History of Japanese Television Drama,* by Kazuhiko Goto, Hideo Hirahara, Katsumi Oyama, and Masunori Sata. Tokyo: Japan Association of Broadcast Art.

Satellite TV tapping Japanese viewers from overhead. 1993. *Asahi Evening News* (February 14): 5.

Sawa, Takamitsu. 1994. Japan may nix multimedia. *Japan Times* (August 29): 18.

Schodt, Frederik. 1986. *Manga! Manga! The World of Japanese Comics.* Tokyo: Kodansha.

Sekai ni ureru nihon no bangumi [Japanese programs are being sold throughout the world]. 1994. *Chūnichi Shimbun* (June 29): 8.

Self, Charles. 1991. The communication improvement initiative and the case of communication policy formation. Paper presented at the Conference on Communication in Japan and the United States, California State University, Fullerton.

_____. 1990. Recent developments in communication technology in the Japanese newspaper industry. *ICB* 25 (1-2): 19- 21.

Sengupta, Subir. 1994. Portrayals of women in television commercials: a comparison between the United States and Japan. Paper presented to the International Association for Mass Communication Research, Seoul.

"Sex" doesn't sell in Japan. 1992. *Newsday* (October 29): 13.

Sherman, Spencer. 1995. Hiroshi who? *Columbia Journalism Review* (July/August): 11-12.

_____. 1990. Pack journalism, Japanese style. *Columbia Journalism Review* (September/October): 37-40.

Shifrel, Scott. 1988. Tokyo: tough news capital. *Washington Journalism Review* (September): 26-33.

Shimizu, Hideo. 1991. The sound growth of juveniles and the responsibility of the publishing, centering on regulation of comics in Japan. Paper presented at the 5th International Forum on Publishing Studies, Seoul.

Shimizu, Shinichi. 1993. Broadcasting and film industries in Japan. Unpublished paper, Hoso Bunka Foundation, Tokyo.

Shinoda, Hiroyuki. 1990. *Kūzen no josei zasshi boom narumono no kyomo* [Illusion of an unprecedented women's magazine boom]. *The Tsukuru* (January): 71.

Shinohara, Makiko. 1992. Ads that compare rival products stir debate in Japan. *Christian Science Monitor* (March 16): 8.

Shiramizu, Shigehiko. 1995. Ethnic media in Japan today. *The Yoke* 13 (72): 6-7.

_____. 1987. *Nichibei terebi niusu hikaku kenkyū* [A comparative study of television news]. *Takachiho Ronso*: 215-29.

Simons, Lewis. 1996. U.S.-Japan scorecard. *Time* (April 22): 18-19.

Six media ordered to pay 4.5 mil yen for murder case libel. 1994. Kyodo News Service, *Japan Economic Newswire* (January 31).

Skov, Lise, and Brian Moeran. 1996. *Women, Media and Consumption in Japan.*

Honolulu: University of Hawaii Press.

Slow march of progress. 1995. *The Economist* (July 15): 49-50.

Smith, Toren. 1993. The world of manga. *Japanese Book News* 2: 1-3.

Soccer boom plays role in newspaper ad PR. 1993. *NSK News Bulletin* 16 (4): 4.

Sonnenberg, Urte. 1994. Mini FM, community radio and local cable television stations. Paper presented at the International Association for Mass Communication Research, Seoul.

Sports magazines face off in popularity race. 1993. *Asahi Evening News* (March 5): 5.

Sreberny-Mohammadi, Annabelle. 1984. The 'World of World News' study. *Journal of Communication* 34 (1): 121-34.

Star becomes first foreign channel in Japan. 1996. *Asian Mass Communications Bulletin* 26 (3): 8.

Stein, Tom. 1993. Porn gets full exposure in Japan. *Toronto Star* (March 27): D5.

Stevenson, Robert. 1994. *Global Communication in the 21st Century.* White Plains, N.Y.: Longman.

Stronach, Bruce. 1992. *Popular Culture in Japan and America.* Tokyo: Seibido.

Success and the "Fuyuhiko syndrome." 1992. *Mainichi Daily News* (November 7): B9.

Suhara, Takeshi. 1992. *"NNN Dokyumento '92" tabako bangumi ga sekai kinen dei ni yomigaeru* [Revival of World No Smoking Day by "NNN Documentary '92"]. *Hoso Report* (July/August): 7-11.

Sun, Marjorie, and James Sterngold. 1994. Correspondents' corner. *Study of Current English* (August): 50-55.

Supreme Court rejects obscenity ruling. 1995. *Mainichi Daily News* (April 14): 5.

Sussman, Leonard. 1993. *Freedom in the World '92-'93.* New York: Freedom House.

Suzuki, Midori. 1993. Charter of TV viewers' rights. *Hoso Report* 120 (January/February): 12-15.

Svenkerud, Peer, Rita Rahoi, and Arvind Singhal. 1995. Incorporating ambiguity and archetypes in entertainment-education programming: lessons learned from "Oshin." *Gazette* 55: 147-68.

Tada, Michitaro. 1978. Broadcasting advertisements and the general public. Symposium on the Cultural Role of Broadcasting, Tokyo. *Summary Report* (October): 43-48.

Takabatake, Kazuya. 1993. Sports papers more popular than ever. In *The Japanese Press '93*, 41-46. Tokyo: Nihon Shimbun Kyokai.

Takagi, Tsuyoshi. 1995. The Great Hanshin Earthquake and media. In *The Japanese Press '95*, 31-36. Tokyo: Nihon Shimbun Kyokai.

Takeichi, Hideo. 1995. Journalism education in Japan: its present state and problems. Paper presented at the Association for Education in Journalism and Mass Communication, Washington, D.C.

_____. 1991. Characteristics of American newspaper reporting on Japan-U.S. trade friction around autumn 1989. *Communication Kenkyu* 22: 31-86.

Takeshita, Toshio, and Shunji Mikami. 1995. How did mass media influence the voters' choice in the 1993 general election in Japan? A study of agenda setting. *Keio Communication Review* 17: 27-41.

Tamura, Susumu. 1993. Medium itself is news. In *The Japanese Press '93*, 31-35. Tokyo: Nihon Shimbun Kyokai.

Tanaka, Hideo, ed. 1984. *The Japanese Legal System*. Tokyo: University of Tokyo Press.

Tanaka, Keiko. 1994. *Advertising Language: A Pragmatic Approach to Advertisements in Britain and Japan*. London: Routledge.

Tanaka, Michiyo. 1993. Yellow cabs: a suspicious definition. *Transpacific* (July/August): 88-89.

Third World faces "information poverty." 1996. *Asian Mass Communication Bulletin* 26 (2): 4.

33 news firms open home pages. 1996. *NSK News Bulletin* 19 (2): 4.

Three electronic newspapers take shape. 1996. *NSK News Bulletin* 19 (1): 6.

Tokuoka, Takao. 1983. How to deal with the Japanese press. Speech at Foreign Correspondents' Club, Tokyo (September).

Topolnicki, Denise. 1991. Why we still live best. *Money* (October): 86-94.

Tsujimura, Akira. 1994. Public opinion and political dynamics in Japan: the tripolar relationship of government, press and public opinion. *Keio Communication Review* 16: 25-48.

_____. 1987. Some characteristics of the Japanese way of communication. *Communication Theory from Eastern and Western Perspectives*, edited by D. L. Kincaid. New York: Academic Press.

Ueda, Yasuo. 1994. Periodical journalism at a turning point. *Japanese Book News* 6 (Spring): 1-3.

_____. 1990. Publishing. In *Japan's Mass Media* (No. 7, About Japan Series): 66-79. Tokyo: Foreign Press Center.

Umesao, Tadao. 1963. *Jōhō sangyo ron* [On information industries]. *Chuō-Kōron* March: 46-58.

U.S. Information Agency. 1993. *Directory of Foreign Correspondents in the United States*. Washington, D.C.: Foreign Press Center.

van Wolferen, Karel. 1993. *The Enigma of Japanese Power*. Tokyo: Tuttle.

Vanden Heuvel, Jon, and Everette Dennis. 1993. *The Unfolding Lotus: East Asia's Changing Media*. New York: Freedom Forum Media Studies Center.

Watanabe, Taketatsu. 1995. *Terebi yarase to jōhō sōsa* [TV manipulations and management of information]. Tokyo: Sanseido.

Watanabe, Teresa. 1993. Japan's press whips up the froth for stories on imperial engagement. *Yomiuri Shimbun* (January 13): 5.

Weinberg, Jonathan. 1991. Broadcasting and the administrative process in Japan and the United States. *Buffalo Law Review* 39 (3): 615-735.

Whipple, Charles. 1991. Japan's "Hanako" girls. *World Press Review* (December): 47.

White, J., and David Dozier. 1992. Public relations and management decision making. In *Excellence in Public Relations and Communication Management*, edited by James E. Grunig, 91-108. Hillsdale, N.J.: Lawrence Erlbaum.

Whittenmore, Edward. 1961. *The Press in Japan Today: A Case Study*. Columbia: University of South Carolina Press.

Women want trendy mags. 1993. *Asahi Evening News* (January 22): 3.

Wood, Daniel. 1991. "Mega-markets" shine on Pacific rim. *Christian Science Monitor* (April 11): 10.

Wray, Henry. 1990. Creating a more international Japan. *Intersect* (March): 17-20.

Yamada, Toshie. 1993. General trends of the Japanese press in 1992-1993. In *The Japanese Press '93*, 15-21. Tokyo: Nippon Shimbun Kyokai.

_____. 1992. General trends of the Japanese press in 1991-1992. In *The Japanese Press '92*, 13-19. Tokyo: Nippon Shimbun Kyokai.

Yamaki, Toshio. 1996. The history of advertising in Japan. *Keio Communication Review* 18: 15-31.

Yomiuri breaks taboo on constitutional change. 1994. *Japan Times* (November 4): 10.

Youm, Kyu Ho. 1990. Libel law and the press in Japan. *Journalism Quarterly* 67: 1103-12.

Index